A. A. WALTERS

THE ECONOMICS
OF
ROAD USER CHARGES

Distributed by The Johns Hopkins Press
Baltimore, Maryland

FOREWORD

I would like to explain *why* the World Bank Group does research work, and why it publishes it. We feel an obligation to look beyond the projects we help to finance towards the whole resource allocation of an economy, and the effectiveness of the use of those resources. Our major concern, in dealings with member countries, is that all scarce resources, including capital, skilled labor, enterprise and know-how, should be used to their best advantage. We want to see policies that encourage appropriate increases in the supply of savings, whether domestic or international. Finally, we are required by our Articles, as well as by inclination, to use objective economic criteria in all our judgments.

These are our preoccupations, and these, one way or another, are the subjects of most of our research work. Clearly, they are also the proper concern of anyone who is interested in promoting development, and so we seek to make our research papers widely available. In doing so, we have to take the risk of being misunderstood. Although these studies are published by the Bank, the views expressed and the methods explored should not necessarily be considered to represent the Bank's views or policies. Rather they are offered as a modest contribution to the great discussion on how to advance the economic development of the underdeveloped world.

Robert S. McNamara
President
International Bank for Reconstruction and Development

August 15, 1968

TABLE OF CONTENTS

PREFACE

Well over a century ago an author, introducing his book to the public, wrote:

"I am aware that notwithstanding my care, nothing will be easier than to criticize this book . . . readers will discover . . . a dominant thought that binds its several parts together. . . . The author who wishes to be understood is obliged to carry all his ideas to their utmost theoretical conclusions, and often to the verge of what is false and impractical. . . . I have not undertaken to see differently from others, but to look further, and while they are busied for the morrow only, I have turned my thoughts to the whole future."[1]

By the nature of our activities we, in the World Bank, are largely "busied for the morrow only." Nevertheless, we keep turning our "thoughts to the whole future." Our large lending operations for transport development in developing countries, particularly for highways, have led us increasingly into policy and practical problems concerning questions of how roads should be paid for, by whom and with what effects. The problems raise questions about the efficient utilization and allocation of resources; the economic coordination of transport; demand on congested urban roads and in uncongested rural areas; the appropriate location of new industries; relevant criteria for new investments; long-term planning; taxation; and public savings, budgetary control, and discipline.

A substantial body of experience and literature exists in developed countries on this subject. It is clear, however, that in the context of devel-

---

[1] A. de Tocqueville, "Democracy in America."

xi

oping countries some basic concepts and practical matters need reexamination. For this reason we asked Professor Alan Walters (of the University of Birmingham) to undertake an investigation into the "Economics of Road User Charges" in such countries. His report is a substantial intellectual contribution to the subject and to transport economics generally. As such, the World Bank is making it available for wider circulation. I wish to emphasize that the Bank in doing so is not expressing a view with respect to the author's conclusions nor is it recommending them as guides to action.

In the above quoted words of de Tocqueville "nothing will be easier than to criticise this book." Each reader will decide whether or to what extent the author in carrying "his ideas to their utmost theoretical conclusions" has provided "a dominant thought" (short-run marginal cost pricing) which constitutes an appropriate guide to policy in the particular circumstances of developing countries. There are some in the Bank, for example, who have serious reservations on this. But whatever his final impression and conclusions, I am sure the reader will agree that Professor Walters has made a stimulating contribution that is worth wider discussion.

Andrew M. Kamarck
Director,
Economics Department

Author's Note

The author wishes to acknowledge the generous help and advice received from friends and colleagues in the course of this study. Colleagues at the University of Virginia, Professors J. M. Buchanan, Warren Nutter, William Beazer, and Roger Sherman, read the first draft and made valuable suggestions on points of theory. At a later stage Professor Paul Samuelson of MIT was consulted on some fine points of the optimizing problem. Professor William Vickrey read the manuscript and made many valuable suggestions for improvement. Colleagues in various departments of the Bank have been most helpful in reviewing both the content and presentation of the theory and in providing data for the author's grist mill. The author is grateful to George Beier, Anthony Churchill, Jan de Weille, Shlomo Reutlinger, Hans Adler, Benjamin King, and Donald Bickers, for particular contributions, and there were many others who contributed to the study by taking an interest in the work. However, the author acknowledges his greatest debt to Herman van der Tak of the Bank's Economics

Department. He was influential in setting out the shape and scope of the study; and throughout the process of developing and testing the theory, Mr. van der Tak not only contributed many ideas but also performed the function of a close colleague in his searching criticism and concern for product quality. Finally, the author wishes to thank Miss Zoe Carson for typing an enormous quantity of difficult manuscript and for managing the voluminous and numerous drafts of the study.

The author is grateful for all this help, without which he could not have completed the study. But he alone, of course, accepts complete responsibility for the study as published.

I

INTRODUCTION

1. *The Purpose of the Study*

1. The origins of this study lie in the dissatisfaction with the current concepts and applications of the theory of road user charges.[1] In the first stages of this research we intended critically to analyze the orthodox theory and practice of user charges. But a survey of existing studies[2] showed that there was no uniform rigorous theoretical structure behind the vast majority of studies of road costs and motor taxation. There was no body of well-defined principles on which there was substantial agreement and that served as a guide in analyzing the data for particular countries.

2. The common denominator of existing user charge theory and practice is the idea that "the user should pay for the roads." A large fraction of the

---

[1] Road user charges are broadly defined as those levies the incidence and payment of which are somehow related to the use of the highway.

[2] See especially Maurice Allais *et al.*, *Options in Transport Tariff Policy*, (EEC, Brussels, 1965); Conference on Rail and Road Transport, (His Majesty's Stationery Office, London, 1932), hereafter referred to as the Salter Report; John R. Meyer, J. F. Kain, M. Wohl, *The Urban Transportation Problem*, (Harvard University Press, Cambridge, 1965); J. R. Meyer, Stenason, Peck, & Zwick, *The Economics of Competition in the Transportation Industries*, (Harvard University Press, Cambridge, 1959); James R. Nelson, *Marginal Cost Pricing in Practice*, (Prentice-Hall, Englewood Cliffs, New Jersey, 1964); Alan R. Prest, *Financing Transport in Developing Countries*, (processed), (The Brookings Institution, Washington, D.C., 1967); and *Road Research, 1964*, Road Research Laboratory, (HMSO, London, 1966).

expenditure on the roads has been incurred only because of the existence of cars and trucks, and so the owners of these vehicles, rather than the general taxpayer, should foot most of the bill for the roads. Several variations are played on this basic theme. Probably the two best known are the benefit principle—that users should pay for the roads in proportion to the benefits received—and the so-called "incremental cost" principle—that users should pay according to the highway construction costs required for their type of vehicle. The basic idea is one of equity; it was thought fair and proper that users pay for the highways.

3. But from this starting point, many investigators have pursued radically different courses. There are wide disparities in the definition of total cost, in the fraction thought to be attributable to the motor vehicle, in the allocation between different road users, and so on. The equity principle has given no guidance on these definitions and allocations; consequently, each investigator has made his own "reasonable" arrangements. Given the premises of the theory, each definition and allocation could be defended in terms of "equity."

4. "Equity" is the most important prop of the current theories, but it has been supported by other subsidiary principles. First, there has been the "need" to "equalize the conditions of competition of road and rail." Second, and I believe more important for developing countries, it has been thought important to expand the tax revenues and to increase public saving; a rationalization for increasing motor taxes was sought and, when found, embraced. It is probably the desire to "justify" higher motor taxation for the purpose of financing public investment that has provided much of the support for existing user charge ideas, however loose and unsatisfactory they may be.

5. Yet dissatisfaction with the vague and equivocal guides of existing principles is probably the least important reason for the reformulation attempted here. More persuasive than the theoretical shortcomings has been the failure of the existing principles of user charges to deal with the plague of the century—the congestion of towns and cities. Indeed, some versions of current user charge practices even make the congestion worse. Less obvious, but of great importance to the developing countries, is the "waste" of rural and interurban road space, and the consequent restrictions on development, occasioned by levying charges for the use of the highway when there are virtually no costs involved in using it. In other words, applications of the existing theory have been seen to involve serious inefficiency.

2. *The Shape of the Study*

6. There are therefore good reasons for examining once more the basic problem of user charges and for attempting to erect anew principles for analysis and policy. This is the main task of Chapters II to V.

7. The main tools used throughout Chapter II, and indeed most of this study, are those of economic analysis. There are two kinds of decision, the vehicle owner's—whether or not to use a road—and the government's—whether or not to build or improve it. The primary criterion by which we judge the various policies is that of economic efficiency—getting the most from the least. The main instruments by which we achieve (or more modestly, approach) this goal are the user charges and other taxes levied by the government, on the one hand, and the road investment policy on the other. Consequently the problem is to find user charges and tax and investment policies that give rise to the most efficient utilization of all resources, including the stock of highways. The solution which we suggest is some form of marginal cost pricing, or, in other words, that the charge for the service of the road should measure primarily the value of the resources (including rents) used up in providing that service. For investment decisions, we resort to consumer surplus criteria, i.e. we try to estimate the amount of money people would be willing to pay for the new facility.

8. There is, of course, nothing new about the basic principle of marginal cost pricing; nor is there any novelty in the principles of investment policy used in this study. All are very old. But there is much room for interpretation, and misinterpretation; so it is necessary to state these principles, their limitations, their interaction, and their application to roads in unambiguous language. The building blocks of the theory must be put together and examined as an integrated model. This is the main purpose of Chapter III.

9. In this detailed discussion of the marginal cost pricing and investment principles in Chapter III, we find it necessary to adopt some slightly new concepts and to sharpen certain conclusions. The "road problem" arises from the indivisibilities or lumpiness inherent in highways, from the joint supply of both quantity and quality of road services, and from the fact that highway services are specific in time and space with no possibility of storing. The implications of these characteristics for pricing and investment policies are worked out in some detail. The main principle of marginal cost pricing, although qualified in some respects, is not compromised by this survey; nor do we find any compelling reason, of principle or practice, to drop the basic consumer surplus criterion in favor of some alternative such

3

as "profitability," "cost covering," etc. In particular, it is shown that on the rural and interurban highways, the revenue collected from user charges at marginal cost is likely to be insufficient to cover the (annualized) investment cost of the roads; whereas in the case of congested city streets it is likely that the revenue from marginal cost pricing will be more than sufficient to meet the total costs.

10. The view that the user should pay for all the costs of the roads is strongly entrenched among many practicing transport economists, and the man-on-the-street accepts this rule as a form of rough justice. In Chapter IV therefore we examine the case for covering the costs in more detail. As far as the economic analysis will take us, we find that there are no grounds for requiring a particular road, a class of roads, or the highway system as a whole to cover its costs by user charges. Of course, it is necessary to examine the usual grounds on which it is alleged that the roads should cover their costs; probably the main arguments are that the location of industry would not be efficient if users were only charged marginal cost for use of the road, that since the railways are required to cover the total costs of rail transport the roads should also cover theirs, and that there is a strong tendency for price significantly to exceed marginal cost in other industries—particularly the railways. We show that the efficient location of industry requires only that the charge levied for the use of the road be equal to the marginal cost; no covering the cost is implied. We also examine the best policy for roads if railways pursue a cost-covering policy; we conclude that there are no grounds for believing that it would then be efficient for the roads to attempt to cover their costs. Similarly, the fact that price exceeds marginal cost for certain other industries in the economy (including again the railways) does not imply that the roads should attempt to cover their costs. Both these latter cases involve some deviation from marginal cost pricing—but the amount and even the direction of the deviation are in doubt.

11. It is important, we believe, that all budgetary rules of whatever kind, including the cover-the-costs variety, should be examined in terms of their effects, and not in terms of the alleged inherent "propriety" or moral principle of the rule itself. Covering the costs of the highways by means of traditional user charges (such as tolls or gasoline taxes) would generally give rise to inefficiency and waste of resources—so, economically, it is a bad rule. Nevertheless, there are good political and institutional reasons for requiring the road users to cover their costs; it helps prevent logrolling over-investment on the one hand, and neglect of the highways on the other. These institutional and political questions are important and need

4

further study in particular environments. But again, to a large extent this institutional and political requirement of a balanced budget does not interfere with the marginal cost pricing rule. For the *use* of the highway each user should be charged the marginal cost. Then if further revenue is required to cover the costs, we ask simply which would be the best way to raise such finance; and if it were decided that, for political or institutional or even economic reasons, the tax would do least harm if raised from the road user, the problem is to create or increase taxes that interfere least with the normal cost-minimizing decisions taken by the truck owner or motorist.

12. One of the main difficulties in discussing the economics of roads is that there is no readily available simple model of the road and the development that it stimulates which can serve as a standard tool for examining the various types of taxes used or proposed. The main purpose of Chapter V is to make a first attempt at such a model and to examine the efficacy of the proposed tax systems. The model is, as it should be, simple and abstract—but we hope to have captured the essential elements of roads and development within the formal geometry, so that the results of the model will be of some use for policy. The main conclusion that we draw is that the best tax is the tax on the increment of rent generated by the road. The tax on the incremental rent would not discourage any land from being cultivated and would impinge equitably upon the beneficiaries of the road construction. On the other hand, the typical user charges—such as ton-mile levies—would reduce considerably the exploitation of natural resources, and are also inequitable in the sense that they allow some people to escape with large gains from road construction and improvement. Contrary to popular belief, road users should not be taxed according to the amount of use they make of the road—for the benefits of a road are not distributed according to the ton-mileage of transport. Indeed it will be shown that, for the purpose of financing the highways, an export tax combined with a market tax is much superior to the conventional ton-mile or vehicle-mile taxes.

13. Chapter V completes the discussion of the theory of road user charges. Admittedly, there remain some unsolved theoretical problems. But the theory as it stands is clear enough and the hypotheses are sufficiently precise to enable one to approach the facts and statistics in order to measure the parameters and check the predictions. The theory of road user charges provides a method of classification that we use in organizing the facts; this is the main purpose of Chapter VI. It must be admitted immediately that in this study we have made only a very cursory survey of the facts.

This is largely due to the fact that nearly all statistics are collected for accounting and administrative purposes; thus they are designed to fit into the financial categories of budget officers, and fit badly or not at all into the classification system suggested by the theory of road user charges. Nevertheless, there are bits and pieces of information and a few statistics that can be used to measure some of the critical parameters of our theory.

14. The linch-pin of the theory is the marginal (social) cost—which we have called the economic user charge, or sometimes, for short, EUC. The statistical evidence confirms the conjecture that for most interurban and rural paved highways the marginal cost of a vehicle journey (the EUC) is virtually zero. But for congested areas the marginal cost is considerable—and perhaps much higher than the existing user charges. Furthermore, the statistics—which appear relatively reliable—confirm the picture of road construction and operating costs sketched in the theoretical discussion of Chapter III. It is indeed consistent and efficient to build and improve rural and interurban highways that are not congested; it is also efficient to construct urban streets that nevertheless are congested—in the sense that vehicles get in one another's way.

15. Broadly speaking, the statistical evidence does not discredit the technological and supply conditions which were suggested by the theory. On the other hand, we could produce virtually no statistics to test the hypotheses about the elasticity of demand for road transport and about the development of cultivation and industry when a new road is constructed. These hypotheses remain as untested assertions, so that relatively little faith should be vested in them.

16. Nevertheless, there is a sufficient basis of factual evidence to support the main tenets of the theory, and so one may proceed to draw up some practical implications for policy. This is the main task of the last chapters of this study; we need to examine what the theory would look like in application. Like any other principle of economics, however, the theory of user charges does not give us a straightjacket to impose on the world. It *is* not and *should* not be interpreted as a rigid orthodoxy; the theory provides only a set of guideposts and very general policy proposals. The detailed application is a task of subtlety and discretion, of nice judgments— both moral and factual—and, above all, of ingeniously fitting suitable proposals into a set of institutional arrangements which are feasible in a developing country.

17. The appropriate instruments for implementing the best system of user charges can only be determined by investigating the institutions and

constraints in each country separately. However, it seemed worthwhile to set out the general characteristics of various taxes, some general orders of magnitude of incidence, and some of the problems ubiquitous in more or less all countries. This is the purpose of Chapter VII. The economic user charges may be at least partly introduced by a rearrangement of existing and tested instruments of user charges—such as the fuel tax, tire levies, purchase taxes on vehicles, and many of the forms of license duties. But it may well be a good idea in some cases to introduce a restricted license for the use of roads in congested areas of large conurbations. Such a system of charging is virtually unknown in practice, and so, much more research is needed. It seems, however, at least a starter.

18. The administrative feasibility of particular types of user charges is only one criterion for their introduction. Another important condition is that on the micro-level they stimulate efficient decisions in all areas of activity. For example, the gasoline tax should not induce the user to employ too small a vehicle, and it should encourage efficient distribution of fuel. All taxes must be examined in terms of their side effects.

19. The final problems examined in this study are those concerned with the institutional and administrative control of road expenditure and user taxes, and their re-distributional and macroeconomic effects—this is the burden of Chapter VIII. The oldest method of budgetary control is through the process of earmarking and through various more or less sophisticated versions of the "road fund." A preliminary survey of the effects of earmarking and road-fund finance suggests that there are no marked disadvantages to this form of control; but that it is difficult to ensure the integrity of the earmarking rule or the road fund. It is possible to devise earmarking procedures that provide the right kind of oscillation in expenditure on roads—so that there is a built-in stabilizer. This will be the case, for example, if the level of road expenditure is fixed by the earmarked finance from an export levy. The basic presumption behind an earmarking or road-fund rule is that such an arrangement will result in a better allocation of funds for road investment and a more suitable user tax system than the alternative of leaving road investment and user charges to be decided annually by the political processes.

20. The political aspects of the suggested system of user charges have implications far beyond the confines of this study. One question is however so important that we give it at least a preliminary examination: who gains and who loses if there is a change-over from the existing system of user charges to that advocated in this study? The only general conclusion we

can draw is that there would be no obvious class of persons who would be unambiguously the losers. Benefits and costs would be distributed widely throughout the whole population. But this does not mean that such proposals would be readily accepted!

21. The main weakness of this study is that we have not carried out an analysis of a country where the efficient systems of user charges suggested here have been employed. There is no case study to which we can refer to show the advantages and disadvantages of the suggested scheme. This is not surprising; persuasion must precede policy. But this does mean that all the evidence on the efficacy of the instruments and their effects is fragmentary and partial. There is no coherently organized system of efficient user charges to which we may refer; we cannot judge the ultimate efficiency of the proposed principles of user charges as they are operating in practice. The policies we propose are new but, one hopes, no longer a step in the dark. The purpose of this study is to shed some light, however pale and diffuse, on the path ahead. The reader himself will judge whether the outlook is any brighter.

II

PRICES, AND ROADS AS PUBLIC GOODS

1. *Costs and Decisions*

1. Cost is the economic bedrock of the user charge. The price for the use of the road should measure the value of the resources expended in providing that service. With a user charge reflecting the cost, the road user can decide whether his interests are best served by "buying" the road journey or by purchasing some other commodity; and the resources will be devoted to the use that most satisfies him. When prices reflect costs, resources will be efficiently distributed between road journeys and other things, and between one sort of road and another, and between one agency and another. This, stripped of the qualifications, is the essence of the case for *economic user charges*.

2. The definition and measurement of the appropriate concept of cost is crucial to this study. Any particular concept of cost is uniquely related to a particular and well-defined decision. The amount of use made of the roads is determined by individuals deciding whether or not to make a journey. Each person takes into account the consequences of making a journey (or perhaps another journey). The cost of a vehicle journey is measured in terms of the resources (i.e. the goods and services) foregone in order to undertake that journey.

3. The individual who undertakes the journey incurs for himself many of the elements of cost; he pays for the fuel consumed, for the wear and tear

9

on his motor vehicle, and for the wages of the driver. These expenses appear in his accounts and he is legally obliged to meet them. They constitute the private cost of the journey.

4. Such a list of private expenses does not comprise, however, the total costs of making the journey. The vehicle will do some damage to the surface of the highway and the responsibility for repairing the damage so occasioned is that of the governmental road authority. The cost of repairing the damage—which we call the *variable maintenance cost*—measures some of the resources used up in making the journey; but this cost appears in the account of the road authority and, assuming no user taxes, does not appear on the books of the motorist. To distinguish it from the private costs borne by the motorist it will be called a part of the social cost of the vehicle journey.

5. When traffic is so light, in relation to the capacity of the highway, that vehicles in no way impede one another's speed and progress, we say there is no *congestion*. In such a case the sum of the private costs and the social costs (of repairing the damage done to the surface) represent in full the costs of the vehicle journey.[1]

6. It is important to notice that this cost does not include the costs of providing the highway; nor does it include those costs of maintenance which are unrelated to the vehicle journey (the *invariate maintenance cost* is the term used to describe them). The resources invested in the highway were committed in the past; they were sunk and the costs are bygones. No fraction of these resources can be saved if the motorist forbears to take his journey; consequently, they are not part of the journey costs. There is no point in discussing the various techniques and methods by which accountants and transport economists "allocate" the historical or replacement costs of the road among the motorists who use it; all methods are arbitrary and all are irrelevant to the problem of defining the cost of a vehicle journey.

7. Superficially there seems to be a better reason for regarding some fraction of the invariate maintenance expenditure as part of the cost of the vehicle journey. Such expenditure is not part of the sunk cost; it can be avoided at any time simply by ceasing to maintain the road. But again

---

[1] Many people would want to include other elements of social costs in this calculation—such as the value of the annoyance caused by noisy motors, the value of lives and injuries in motor accidents (over and above the valuation in the insurance premium), the costs of pedestrians being further impeded, etc. Although there is no objection to including these costs, if they can be measured, it is necessary also to add a list of social benefits which do not accrue to the motorist himself.

we ask the elementary question; is there any variation in this expenditure as one uses the road for an additional vehicle journey? By definition, all maintenance costs that vary with the number of road journeys have been excluded from the invariate maintenance expenditure. Consequently, these expenses are not part of the costs of the vehicle journey.[2]

8. Up to this point we have supposed that traffic was so light that no vehicle impeded any other; each could choose whatever speed he liked. This assumption is approximately correct for most rural, farm-to-market, and interurban highways. But it is clearly incorrect for urban streets, for most of suburbia, and for some interurban highways. Vehicles do get in one another's way. There is much congestion.

9. Under congested conditions an additional vehicle journey will add to the congestion. The vehicle will get in the way of other vehicles using the road and will cause their costs to increase as they waste more time in traffic jams and incur higher maintenance costs per mile in the dense traffic. Thus the decision by a vehicle owner to use a congested highway involves all other users in increased operating costs. They are not the accepted responsibility of any particular motorist who decides to use his vehicle on the congested road; they do not appear in his accounts. But these "congestion costs" are clearly attributable to the vehicle journey; if the vehicle journey had not taken place they would not have been incurred.

10. To sum up, therefore, the costs of a vehicle journey consist of:

Private cost (a) operating cost—borne by the motorist himself

Social cost
(b) variable maintenance cost—borne by the public road authority

(c) congestion cost—borne by all other users of the road

The central problem in formulating a policy for user charges is to deal with (b) and particularly (c). Henceforward (a) will be generally disregarded: it is self-financing.

11. Since the sum of these three elements comprises the resources (i.e. the goods and services) foregone because of the vehicle journey, it is clear that all three costs should be reflected in the user's accounts. If these costs are not properly exacted from the motorist, he will be induced to undertake too

---

[2] There is one odd case where all maintenance expenses are part of the costs of the vehicle journey; this is the case where there is only *one* journey undertaken. Then the road is kept open only for that journey.

many journeys, to add unduly to the congestion. While it may be efficient to have *some* congestion on the highway, the fact that the motorist is not required to pay for the congestion he causes will induce too many motorists to use the road and there will be too much congestion. These conditions are probably typical of large conurbations throughout the world. Rarely do user charges reflect adequately the congestion cost in large cities— traffic jams and snail-like speeds are the consequence. These are the wastes of user charges that are too low.

12.   If, on the other hand, user charges exceed the sum of the variable maintenance cost and the congestion cost, then the vehicle owner will be dissuaded from undertaking certain vehicle journeys although the true cost is less than the returns. Taking into account the user charge, he may find that the sum of the operating cost and user charge exceeds the returns he expects from the trip. The journey is actually worthwhile but the unduly high tax prevents him from making it. Consequently, potentially valuable services of the road are wasted. Such conditions are probably typical of most interurban roads and rural highways. The waste is less obvious than in the case of the congested cities—but it is there and just as pervasive. In particular, examples are available of the under-utilization of toll roads.

13.   There are therefore good reasons for arranging user charges (or motor taxes) so that they reflect the two elements of the cost of a vehicle journey—the social costs—that are not reflected in the accounts of the road user. The user charge should be the sum of the variable maintenance cost (per vehicle-mile) and the congestion cost (per vehicle-mile). Then the private cost of the vehicle owner—including the user charge per vehicle-mile—will reflect all the consequences of his decision to use the road.

14.   The importance of linking costs to the decision about road use can be illustrated by considering what is probably the most common mistake in the cost approach: as the additional vehicle journey causes the road authority to undertake new investment in the highway, the costs of the new investment are often thought to be part of the costs of the vehicle journey. The fatal fallacy in this chain of reasoning is the allegation that the vehicle journey "causes" an increase in road investment. It does not. The government decides on the level and distribution of road investment. Even though traffic has increased, it might decide to spend the same amount as before, it might decide to invest more, or it might even reduce investment in roads. All these decisions may be perfectly rational. There is nothing automatic about an increase in traffic and the road investment

12

decisions of the government.[3] An additional vehicle journey does not ear-mark a certain amount of investment money and convert it into road space. Decisions about expanding and improving the road are quite differ-ent from decisions about whether or not to use the existing highway, and can be made quite independently. To confound them merely spreads confusion.

15. What is worse, the wrong analysis leads to uneconomic user charges and uneconomic use of the available road space. If user charges are fixed according to the measure of the investment cost erroneously deemed to be "caused" by an additional vehicle, one can easily see that the charges will be too high on the uncongested interurban and rural highways, and will probably be too low on the urban streets. Consequently, the urban high-ways will be over-congested and the rural and interurban roads will be under-utilized. These wasteful effects of such definitions of costs, and of the derived system of user charges, are the really telling indictment against them. User charges are based on "cost," but the "cost" concepts are wrong; they do not pertain to the decision of the motorist whether or not he will use his motor vehicle for a journey along the road. The relevant costs are those that are incurred due to his particular use of the road.

2. The Functions of Prices

16. Prices that reflect costs perform the task of rationing scarce resources. They encourage a purchase if the benefits exceed those of alternatives and they provide incentives for resources to move to those uses which people value most highly. The efficiency of the price mechanism, however, de-pends on certain conditions being met. The first is that there be no monop-oly or monopsony power. The competitive producer takes the price as given and produces the commodity if the price just exceeds the value of the resources used up. The monopolist entrepreneur, however, will take into account the fact that the price *falls* when he expands output—the additional benefit he receives is then smaller than the price. The second condition is that all the consequences of a person's decision be his legal responsibility and be reflected in his accounts. If, for example, I conduct a business that emits much soot and smoke so that there are unusually large laundry costs in the vicinity of my factory, the responsibility for those excess costs is clearly mine. But they do not appear directly in my ac-counts. These costs are the legal responsibility of the population near my factory and are borne by them. I will therefore not consider these costs

---

[3] It may well be argued, however, that there *should* be such a relationship. This is the sub-ject of the discussion in Chapters IV and VIII.

13

when I decide on my output or my plans for smoke reduction.[4] These costs are "external" to my activity. They may be called the *social costs* of my production. It is, of course, true that many external effects are not costs but benefits—these are the social benefits of carrying out an activity.[5]

17. The price system should properly reflect all the consequences of our decisions. There are, however, important limitations to this general rule—and some of these qualifications apply with particular force in road transport. In many cases the administrative cost of using the price mechanism may be too great. There are real costs of introducing a price system—and we should never assume (as is often done in much economic theory) that they are zero. It may, for example, be more efficient to have free parking spaces and let people pay the costs of queueing for parking lots rather than incur the higher costs of administration and enforcement of a price for parking.[6]

18. The alternative to using the price system is a set of administrative exclusions. People are excluded from a road not because they are unwilling to pay the price but because they fall into a category of excluded persons (or firms or commodities or nationalities, etc.). Many administrative regulations apply to all and do not much discriminate between persons and trades. For example, any driver (other than that of a fire engine or ambulance) is precluded from driving on the left-hand side when the national rule is to drive on the right. This obviously is not a form of rationing by administrative fiat. But if the truck is permitted to carry only certain goods, in certain areas, for specified customers, etc., then there is rationing by administrative regulation. The exclusions are legal (or, in the case of much administrative regulation, extra-legal) rather than economic.

19. All countries practice non-price rationing to some degree. And the method of administrative rationing cannot logically be shown to be inferior to the use of the price system. In principle it is obvious that a pure admin-

---

[4] It will be observed that the burden of the laundering costs will be passed on to the property owners in the vicinity—since the rents of houses in the area will be lower to reflect the laundry costs. It seems that it may pay the landlords to get together and pay me to introduce smoke control devices—and for me to accept such an arrangement. But this does presuppose that it is easy for landlords to come together and express their preferences. The costs of forming a landlord society may be larger than the gains.

[5] An example of this is when a firm trains men in certain skills. It incurs the cost of training them but it does not reap the whole of the benefit since the man might leave the firm's employment. Ignoring the possibility of severance pay, the new employer and employee get the benefit.

[6] In *Road Pricing: The Economic and Technical Possibilities*, (HMSO, London, 1964), hereafter referred to as the Smeed Report, the real costs of introducing various road pricing systems are examined in some detail.

14

istrative system, where the administrators have perfect knowledge, zero self-interest and a detached attitude, could correct for the inefficiencies of the price system. In practice, however, no one is perfect. The choice between more or less reliance on the price system must be made by a survey of the practical *results* of different systems. Only the facts can decide the issue.[7]

20. The price system and its (uglier) twin sister, administrative exclusion, should be used only to ration commodities or services that are scarce. If we charge a price for something that is not scarce (for example, air) then we exclude people from enjoying it and no one gains as a consequence of their frugality. It is clearly important to decide on precisely what is and what is not scarce. Air depollution machines, for example, are scarce commodities. But clean air to the individual is not a scarce good. If I consume clean air in great volumes and do not emit polluted air, it makes no difference at all to anyone else. To the individual there is no scarcity and the price should be zero. This defines clean air as a pure public good.[8] Society as a whole determines the degree of cleanliness it wants in the air and invests accordingly. But each of us as individuals gets the same quality of air and, due to the technology of air supply, we cannot contract with the public authority to buy a different quality.

21. It is difficult to decide how much should be spent on such investments as anti-pollution machinery and who should bear their cost. Each person would have an incentive to push the costs onto someone else and become a "free-rider." For in large communities the individual can ignore the strategic effects of his behavior on the others, and in small communities he will conceal his true preferences.[9] This is essentially the "investment dilemma" of pure public goods. There is no price which can be used to indicate whether more or less investment is desirable.[10] Other criteria are needed.

3. *Roads as Pure Public Goods*

22. What is the relevance of the "public goods" issue for road user charges? A "pure public good" means that my enjoyment of the good or

---

[7] For a survey of the evidence see A. A. Walters, "Economic Development and the Administration and Regulation of Transport," *The Journal of Development Studies*, (London, October 1967). The suggestion there is that the price system should be the main allocative mechanism.

[8] Of course, there is a certain scarcity of towns with clean air.

[9] Paul A. Samuelson, "The Pure Theory of Public Expenditure," *Review of Economics and Statistics*, Vol. XXXVI, (Cambridge, Massachusetts, November 1954), p. 388.

[10] With the pure air case it is indeed difficult to see how one *could* conceivably charge for air consumption!

service in no way inhibits anyone else from enjoying it. A typical example of a "pure public good" is a radio service; the fact that I join the existing listeners in no way interferes with their pleasure or with anyone else's behavior (provided I do not turn it on too loud). When I tune in it adds nothing to the cost of running the radio station. In this sense then radio listening is a pure public good.

The Single User

23. But, it might be asked, suppose that you *and you alone* were beyond the range of the radio station. By increasing its wattage, and so its expenditure, the radio station could reach you. A radio station should employ resources in this way only if you are willing to pay the costs. The resources have alternative uses and it is efficient to use them to increase wattage only if you value such a service more than the alternative uses to which the resources could be put. Suppose that all the costs of increasing the wattage are plant costs; then it is efficient to pay annually for the right to listen, or commute once-and-for-all, if you prefer. Whether you do actually listen or not will not affect costs so it is clearly not efficient to charge a "listening fee" in addition.[11] In other words, if we assume the technology of radio operation is such that costs have to be incurred for the whole period, whether I listen or not, it is efficient simply to levy an annual rent for the privilege of listening and no charge for actually listening. In principle, the variations in service can be extended even further. Different wattages can be compensated by changes in the height of my antenna (with changes in my private cost); the wattage may be higher just for part of the day, etc. These infinitely small variations affect the annual rent I would pay—but they do not affect the principle that no price should be charged for actually listening.[12] The act of tuning in imposes no costs on anyone—consequently it is inefficient to use a price to discourage anyone from listening.

24. Some roads have similar "public good" characteristics, but the case is now more complicated. If there is a road system on which my car does not in any way interfere with anyone else's car (or pedestrian or cyclist, etc.), and if it doesn't damage the road surface, then we can all independ-

---

[11] Note that if the costs of the higher wattage were solely power costs (at a constant price per unit) and that if it were possible to switch the higher wattage in and out at will, the efficient solution would be to link my receiver to the power switch at the radio station—by some suitably cheap device.

[12] Note also that different rents might be paid for different program mixes. The actual choice of programs is in principle determined by the rents which people would be willing to pay for the right to listen.

ently enjoy the services of the road.[13] Roads are then a pure public good. If my car gets in someone's way, however, my enjoyment of the road reduces someone else's enjoyment. The services of the road are then *not* a pure public good; they exhibit some degree of congestion. In practice, it seems that many rural and interurban roads do in fact approximate to being pure public goods; congestion is so infrequent and small that it can be ignored. For these roads, therefore, no price should be charged *for their use*. Any price exacted would discourage someone from enjoying road services and so it would amount to throwing these valuable services away.

25.   Consider now the analogy with the "new subscriber"—like the single new listener who *alone* was brought into range by the increase in wattage. For roads one would naturally examine the case of the owner-occupier of a piece of property who wishes to have access to his property from the road system. As we assumed with the radio antenna, he and he alone will use the access road. Again the solution is similar to the radio case. The road building authority will build the road and charge him an annual rent over the life of the road; or, alternatively, a capital sum in commutation of future rent charges. It would not be efficient for the authority to charge the owner of the property a fee according to the number of times he actually uses the road. The *use* of the road is a pure public good. It should be free. *The provision of the road* however involves alternatives foregone. If the owner is not prepared to pay for construction of the road then he must judge that the services of the road to him, when supplied at zero price, are worth less than the annual rent for the road. Then the road is not worth building.

26.   The examples of the additional single radio listener and of the single user of the new road are extreme ones and of limited use. In most practical cases a number of new listeners will be brought into range, and new roads or improved roads will generate more journeys by a number of vehicle owners. Nevertheless, the example does emphasize that, even though one can invest efficiently in very small amounts at a time so that we cater for the individual listener or property owner, it is still efficient for there to be a *zero* price for tuning in or for actually *using* the road. The services of radio or road involve no one else's disservice; therefore, no price should be levied for use. Once-and-for-all charges or equivalent annual payments are however appropriate as measures of the desirability of *investment* compared with alternative uses of the resources.

---

[13] For simplicity let us neglect the wear and tear on the surface of the road caused by the passage of vehicles.

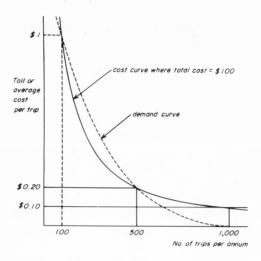

$1 ----

Toll or
average
cost
per trip

cost curve where total cost = $100

demand curve

$0.20

$0.10

100   500   1,000

No. of trips per annum

Figure 1.

27. A numerical example may help illustrate this argument. Suppose that it costs $2,000 to construct an access road of which I am the sole user. Suppose also that the equivalent annual cost of $2,000 now is $100 a year. Then if I am willing to pay for the road a sum of either $2,000 now or $100 a year, it is clearly worthwhile. Suppose, however, that an economist insists on financing this investment by a user charge rather than by an annual rent. Then we must take account of my demand for travel (i.e. actual journeys) over the road. If a price or toll is charged each time I use the road, the relationship between the toll and the number of trips I would take is shown by the *demand* curve. The locus of average costs and trips that *just* give the total annual *costs* of $100 is also shown. It is clear that a toll between 20 cents and $1.00 will produce as much, or more, revenue than the costs of providing the road. Suppose that the economist who insists on *user* charges also believes in choosing the toll that gives the larger volume of traffic *and* covers costs, then our user-charge-economist chooses a toll of 20 cents. He collects over the year $100 from me and I take about ten trips a week or five hundred a year.

28. But it is obvious that this is a wasteful solution. It would pay me to come to an agreement with the government. I will pay the rent of $100 and the government will abolish the user charge (and fire the user-charge-economist). I will now enjoy one thousand journeys a year at the same total cost. The net gain is an extra five hundred journeys—and no one else suffers. The lesson is clear: even if there are no expenses involved in levying tolls or user charges, it is inefficient to do so. The corollary is that under

18

free competitive conditions, I would find it efficient to rent the road. It does not matter if the quality of the road can be varied continuously; this merely results in a variation in the cost and in the equivalent rental charge. The user charge should still be zero.

Benefit to a Large Number of Users

29. Now consider the case where investment can only be done in lumps. The enlargement of the listening area may then extend to a large number of households. Analogously, building a road, or improving one, may benefit a large number of road users. The principles of pricing road services and listening remain the same. As long as there is no road congestion, road services are a pure public good. The price of the services should then be zero. The marginal cost of any car *using* the road is zero and it is silly to deny any motorist the pleasure of using the road by charging him any positive price. No resources would be saved thereby—the potential benefits of the journey would simply be foregone, and for no purpose at all.[14]

30. The real difference between this, the lumpy case, and the previous one where we invested for one listener or one property owner is that we have now no ready-made rule which tells us how much to invest in radio output or in road construction. The problem is now not the previous simple one of making small adjustments for each person and asking whether he would pay for the installation, but involves many people with conflicting interests.

31. The general principle of investment choice remains, of course, the same: roads should be built so as to maximize the surplus of total benefits over total costs. It is easy to define, and not too difficult to measure, costs. With benefits, however, the difficulties are great. In measuring the benefits of a "lumpy" extension of a road system there is one rough and ready rule which has stood the test of time if not the test of practice; this is the consumer surplus criterion. It measures the benefits as the maximum that people, as a group, would pay if they were subject to the most skillful blackmailer. This unsavory character would extract all the consumer surplus which is the maximum amount they would be willing to pay rather than do without the road. The consumer surplus criterion is however only a rough tool and we shall have occasion to examine the limitations on its use later in the next chapter.

---

[14] It will be observed that this conclusion is quite independent of the technical difficulties of excluding the "free riders"—by licensing or other methods. Since the price should be zero, the technical feasibility of such price schemes is quite irrelevant.

32.   It is useful briefly to examine other investment criteria which might be employed. Probably the most common procedure is to vote on whether the investment should or should not be undertaken. The simple democratic model serves as a prototype. Each participant has a vote and the issue is decided by a simple majority. Now it can be shown that if the benefits of road extension are more concentrated than the taxes or charges raised to finance them, "logrolling" will tend to result.[15] Since I benefit greatly from a particular improvement and only have to pay small taxes for improvements which greatly benefit others, I have an incentive to form coalitions and vote for extensive road investment. The result is that I have to "buy" the support of only 51 percent of the voters to get "my" project approved. I do not have to take directly into account the effect on the other 49 percent minority. This voting system will, of course, give different results from the consumer surplus criterion; and it will tend to give rise to more investment than is ideal. The voting system and majority rule are the villains of this set piece.

33.   When there are discontinuities in road investment, the costs of expansion cannot be nicely allocated to any one person. There is no general rule by which we can allocate the costs of expanding the road network. Some additional rules must be devised in order to finance the cost of the extension of the road system. For example, equity suggests that we should levy a charge in proportion to the benefits derived from the extension. But this is just one arrangement; many other methods of finance are feasible. It is of the utmost importance, however, to note that the method should avoid, as far as possible, imposing any price on the *use* of uncongested roads. As long as there is neither wear nor congestion, the services of the road should be free since they are pure social goods. If we *do* impose a price for a free good, then it must be justified by arguing that the best alternative would be inferior.[16]

34.   To illuminate the argument we might imagine an extension of the example of the road for the single individual. Now the road system is extended or improved for the use of many individuals—and still no one gets in anyone else's way; so there is no congestion and marginal cost is zero.[17]

---

[15] See James M. Buchanan and Gordon Tullock, *Calculus of Consent: Logical Foundations of Constitutional Democracy*, (University of Michigan, Ann Arbor, 1962), pp. 135–145.

[16] It might be worth having an inefficient price system if, as a trade-off, one gets considerable assistance in making investment decisions. The pricing inefficiencies might well be counterbalanced by the additional information and so greater efficiencies of investment. This choice too must be made in terms of its practical advantages.

[17] It is tempting to stop the argument at this stage by saying: surely if there is no congestion we have overextended or overimproved the road system. This is, however, for rural roads not necessarily and perhaps not usually the case, as we shall show in the next chapter.

The (reinstated) government's user-charge-economist may now proceed to levy user charges that will repay the investment costs. But this will cut down the traffic and the benefits of the road. It is obviously better for the beneficiaries *as a group* to pay the government a capital sum (or an equivalent annual sum) and for the roads to be free. Everyone will then be better off than under the user charge regime. There are many ways of levying payment of this kind—and by the same token many of these ways will be superior to the user charge system. The essential difference between this group case and the example of the individual beneficiary is that there is now a distributional problem of levying the annual charges.

35. To summarize, then, it seems clear that a *prima facie* case exists for treating road *services* of uncongested wear-free highways as pure public goods. As a consequence the price of the road service in such cases should be zero. And this involves us in difficult problems of finding the optimum investment in roads and in allocating the financial burden of road building. The investment criteria, though difficult to apply, are not arbitrary—there are clear, but complicated, rules, which will be discussed later (see Chapter III, paras. 73–85). The allocation of the financial burden, however, *is* arbitrary. We can develop general "guidelines" from concepts of equity—"he who benefits should pay"—but there are no neat rules available.

36. The important question remains, however, whether one may properly regard many roads as "public goods." What are the characteristics of roads that make them "public goods"? Before we can answer this question it is necessary to set out a standard model of a road. We need to define the cost concepts, the "capacity" of a road, and the speed-cost-density-flow relationships. This standard model is presented in the next chapter.

III

COSTS, PRICING, AND INVESTMENT

1. *A Standard Road Model: Costs, Capacity, Congestion*

1.   We make one fundamental assumption about the ownership and operation of the vehicles and road which we shall retain throughout the whole of this study. The road is owned by one authority—and we shall normally suppose that it is a governmental authority—while the vehicles are owned and operated by a large number of independent agents. The crucial assumption is that the owner of the road does not at the same time own and operate the vehicles that use the road; the second implication is that there is no monopoly in the use of the road. This is the essential difference between the public roads and the railways.

2.   The costs of road transport may be divided into two parts. First there are those costs for which the road authority is responsible. The time-honored name for these expenditures is *track costs*, although sometimes they are called *highway costs* or *road costs*. They are legally the responsibility of the highway authority and are not part of the accounting cost of users. Secondly, there are the costs incurred by users of the highway, which we might refer to as *vehicle costs* or more generally *user costs*. These are the responsibility of the motorist.

3.   The *track costs* to the highway authority may be classified into:

Fixed costs of constructing the track.

These include any long-term contractual (capital) commitments—such as the purchase of land, the laying down of the track, etc. Once committed they are inescapable except in the very long run. The degree of commitment varies enormously in roads—from two or three years for a jungle track to thirty or even fifty years for modern motor highways.

Maintenance costs that vary with the amount of traffic.

These include the current expenses in making good the wear and tear to the surface of the highway that is caused by the passage of vehicles. We should also include here those policing costs that vary with the level of traffic—over wide ranges they seem to be roughly proportional to the volume of traffic.

Maintenance costs that do not vary with the amount of traffic.

This category includes the vast majority of maintenance expenses since, according to engineering opinion, most of the damage to a paved highway is caused by weather and time, and not by use.

The distinction between the two types of maintenance costs is fundamental for all analytical purposes, but is unfortunately not made in the accounts of road authorities. To distinguish between the two types of maintenance costs we shall call the first the *variable maintenance cost* and the second the *invariate maintenance cost*. Both of them are however variable in the sense that the road authority, assuming it does not have long-term maintenance contracts with a private firm, can simply stop spending at any time.

4. The *user costs* are those classified (a) and (c) in Chapter II, para. 10 when we were discussing the costs of a vehicle journey.

Operating costs. As the motorist travels he incurs operating costs in terms of fuel used, tires worn, vehicle depreciated, repair bills increased, etc. Time also is a cost. If a driver is employed the wage costs increase according to the time spent on the road.

5. When there are very few vehicles on the road they will not get in one another's way. Each vehicle may choose the particular speed that minimizes costs. But as the number of vehicle journeys increases, they interfere with one another. Each vehicle has to adjust its speed according to other traffic on the road. The costs incurred by a vehicle rise above the level which he enjoyed on the empty road. Thus the operating costs of vehicles rise as the volume of traffic increases.

6. *Social costs.* The addition of another vehicle journey will incur for me, the owner, the additional operating costs of my own vehicle—for which I

am legally responsible. But by running my vehicle on another journey I add to the congestion on the road, so that all other vehicle operators using the road suffer an increase in their costs. These consequences of my decision to take a trip do not appear in my accounts; they are dispersed through the accounts of all other vehicle owners. The true costs of my vehicle journey should include the costs of all resources used up as a consequence of my decision. The true costs include my operating costs and, in addition, the social costs which I impose on others.

7. We can set out the typical form of the various cost relationships diagrammatically. Let us imagine a road of given dimensions and other characteristics and let us suppose that all vehicles and drivers are homogeneous—so that all vehicle journeys cost the same for any given level of traffic. The cost curves are more usefully described in terms of *unit* cost rather than total cost, so that one may illuminate the marginal relationships involved. The variable maintenance costs of the road are constant for each vehicle; each car does as much damage to the surface of the road whether it is in a dense or sparse traffic stream. This is shown by the broken line AB and the variable maintenance costs per vehicle journey are OA. To these maintenance costs we add the operating costs of a vehicle journey—these are shown as AH for volumes of traffic up to q_o. After q_o however, operating costs increase as vehicles get in one another's way. Speed declines, costs increase, but the flow of vehicles continues to increase. But as the density of vehicles on the road increases, speed is reduced so much, that the *flow* of vehicle journeys reaches a maximum—shown as

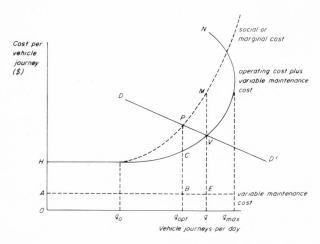

Figure 2.   Costs of a Vehicle Journey in a Homogeneous Traffic Flow.

24

q_{max} in Figure 2. If the density of vehicles on the road is increased further, the reduction in speed will be so large that the flow will be reduced.[1] Thus there is a maximum *flow* q_{max} that is physically possible on this road. The operating cost curve then "bends backwards" as the density of vehicles increases, and one gradually approaches conditions of a complete traffic jam.[2] The curve describing the path of operating costs *plus* variable maintenance costs is shown by *HCN* in the figure. Fixed costs and maintenance costs which do not vary with traffic—the invariate maintenance costs—do not appear in this figure.

8. We are assuming that the fixed costs have been sunk and that the road authority has decided to maintain the road; then the question is—what price should be charged for road services and what quantity of traffic should be carried? If the authority levied charges of *OA* per vehicle journey, and if the demand for vehicle journeys were represented by the line *DD'*, the quantity of traffic on the road would be q and its price V. But with this quantity of traffic there is congestion on the road, and the true costs of an additional vehicle journey must include the extra costs of congestion which it imposes on others. These costs are shown by the broken curve *HPM*, and this is simply the curve which is *marginal* to the curve *HCVN*.[3] At a level of traffic q the true cost is M whereas the "private" cost (including the *OA* paid to the public authority) is V.

9. The charge levied per vehicle journey by the public road authority should obviously include the costs *OA* it incurs in respect of maintenance for each journey. But there is still a difference of *MV* between the operating cost *VE* that is reflected in the account of the motorist and the true cost *ME*. To make the marginal valuation of a vehicle journey equal to its true cost we must raise a congestion levy equal to the difference between the true cost and the private cost of a vehicle journey. Thus when the authority imposes a levy per vehicle journey of *PC* (as well as extracting *OA* per vehicle journey in maintenance cost), the volume of traffic will fall

---

[1] Note that: flow = speed × density and that speed is an inverse function of density. When traffic is very dense, a small proportionate increase in density will give rise to a larger proportionate decline in speed—so the flow goes down.

[2] Although derived from the theory of fluid dynamics, there is much evidence to show that actual speed (cost) density and flow relationships are of this form. See: A. A. Walters, "The Theory and Measurement of Private and Social Costs of Highway Congestion," *Econometrica*, Vol. 29, (Amsterdam, 1961). A more readable account will be found in Christopher D. Foster, *The Transport Problem*, (Blackie, London, 1963).

[3] It can be proved that:
Marginal cost (or social cost) = private cost × (1 + elasticity of cost curve)
See Walters, "The Theory and Measurement of Private and Social Costs of Highway Congestion," *Econometrica*, Vol. 29.

to q_{opt} and the price P which users pay for the journey will be equal to the additional true cost of another journey, i.e. the sum of variable maintenance costs, private vehicle operating costs, and congestion costs.

10.   The amount of revenue raised by the congestion levy may be thought to be a contribution from which we may cover the *invariate* maintenance costs and the fixed costs of the highway. There is no inherent reason why the tax should just cover these costs; it may be a good idea to earn a profit or to run at a loss. These questions will be examined later (paras. 86–93).

11.   It is worthwhile observing that there is no useful concept of capacity which is independent of the demand curve. The natural concept of capacity, the maximum flow of vehicle journeys, q_{max}, is clearly not a suitable concept for most purposes. If the number of vehicle journeys does rise to this level there is clearly inefficiency—since the marginal true cost of an additional vehicle journey is infinite! Only in the case when congestion is zero and then suddenly jumps up to a very high level, would it be efficient to operate with a road very close to maximum capacity.

12.   There are as many definitions of the concept of capacity as there are demand curves. To develop a useful definition one might suggest that for any given demand curve there is an optimal road which would be constructed according to the efficiency criteria mentioned in Chapter I and to be discussed at length later in this chapter. For each combination of demand and optimal road we might define the optimum level of traffic on the road as its *design capacity*. If there were no discontinuities in road construction and no joint-product aspects, this definition would be most useful. It would tell us the size of road that minimizes cost for that particular flow of traffic. Unfortunately in the real world of discontinuities and joint-products the design capacity is meaningless. A given size of road may serve as efficient for a wide range of traffic flows. It is natural then to define the *maximum* efficient traffic flow for a road as its *feasible capacity*. This term seems to be a useful one for practical purposes. When we refer simply to the "capacity" of the road we shall in fact mean the feasible capacity. Unfortunately this quantity still depends on the shape and shifts of demand curves over time. In principle one ought to specify the whole set of demand curves for different times of the day, different years, etc.; in practice we shall take this as given—as a *ceteris paribus* of the discussion.

Some Simplifying Assumptions

13.   There are many other problems to complicate this description of the cost conditions. We have yet to deal with diurnal, seasonal and annual

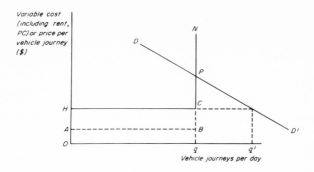

Figure 3.

variation in traffic flow, with the problems of uncertainties, probabilities and likelihoods, and with the various consequences of the changes in price. These will be discussed at the end of this chapter. For a start there are too many complications in the picture, in which one might get bogged down. We propose a basic simplification. Operating and variable maintenance costs are assumed to be constant up to a certain traffic level; then these costs increase very sharply indeed. In other words we approximate the smooth curve $HCVN$ of Figure 2 by the right-angled cost curve, such as HCN in Figure 3.

14. This simplification will enable us to sharpen the discussion of the principles of road pricing without ignoring essential elements of the problem. We can talk about *the* capacity of the road and *the* operating *plus* variable maintenance cost, without having to trouble about the level of traffic and demand conditions. These artifices are useful only for discussion of principles; to employ them in any practical case where measurement and application are required would be to court serious error.[4]

15. With the demand curve DD' as shown in Figure 3, the solution which the authorities must attempt to achieve is described by the point P. If the authorities charged only OA, the variable maintenance cost for each vehicle journey, and each vehicle incurred operating costs of AH, the demand would exceed the capacity of the highway—people would attempt to make q' journeys. The road would get jammed with traffic and each motorist would pay an enormous amount in congestion costs. If, however, the authority levied a congestion charge of PC (plus the variable cost of Bq) for a vehicle journey, the quantity of traffic would just be equal to the capacity of the road at q.

---

[4] These assumptions were used by a group of experts in the study *Options in Transport Tariff Policy* for the European Economic Community in 1965. It seems that the authors *did* think that this linear model was a good approximation to real situations, however.

27

16. In this simplified model the congestion levy PC plays the same role in limiting the use of the road as the *rent* or *surplus* earned by a scarce facility. It is often convenient to think of the congestion levy as a *non-cost* outlay by the motorist. But a look at the general model of Figure 2 shows that this is not the case. Although the congestion levy is a transfer income to the government, it does in fact measure the *real costs* of an additional journey along the road. It measures part of the marginal real costs of congestion—in terms of fuel consumed, tires worn, time expended in jams and so on.[5] This is an important difference between the general model of Figure 2 and the simplified model of Figure 3. But fortunately the difference is not crucial for any of the purposes for which we use the simplified model in the remainder of this chapter.

17. There is one other assumption that is almost universally made in economic analysis—and very often in economic policy—and needs emphasis in this study. We normally suppose that the price can be changed quickly whereas it takes a long time to make changes in investment. Indeed in the ordinary model of market behavior one supposes that price can be changed immediately, and there is quite a lot of evidence to show that this proposition is near enough for most practical purposes in private markets. But the roads are not a private market. Changes in motor taxes are often brought about by a budgetary process. There is no automatic mechanism by which price is nicely adjusted to prevailing and expected conditions. Indeed changes in the *structure* of prices, and sometimes even simple changes in the level, can be achieved only by lengthy processes of political bargaining. Whatever results emerge from such maneuverings certainly are not produced quickly.[6]

18. Thus it seems that the price may take a long time to adjust to the new situation—so long, in fact, that the period of adjustment for price may be longer than that for investment. The administrative constraints on price movements may be so severe that, for very long periods of time, we must regard the price as a constant. Indeed it may be quicker to adjust the size of the road through investment than to change the user charge. Then the roles of price and investment are reversed; the stock of roads is adjusted to the administratively (or politically) *sticky price*.[7]

---

[5] In the model used in *Options in Transport Policy*, the authors emphasized that this component was not a cost—"nor can it be interpreted as a cost. It is a pure scarcity price, serving to limit demand to the available capacity . . . ." p. 65 (English version).

[6] The need to court popular support has led many governments to delay for many years increases in gasoline taxes which were acknowledged to be necessary.

[7] See A. A. Walters, "The Long and the Short of Transport," *Bulletin of the Oxford University Institute of Statistics and Economics*, Vol. 27, No. 2, (Oxford, May 1965).

19.   Throughout all the discussion of this chapter, and through most of this study, we shall, however, assume that price *is* flexible—and, in particular, that price is more flexible than the capital stock of roads. This is not simply (or perhaps one should more modestly say solely) the aberration of theoretical economists whose concern is more with ivory towers than with the road problem. It is of great importance that the price *should* be as flexible as possible. Sticky prices should not be accepted as an inevitable part of a policy of user charges.[8] One must try to develop appropriate administrative arrangements that will give rise to flexible user charges (and it is unfortunately necessary to add, flexibility in the right direction). These have been extensively explored in recent years and new administrative techniques are rapidly being developed.

20.   In developing countries the administrative instruments are much cruder and less reliable than in developed countries. The execution of policies is likely to be erratic, and adjustments more difficult. A very rough approximation to efficient solutions is all that can be expected. Nevertheless, it is important to understand the *aims* and *objectives* of policy. This is the purpose of the analysis of this chapter. Administrative measures for approximating those aims will be discussed briefly in the chapters that follow.

2. *"Divisible" Roads and Perfect Divisibility*

21.   It is relatively easy to set out the consequences of road services being a pure public good. But the question remains, of course, are the services of roads really pure public goods? Is there anything inherent in the nature of the services of the road that makes them more likely to approach a pure public good than any other form of service? No answer can be derived from pure logic. We must study the facts to see whether the services of roads do or do not exhibit the essential characteristics of pure public goods. Only empirical evidence can decide whether it is sensible to treat the services of roads as if they were analogous to radio listening. But it is important to recall that we are here talking about the *services* of the road— which is the *raison d'être* of the construction. Roads, as pieces of equipment or plant, are not public goods; for if we increase the number of *roads* we shall have to reduce the output of something else.

22.   If a certain quantity of roads could produce uniquely and *exactly only one quantity* of road *services*, it would obviously follow that road

---

[8] It will be observed that it is economic flexibility that is so desirable. In practice the variations in user charges are the consequence of the financial requirements of the treasury.

services were not a pure public good. To increase road services we would have to build more roads, and roads cost resources; therefore, road services would not be a pure public good. But this is clearly quite inconsistent with the evidence. A large variation in the quantity of services derived from a road is clearly possible; we observe it every day. There is no unique road/road-service relationship; the road "plant" is flexible and can produce a wide variety of quantities of services.

23.   Now suppose that in the example of the access road of which I am the only user there is not just one kind of road which the government may construct—there is a whole spectrum of roads. Suppose that there is effectively an *infinite variety* of roads; some are straighter than others, some have steeper gradients, some have better surfaces, some are wider, enabling me to drive faster, etc. The particular type of road that is built will affect my private costs of operating my vehicle over this road. Thus I shall be able to judge a nice balance between the increase in construction costs and the discounted future reductions in operating costs. When these two are equal the road investment is at the right level. But we see that the variability of investment in no way amends the pricing rule. Since I do not get in anyone's way when I use my own access road, no toll should be charged for the actual *use* of the road.[9] This result arises because with one vehicle only I never get in my own way (except perhaps on very dusty roads). The road is built to reduce the costs of operation. Surfacing, for example, may well increase the feasible number of vehicles that can use the road without getting in one another's way. But since the services of the road cannot be transferred or made available elsewhere, where there is a scarcity of road space (for example, in downtown Washington), the feasible capacity of the road is irrelevant.

24.   Now consider an extension of this model of the access road. Suppose that, instead of one vehicle, I own a fleet of vehicles serving a factory at the end of the access road. Then, since a number of vehicles use the road there is a possibility that they will get in one another's way. Under these circumstances one must take into account *two* margins when planning the optimum road. First, a better quality road may give rise to reductions in operating costs even though vehicles do not get in one another's way. Secondly, a better (wider) road may reduce the delay experienced by each vehicle as it reduces the amount of congestion on the road. Thus the improvement reduces congestion costs (assuming, of course, that such congestion was present before the better road was constructed). If, on the

---

[9] We ignore for the moment the variable maintenance cost.

other hand, there were no congestion before, it does not follow that a better road should not be constructed. As we saw in the simple one-vehicle case discussed above, it may nevertheless be worthwhile investing more in the road—simply because operating costs of vehicles are reduced. Indeed, to state the perverse case, it *may* be efficient with uncongested traffic flows actually *to reduce* the feasible capacity of the road, as when an earth road is turned into a narrower paved road for example.

25.   In principle an enormous variety of combinations of feasible capacity, operating costs and capital costs may be possible. The unique importance of the *capacity margin* however arises from the fact that we may be able to adjust the road investment nicely to the quantity of traffic. It is easy to imagine a technology where the capacity variation and the operating cost variation are each *independently* achievable. Then we can purchase (or sell) *separately* an increase in capacity on the one hand which would not affect operating cost or, on the other hand, a reduction in operating cost that would not affect capacity. Symbolically we may think of this type of road as a piece of putty. It has infinite malleability. The putty can be stretched to any length and be squeezed to any width we require at any time.

Long-run and Short-run Marginal Costs with "Putty" Roads

26.   The extreme case of flexibility is when the road is like pure putty. The capacity can be increased immediately and by very small fractions at a time. The cost of the increase in capacity of one vehicle journey, on the simplest assumption of the putty model, is constant. Similarly, the cost of improving the road to reduce operating cost by a certain amount is constant. Each of the two economic dimensions of the road—the capacity and the quality of the service—can be *independently* varied in either direction.

27.   The reason for using this highly abstract and unrealistic model is to show that the real fundamental reason for the "road problem" is the fact of joint-products and discontinuities[10] in road building. If the roads were like putty, we can demonstrate that the solutions would be simple: we should levy user charges equal to the cost of extending the road system to cater for one additional vehicle journey at the current level of congestion. And in equilibrium this same user charge would be exactly equal to the optimum congestion levy plus the variable maintenance cost. If the optimum congestion levy exceeds the cost of expanding capacity to cater for

---

[10] Discontinuities, indivisibilities, or lumpiness—the three terms are used here as synonyms.

additional vehicles, then investment in the road should proceed until they are brought to equality. The construction of roads which can be built a little more, or a little less, at the margin should be judged by the price which people are willing to pay the authority for providing this capacity.

28. Let us begin with the pricing rule. This remains the same whether investment is lumpy or continuous; price should be equal to the marginal cost (including marginal rent in the simplified model) of supplying the service. And this marginal cost is the *short-run* concept; the pricing rule tells us how to make the best use of existing resources, including the existing stock of roads. It allocates the limited services of the road to those willing to pay for them.[11] If, for some reason, there is no effective limit to the number of journeys to be extracted from the road in a given period at the same quality of service and operating cost per vehicle, then the price should be zero, so that each may use the road to his heart's content.

29. But with continuous and divisible roads such a zero price and excess capacity would only occur if there had been a mistake of overbuilding on the part of the road authority, or if there had been an unexpected drop in the demand. This would be a transitory situation in which the road authority would permit part of the road to wear out without replacing it. When that transitional period is over, some congestion will exist again on the remaining road and the congestion levy will measure the marginal costs of using the smaller road. If the road authority let too much road wear out, this would be indicated by the fact that the congestion levy—the rent per vehicle journey which users are willing to pay—would exceed the cost of adding just sufficient road space to accommodate one more vehicle journey. If the congestion levy exceeds the cost of adding to the road, the authority should invest more in the roads until the two marginal quantities are equal.

30. In this happy state of continuous and divisible road investment, there is a long-run equilibrium when the road authority has expanded the road system to the point where the cost of further extending (or reducing) the road system by a small amount is just equal to the rent of the existing system. Thus the long-run marginal cost is brought to equality with the short-run marginal cost (or rent in the simplified model). This is brought about by an optimal investment policy with stable demand conditions. Under these conditions—and, at this point of our inquiry, we leave it for the reader to judge their relevance—the price charged for using the road

---

[11] There are some qualifications to be added later in this chapter to the concept of short-run marginal cost which must be interpreted carefully in each practical situation.

equals both the long- and the short-run marginal cost (rent).[12] Any deviation of demand from the expected value, and any mistakes in investment policy, will automatically render the long-run marginal cost concept irrelevant for pricing policy. The *short-run* marginal cost (rent) is *always* the appropriate guide for pricing policy, whether or not there have been mistakes in investment policy and whether or not the investment program is up to date.[13]

31. With divisible investment, the rules of investment behavior are analogous to those of private competitive industry. The road authority should take the price as given—just as the firm does in a competitive market. It should invest if the revenue obtained for the extra journey produced exceeds the investment cost. The extra journey will be valued at the going price. The road authority should not take into account the reduction in revenue due to the fact that, as the number of vehicle journeys expands, the *price* must be reduced, because there is a downward sloping demand curve. Such concern would be appropriate for a private monopolist running the roads. But the job of the road authority is to *simulate* the behavior of competitive industry. It must behave *as if* it were a perfectly competitive industry in supplying road services and in investing in roads. We simply translate the rules obtained from an analysis of competitive industry into the framework of road costs and demands.

32. With investment perfectly divisible, the only difference between supplying more or less services from a given highway and expanding or contracting the roads a little bit, is that investment takes time whereas price changes and variations in the amount of services can take place immediately.[14] Apart from this admittedly important difference, the marginal adjustments are the same: with the bit-by-bit adjustment to the roads the road authority can invest and read the price and cost signs correctly all the way to the new equilibrium. No large jumps are involved; at no time does the authority lose sight of the price and cost signals.

33. With investment taken as divisible, it might reasonably be suggested that there is no need for the roads to be produced, maintained and operated by the public authorities. Could not roads be supplied and operated by

---

[12] For a geometrical illustration, see Annex Note i at the end of this chapter.

[13] It is odd that many economists continue to argue that *long-run* marginal cost is the appropriate magnitude for pricing purposes. The experts of the European Economic Community, however, carefully formulated their pricing rules correctly; see *Options in Transport Tariff Policy*.

[14] On this point see paras. 17–19.

private entrepreneurs in competition with one another? Competitive private turnpikes could be an answer.

34. But what prevents such a radical solution is simply the minimum scale of roads compared with the narrow scale of the local market for transportation. Despite the evocations of the putty model one cannot imagine half or one-tenth lane roads which are in competition with one another. There *are* economies of scale over low traffic volumes. Roads are *natural* monopolies.[15] The state must regulate and control them—even if they are nicely divisible investments—wherever there is local monopoly of this kind.[16]

35. The only excuse for analyzing the divisible-investment case at some length is because, by contrast, it throws the road problem into sharp relief. The divisible case as such is, I believe, of little direct use. But this is not because the *assumption* of divisible "putty" is unrealistic; all assumptions trample roughshod over reality. The compelling reason is that the *predictions* of the "putty" model are contradicted by everyday experience; each of us does not "buy" his own tiny road service—nor are roads supplied by competitive private enterprise. And it is difficult to imagine a world in which this could be the situation.

36. Of course, roads are not putty. Road capital is not a malleable quantity which can be kneaded at will into just the right shape. I am not suggesting that it is *impossible* to produce a road of exactly the shape required, beginning from scratch, for each perfectly predicted pattern of traffic. It is perhaps always possible to do so; but it would almost always be the *wrong* policy. It is difficult (though again perhaps not quite impossible), to imagine that such a policy would give the best or cheapest way of providing road services.

3. *Indivisibility and Joint-Products*

37. We may at this stage list some of the reasons for treating roads as different from putty. The first is that there are *irreversibilities* and *historical antecedents*. Put simply, roads are baked clay, not putty. What we should do now depends primarily on what has been done in the past. A second reason is that there are economic *indivisibilities;* the clay is expensive to buy in very small amounts—it comes cheaper by the ton.

---

[15] If one imagines that the segments of the road are controlled and operated by independent owners, then the monopoly is even more local and invidious.

[16] It must also be recalled that we are supposing that charging a price involves no administrative cost. The cost of excluding people from using the road must be zero.

38. The third reason, however, is the most interesting because it concerns the concept of capacity, and its variation. As we have argued above, if the roads were putty there would be no need to analyze separately their quality (in the sense of reducing operating costs) and their capacity (in the sense of the maximum feasible number of vehicle journeys per day). By rerolling the putty we can have whatever combination we want, at a constant trade-off of one against the other. A diagrammatic representation of the putty model may help. For quantity of putty C_o the line K_oC_o describes the constant rate of transformation between operating costs of a given volume of traffic and capacity. The line K_1C_1 describes the trade-off for an increased quantity of putty, and since putty is putty it has the same slope. Again this trade-off is for the same given traffic volume. Professor James Buchanan has pointed out that this diagram simply uses savings in operational cost as a surrogate for "quality."

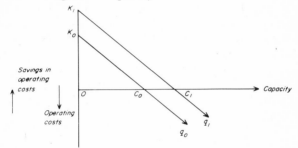

Figure 4.

39. Clearly, this putty concept is irrelevant for almost all problems involving road investment.[17] We must, in fact, review investment in roads as having at least two "dimensions"—first the *quality* of the road and secondly the *capacity* of the road.[18] There is no constant trade-off as in the putty case. For a given expenditure on a mile of road one cannot assume that there is a constant rate of exchange between reduction in operating cost and capacity. The technology of road construction and traffic suggest that the rate of exchange varies considerably and continuously. We must treat the two "dimensions" of the road as *joint-products* of the investment.

Capacity and Quality as Joint-Products

40. Both capacity expansion and quality improvement, in practical experience, are joint attributes of spending on the highways. *Some* variation

---

[17] The exceptions are, of course, at the aggregate level; it may then be sensible to treat road capital as a homogeneous putty.
[18] These dimensions are *not* physical dimensions.

between the two is possible. But as a very rough approximation it may even be sensible to treat the roads as giving a joint-product with *rigid* proportions. When we spend money on road improvements, we get then an expansion of capacity and an improvement in quality in the *same* proportions. Thus we may find that, with a given road, the response to expenditures can be represented by single points showing the savings in operating costs on the one hand and, on the other, the expansion in capacity (see Figure 4).

41. If every expenditure that results in a saving in operating costs for existing (uncongested) traffic also results in an increase in capacity, there is the problem of "allocating" the investment cost between capacity creation and operating cost reduction. With rigid proportions no such allocation can be carried out. The price or value of each of the dimensions of the road is set by the demand. If the road is uncongested an expansion of capacity will be worth nothing; such capacity cannot be sold to motorists for use elsewhere. It is specific both in time and place. It cannot be stored or transferred like electricity to a place where a demand exists. But it is possible, and indeed likely, that although there is spare capacity it is still wise to invest in roads since the reduction in operating costs may offset the capital cost. Capacity here is a by-product—a free good with a shadow price of zero. The only margin that matters is the reduction of operating costs—and this improvement in quality is the only *raison d'être* of investment.[19] To reduce the road capacity by disinvestment we should have to reduce the quality and increase the operating cost; this will be inefficient since the reduction in operating cost alone is worth the investment.[20]

42. Even an earth track between two points in the countryside cannot be laid down without offering more capacity than is needed for the traffic using it (say ten vehicles a day). Low-quality roads have relatively large capacities. As a result, quality improvements of low-volume roads become justified by savings in operating costs before traffic reaches capacity. But such quality improvements automatically increase capacity. Beyond a certain point of traffic growth however, further quality improvements be-

---

[19] Note, however, that under conditions of uncertainty with unbounded probability distributions the increase in capacity will *always* be worth something. The rule of zero price only operates if there is complete certainty.

[20] We can drop the assumption of rigid proportions by supposing that it is possible to choose different *kinds* of road investment, so that over a limited range an increase in capacity may be "bought" at the expense of lower quality. This merely means that with the uncongested roads it will be profitable to trade capacity for higher quality to the limit of this range. If then the road is still not congested the case is essentially the same as the rigid proportions case.

come increasingly expensive and difficult, and on high-volume roads, only capacity restraints are binding.

43. Let us therefore leave the putty model and let us develop a more appropriate model which portrays this joint-product pattern and attempts to reflect more closely the real-life choices which face a road authority in making road investments. Roads are each joint-products of so much capacity and specified quality. On the Y axis of Figure 5 we record the total costs of a vehicle journey—lumping together both the costs incurred by the authority and the costs of the road users. The capacity of the various roads in which the authority may choose to invest is in ascending order C_1, C_2, etc. The fixed cost of each is shown by OF_1 for road 1 and OF_2 for road 2, etc. The increase in cost as traffic expands to capacity is shown by the slope of each road cost line. The traffic flow where the cost slope becomes vertical indicates the capacity flow of the road. As traffic increases, the authority switches from road 1 to road 2 and from road 2 to road 3 because the costs are lower, not because traffic on road 1 has reached capacity.

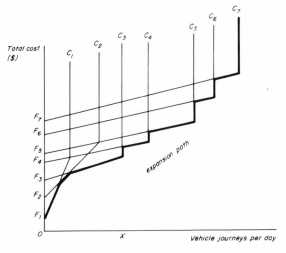

Figure 5.

44. We may imagine a series of cost curves of this kind; the expansion path will follow those parts of the curves which offer least cost for a given traffic. Along this path we do not reach the capacity of either road 1 or 2. Ultimately, however, beginning with road 3, we encounter capacity constraints. We switch from road 3 to road 4 at X because road 3 is at capacity at X, and alternative uncongested roads (such as roads 5, 6, 7 in the figure) are at much higher cost. For low volumes of traffic it will be effi-

cient to choose roads that do not involve congestion, but for volumes of traffic above a certain point it may be efficient to have roads that are congested.

45. It should be observed that these effects do not require the assumption of discontinuities as normally defined.[21] Even if we could vary the size of the road continuously, so that the expansion path was smooth, efficient low volume roads would be uncongested, and efficient high volume roads congested, provided quality/capacity and joint-product/cost relationships were those assumed in the diagram. The technical character of road costs, for instance that below a certain level of traffic (X) it is often efficient to build a road that is not congested, suggests that rural and intercity roads in developing countries, for this reason alone, will often approach "pure public goods." User charges on such roads should be approximately zero. Although perfectly efficient investments, such roads will incur a budget deficit.

46. But budget deficits may occur for other reasons. In Figure 5 above, roads for low traffic volumes show decreasing costs (economies of scale), and roads for high traffic volumes show increasing costs (diseconomies of scale). Schematically, and *ignoring discontinuities*, this may be represented by the familiar S figure, illustrated in Figure 6.

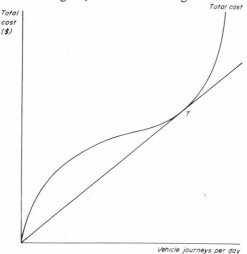

Figure 6.

---

[21] It may, however, be argued that the joint-product hypothesis itself implies discontinuities; this is a matter of semantics.

47.   The supposition that there are decreasing costs over the low-volume range rests on the capacity/quality characteristics of low-volume roads. That there are increasing costs over a high-volume range rests on the evidence that a high volume of traffic normally reflects a high density of population and that to displace dwelling-houses and the mass of urban real equipment for roads carrying a given traffic volume is more expensive than to displace open fields. But we are here only advancing hypotheses; the critical test is whether they are discredited by the facts to be reviewed in Chapter VI.

48.   Congested high-volume roads do not necessarily have increasing costs. For example, in Figure 5, roads C_3 to C_5 show decreasing total costs. To carry a 10% increase in the volume of traffic it may be necessary only to incur an increase in costs of less than 10%—by adding another lane, for instance. Where there are such economies of scale, i.e. declining long-range average cost, the appropriate marginal cost pricing policy (combined with the optimum investment policy) will give rise to deficits—even though there is no excess capacity on such highways.[22]

49.   We have suggested that for rural and interurban roads there are typically increasing returns to scale. At the other extreme, however, in the congested urban areas there are likely to be decreasing returns to scale— partly because of the difficulty of building roads in urban areas and partly because of the increasing rents of land. Thus an optimum pricing policy on both rural and urban roads will result in a surplus on the urban highways and a deficit on the rural roads. Whether or not there will be a surplus or deficit on the road system as a whole will depend on the balance between urban and rural (including interurban) traffic.

50.   To sum up the discussion thus far, the broad description of the cost and capacity/quality characteristics of roads which we have suggested as a model of reality, has the important consequence that, even without lumpiness in road construction, uncongested roads are likely to be efficient for small volumes of traffic. It also follows that uncongested roads are public goods, and will show deficits if one follows the policy for road user charges outlined above. For large volumes of traffic, however, congested roads will be efficient, and with diseconomies of scale, are likely to yield a surplus.

"Lumpiness"

51.   When we consider the other characteristics which are alleged to apply to road investment, we find that in general they support the public goods

---

[22] Provided that the authority pursues an optimum investment policy.

aspect of road pricing. The indivisibility or "lumpiness" of road investment arises from technological reasons. It would clearly be inefficient to add an inch to the width of a road every month; the efficient policy is to add a new lane (and resurface, etc.) after five years. The lumpy adjustment in fact adds to the pure public goods character of road services. The general effect of discontinuities is, as in our simple examples, to give the inherent economies of scale which are the essence of a pure public good. But "lumpiness" is a difficult concept to define and analyze. What is meant by lumpiness, indivisibilities and discontinuities? Clues can be found only in the characteristic "market" situation in which road services are supplied.

52.   Road services are supplied to a local market. They are exactly specified in space and time; spare road capacity in Timbuktu cannot be sold to the London commuter. Vehicles can be switched from one route to another at various times; the road cannot. For most manufactured goods there is a world market which, when goods can be stored, may be extended over a lengthy period of time. With road services the market is local and momentary. The immobility of a road is monumental. If one compares roads with other classic examples of "natural monopolies"—electric power supply and water—it is clear that an excess supply of power or water may be sold, at some cost, to other markets. But virtually no such opportunities exist for roads. If it is not used locally at that particular time, the capacity of the road is wasted.

53.   In manufacturing industry there are many striking examples of indivisible inputs—blast furnaces, giant presses, the entrepreneur himself—but normally these indivisibilities may be considered negligible in relation to the size of the market. Even large absolute indivisibilities may then be ignored. But given the limited, local market of roads, even small indivisibilities may be large in relation to the size of the market. It is primarily the limitation of the market that makes indivisibilities in roads of far more moment than in other areas of economic activity.

54.   Indivisibilities may arise in two ways. First, there is lumpiness in the inputs of the road building industry. Large surfacing machines and giant pieces of earth-moving equipment are typical examples of indivisible inputs. There is much evidence that for large roadworks costs may be diminished considerably by using large machines of this kind instead of small machines and much labor. Even in countries where labor is relatively cheap (in many countries in West Africa for example) it is still efficient to employ large specialized machines provided that the roadworks are large enough.

55.   These indivisibilities of inputs are not essentially different from those encountered elsewhere in the economy. They give rise to increasing re-

turns—over a certain range—in the supply of roadworks. The equipment itself can be moved around from road to road but many rural roads are so small and of such low and cheap quality that it is not worth employing a large machine. If the road authority needs to produce many stretches of low quality road, it must necessarily forego the increasing returns to scale (or decreasing costs) obtained from the use of large machines for a few big roads.

56.   This emphasizes the second aspect of indivisibility—the lumpiness in the output in the road itself. This is probably the more common concept of indivisibilities in roads. Certain restrictions are imposed by the technology and size of the motor vehicle on what one may usefully call a "motor road." If, for example, its width were less than that of the narrowest motor car, the road would not be at all useful for four-wheeled motor vehicles. A road of the width of one car, however, will be of some use—although it will still cut out most truck traffic. Single-lane highways on which most varieties of vehicle can travel are better; and two-lane highways are a still greater improvement. They eliminate delay and allow considerably greater speeds. Similarly, with improvements such as surfacing it is technologically silly to put pavement down 1/100th of an inch at a time. The road authority can pave the whole road to a sensible minimum depth, or it can pave sections of the road one after another. Both involve discontinuous or lumpy improvements.[23]

57.   The essence of these technological facts is that there are certain preferred sizes or types of road—just as there are technologically desired sizes for blast furnaces. This does not mean that it is impossible to construct very narrow roads or tiny blast furnaces. But the overly narrow road and the midget blast furnace are so costly to operate that no one would suggest building them. Technology polarizes size. Roads are typically classified in terms of the number of lanes, and road engineers think of highways in these terms. It is true that one can vary the width of the lanes within certain limits—but the main quantitative unit of highway output is the lane. Qualitative improvements are also polarized—earth, gravel, and paved. Rather more variations are possible here—but again economically desirable variations are contained within a limited range. Improving alignment is similarly lumpy. The polarization of technology is much more

---

[23] The sectional approach seems to approximate to a continuous case; but such appearances are deceptive. People will use different segments of the road in different proportions—and the net effect will make for discontinuous improvements as far as the traveling public is concerned. The exception is when there are no inhabitants or development along the road (it may go through a waterless waste)—thus everyone always travels all the way from one end of the road to the other.

restrictive in roads than in blast furnaces because of the localized small market for road services.

58. The concept of lumpiness or discontinuity may indeed be thought to comprehend the concept of the *joint-product* model which we suggested above. We argued there that for roads on which traffic was so light that there was essentially no congestion, an improvement in the quality of the road would usually extend the capacity of the road as well. The quality and capacity of the road are joint-products of optimum road investments. The inability to vary these two "products" independently may be thought to be a discontinuity of the road technology. As we shall see, the joint-product characteristic and discontinuities produce similar problems and effects.

Irreversibility

59. The irreversibility of road investment enhances these effects. Once we have built a road it is sunk in a particular location for a long time. Furthermore, and this is where it differs from the majority of investment models, the irreversibility occurs in *increasing* the capacity of the roads.[24] For example, if the road authority has already built a two-lane highway, the cost of widening it into a four-lane highway will differ from the cost of starting a four-lane road from scratch. There are as many costs of a four-lane highway as there are paths to it. Indeed, if for some reason a three-lane highway had been built, it might not be worth extending it to a four-lane road; only if we are starting with a two-lane road may it be worth building the high-capacity four-lane motor way.

60. In one sense the irreversibility argument is nothing more than the old adage "bygones are forever bygones." But applied in practice, it implies that each expansion path is defined in directional terms. There is no such thing as *the* minimum long-run cost curve. We have illustrated the example of the two- to four-lane and the three- to four-lane options in Figure 7. The broken line indicates the two to four expansion path, and the continuous line shows the three to four expansion path. There are two fixed costs for the four-lane highway, F_{24} and F_{34}, according to whether one

---

[24] In my view this irreversibility is typical of virtually all economic processes. The path of adjustment affects the final desired outcome; there is no unique long-run equilibrium—there are as many long-run equilibria as there are paths to it. This suggests that the general analysis of the long-run needs considerable revision—but, of course, this task is not attempted here. Again, one may contrast this situation with that in a "simpliste" manufacturing industry—we can simply add spindles and the appropriate floor space to the existing stock; no redesign is required. (The reader may well wonder, however, how close this characterization is to any process in the real world.)

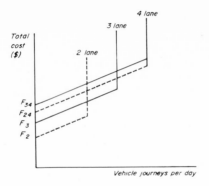

Figure 7.

begins with a two- or three-lane highway; but we have supposed that the variable costs are the same.[25]

61. It is obvious that this irreversibility argument does not depend on discontinuities in the production relationships. One could generate similar families of long-run cost curves with ordinary continuous functions. But one suspects that the combination of discontinuities and irreversibilities is characteristic of roads. We have emphasized here the irreversibilities of expansion paths; but there is also the usual *time* asymmetry in the contraction path. It takes many years for roads to wear out—far longer than to build them. This asymmetry plays an important role in optimization policies.

62. The length of life of roads, and the discontinuities associated with them, give designers and planners an incentive to construct roads that are adaptable to wide ranges of traffic conditions. Adaptability to changes in future conditions as well as to the expected variation in traffic flow is one of the hallmarks of efficient decision making. This may take the form of routing the road through potential growth areas at the cost of extra mileage unjustified by present traffic. More specifically one may complete the earthworks and foundation of a three-lane highway—but pave only two of the lanes. The road can then easily be adapted to take on a heavier traffic flow. Such adaptable planning is often associated with obvious discontinuities and economies of large scale earthworks. Indeed such arrangements may be part and parcel of the irreversibility effect discussed above.

The Consequences of Lumpiness and Irreversibility

63. This completes our description of discontinuities and associated phenomena; we now turn to examine their consequences for the pricing

---

[25] See Chapter VI for empirical evidence on this aspect of highway costs.

and investment policies of the road authority. As we shall see, the price policy is not affected by discontinuities—but the investment criterion needs modification.

64.   Let us begin with the extreme case when we can either have *one* specific road or no road at all. This all-or-nothing case is unrealistic but it will highlight the problems involved. In Figure 8 we show the marginal cost conditions for the all-or-nothing road. OA describes the variable maintenance cost per vehicle journey, and AH the operating cost of a vehicle journey. The capacity of the road is given at q vehicle journeys a day.

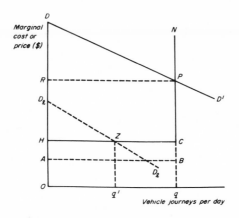

Figure 8.

65.   Now let us suppose that the road is actually in existence. Whether it was built as a consequence of a "correct" or "wrong" decision does not matter—it is there. The basic price argument is easily applied here. Price should be fixed at short-run marginal cost (including rent), and should be consistent with the demand conditions. With the demand curve DD', the price of a road vehicle journey should be qP. A part is paid over to the road authority in respect of the damage done to the surface by each vehicle journey—this is qB. Similarly, there is a congestion levy raised on this highway—this is measured by the distance CP. Finally there is the operating cost incurred by vehicle owners on each vehicle journey—this is CB.

66.   The road authority will receive a daily revenue (net of payments for variable maintenance expenditure) represented by the rectangle $HRPC$. It is often convenient to think of this daily revenue as a fund from which the invariate maintenance costs and the fixed (accounting) costs of the road are met. But this is merely an accounting or administrative conven-

44

tion. There is no good economic reason why the revenue so raised should not exceed or be less than the invariate maintenance costs plus the fixed costs. The road is there and we are simply concerned with making the best use of it. This is exactly the same as the pricing policy of the continuous case in the short run.

67. Now consider the extreme case, where demand is very low—$D_l D_l$ in Figure 8. With the efficient pricing rule the road authority would charge only the variable maintenance cost so that the number of vehicle journeys would be q'. Let us assume that the invariate maintenance costs are required to keep the road open; if they were not incurred daily the road would have to be closed. If the road authority closed the road it would save the real resources required for this invariate maintenance expenditure.[26] Should the road therefore be closed?

Close-down or Continue Problem

68. The value which people place on the services of motor transport are at least as large as the amount of money paid for them. This is represented by the rectangle $OHZq'$. But we know that the amount which most people would be *willing* to pay is larger than the amount that they actually pay. One vehicle journey would be worth as much as OD_l to a certain user— since the demand curve $D_l D_l$ tells that such a valuation would be placed on the first vehicle journey. The value which consumers place on the services of the road over and above the amount they have to pay for them is represented by the area $HD_l Z$. This is the *consumer surplus* and it tells us how much money could be extracted from users of the road if the road authority acted like an unscrupulous blackmailer—offering the services one by one and extracting the maximum amount which consumers would be willing to pay.

69. Now we can answer the question: should the road be kept open? If the value placed by the users on the services of the road exceeds the cost of keeping the road open then there is a good case for maintaining the highway. Thus if the consumer surplus exceeds the invariate maintenance cost, the road should be kept open, and the price of using it should be equal to the variable maintenance cost per vehicle journey so that the number of vehicle journeys per day is q'. The road will then obviously incur a budgetary or accounting deficit—even on current operating account—since only variable maintenance costs are covered by receipts;

---

[26] The reader is reminded that this maintenance expenditure is invariate with respect to the volume of traffic—not with respect to time.

invariate maintenance expenditures, although judged worthwhile by consumers, are not actually paid by them directly according to the number of journeys they make.

70. The common sense of this rule becomes clear if one considers what would happen if the road were closed. Those resources that were employed on invariate maintenance would seek employment in other industries. Each small unit of resource would contribute marginally to the output of other products. Thus the total contribution of these resources in other industries would be the sum of their marginal productivities which, under competitive conditions, is measured by the sum of their prices. Since only marginal adjustments are involved in all other industries the value of goods foregone by keeping the road open is simply the value of the resources used for that purpose: there is no consumer surplus in other industries to compensate for that generated on the "lumpy" all-or-nothing road.[27] The value to consumers of the resources set free by closing the road is measured simply by their price, while the value of the open road is measured by more than the price paid for its services.

71. In the above narrative we have slipped in the assumption, almost surreptitiously, that the "invariate" maintenance cost required to keep the road open is an all-or-nothing proposition. This may not be the case—it may be possible to adjust maintenance expenditure to keep the road in various degrees of repair, or to maintain a variable width of road. The consequences of a skimped maintenance program will be manifest in increased operating expenses and perhaps also in increased variable maintenance expenses. Clearly these margins need to be balanced one against the other. This reduces, but does not eliminate, the need for a consumer surplus criterion when deciding whether or not to keep the road open.[28]

72. The importance of the above discussion stems from the fact that one must use a consumer surplus criterion even in the *short-run* decisions. It

---

[27] This statement needs qualification according to the extent to which resources used are particular and specialized; see para. 125 below.

[28] It should be noted that the consumer surplus criterion might be required even if roads were continuously divisible and variable in the *long run*. If in the *short run*—through some unexpected change in demand—we had the road of Figure 8 associated with the demand curve D_lD_l, it simply would not matter that it was possible to vary continuously the size and character of the highway. The decision whether or not to renew the road would be irrelevant for present purposes. (Again this must be qualified. If the road were intended to be renewed it might be worthwhile to maintain it. On the other hand the pavement of a road about to be completely repaved might be allowed to go to pot.) The present reality would be that we had a road and we wished to know how to make the best use of it—or indeed whether it would not be better to close it. For this latter purpose one would again need the consumer surplus criterion.

must be admitted that it is used for only a limited class of "close-down-or-continue" problems—but for this limited purpose it is a correct approach.

All-or-Nothing Expansion

73. The main use of the consumer surplus criterion, however, is for investment rules in cases with discontinuities and lumpiness. Let us return to Figure 8, where we supposed that there was only *one* type of road which could be constructed—the all-or-nothing case. Either we build the road described by the cost function of Figure 8 or nothing. Suppose that the demand curve is *DD′* and that this is expected to be the demand in perpetuity. (Correspondingly it is supposed that the cost conditions will last forever.)[29] Suppose the road were built by charging the users a congestion levy of *PC*, the road authority would raise a total revenue (excluding variable maintenance costs) of *HRPC*. If the revenue from the congestion levy is expected to exceed the invariate maintenance costs and the fixed costs of the road, the investment in this all-or-nothing highway is clearly worthwhile. There will be no budgetary deficit—there will only be the problem of how to spend the surplus!

74. But what if the expected sum of the congestion levies paid by users is less than the total of fixed and invariate maintenance costs? Let us continue to assume that the correct pricing policy is adopted so that the ideal congestion levy is extracted from users. (We shall drop this assumption later in the study but it will be retained for most of this chapter.) The second assumption is that the road in question is a very small part of the national economy. The third assumption is that the alternative uses of resources are in a highly competitive industry or in divisible investments in the public sector. This means that the value of the resources to the consumer, if used not for the road but elsewhere, is measured by their price; lost consumer surpluses are not involved.[30]

75. The use of these resources in constructing the road, however, *does* give rise to a surplus. Resources are concentrated in one particular use. Most users would be willing to pay higher charges than the road authority levies for the use of the highway, a few as high as *OD* (including operating and variable maintenance costs); only the marginal user would be willing to pay no more than the price actually levied by the road authority. Thus the users value the road more than they actually have to pay for it by an amount represented by the triangle *DRP*.

---

[29] This assumption of unchanging conditions will be waived in subsequent sections of this chapter. Here it is made for simplicity.

[30] This will be reconsidered in a later section of this chapter, paras. 125–126.

76.   Clearly it will be good policy to build the road if the value which consumers place on the services of the highway exceeds the value which they would attach to the goods and services which could be produced if the road were not constructed. Thus if, after suitable discounting, the investment (and invariate maintenance) costs of the road are less than the sum of the revenue from the congestion levy *and* the consumer surplus, the all-or-nothing road is worth constructing. Consumers would be better off with the road than without it.

77.   Exactly the same sort of argument applies even when there is little traffic on the all-or-nothing road, i.e. if demand is D_1D_1, in Figure 8. Then no congestion levy is extracted from users. The road authority collects only the variable maintenance costs and the road is bound to incur a deficit in the accounting sense. But even so, it is clearly a good policy to build the highway *if* consumers value the services of the road more highly than they value the increments in other goods and services foregone. Thus if the consumer surplus measured by the triangle ZHD exceeds the costs (invariate maintenance costs and fixed costs) the road is worth building.

78.   This completes our introductory discussion in terms of all-or-nothing cases. We now turn to more useful cases, with a number of discrete possibilities in building roads. There is then a choice between various sizes and types of road; and stage construction may become feasible.

4. *Multiple Discontinuities, Urban Deficits, and Stage Construction*

79.   We have examined in some detail the theory of the all-or-nothing road, and showed that the investment criterion depended critically on the calculation of the whole consumer surplus—from the price which would be extracted if there were only one vehicle journey through to the valuation of the marginal journey. A formidable task. But, fortunately, these examples are figments of the imagination. For it is difficult to imagine the all-or-nothing road having any practical significance. In the real world there are always many possible schemes. We rarely if ever start from scratch. Some form of highway always exists; the problem is to what extent and in what way it should be rebuilt, replaced, extended, or improved.

Multiple Discontinuities

80.   The role of the consumer surplus in such conditions is the same as before—but its quantitative importance is much reduced. There are two basic problems: first, one may have the choice of starting a number of roads from scratch; secondly, the choice may simply be to extend the capacity

of the road by certain intervals or to improve the quality by surfacing the complete length. The following example shows, however, that the first problem can be turned into the more manageable second.

81. Suppose there are two possible roads which may be built from *scratch*. Both have exactly the same operating costs of motor vehicles up to capacity—so these do not affect the analysis. Suppose also, for simplicity, that the two roads have the same variable maintenance cost per vehicle journey. These cost conditions are illustrated in Figure 9. Let us suppose that the present (capitalized) cost including fixed costs and invariate maintenance costs of Road I is $150 and that this road has a capacity of 1,000 vehicles a day; and that for the second highway, Road II, the capitalized cost is $200, and the capacity is 1,500 vehicles a day. Thus there are economies of scale, suitably defined, in the provision of road services.

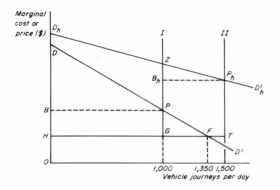

Figure 9.

82. With the stable demand curve DD' the authority would charge a congestion levy of BH per vehicle journey. Now let us suppose that the tax revenue collected from the congestion levy, duly capitalized, exceeds the cost of Road I, and thus there is a clear indication that Road I should be built rather than leaving things as they are. It does not follow that Road I is necessarily preferable to Road II.

83. The only sense in which the "worth" of Road II can be interpreted is by comparison with the two situations where we have either no road at all or Road I already. If we compare Road II with no road at all, it may well be sensible to build it. This will be the case if the consumer surplus DHF exceeds the cost of $200m. But a choice also exists between Road I and Road II—and so a comparison must be made. From Figure 9 we can

49

see that Road II will add to the total surplus value (consumer surplus plus revenue from a congestion levy) an amount represented by the triangle *FPG*. By building Road II we shall have no congestion and so the road user charge will be zero (other than the charge for variable maintenance cost per journey). At this charge the number of vehicles using the road will be 1,350 a day. The question is whether the valuation placed by users on the additional 350 journeys a day exceeds the additional $50m cost involved in choosing II rather than I.[31]

84. The practical importance of this argument is that once we have a low-capacity road, actually existing or in project, that could be supported financially by congestion levies, this road may be used as a *base line* from which to calculate additional, and less intractable, consumer surpluses on the road increment only. To that extent one can deal with conceptually much easier measures—such as the congestion toll on the low capacity road—rather than with the highly abstract hypothetical valuations of consumer surplus.

85. Now let us ask a different question, using the same basic model of Figure 9. Suppose that for the expected level of traffic the consumer surplus on Road II does not warrant the additional costs;[32] Road I is therefore chosen (without consumer surplus considerations) and actually built. But immediately afterwards demand expands suddenly and unexpectedly to $D_h D_h'$. At this new high demand Road I earns a very fat profit indeed. Is it now worthwhile to build Road II even though Road I has already been built? It is realistic to assume that Road II will cost more than if we had started from scratch; let us suppose that the discounted *additional* cost of construction of Road II given that Road I exists is $100m rather than $50m. The correct criterion is now to compare the *additional* benefits of Road II with the additional $100m cost. The additional benefits are measured in Figure 9 by the net revenue of the additional traffic (i.e. $500 \times P_h T$) plus the consumer surplus $ZB_h P_h$.[33] It will be observed that no deduction is made for the decline in profits per vehicle journey from that on Road I. This is merely a transfer of rent receipts from the road authority to motorists. The traffic of 1,000 vehicle journeys a day was carried before

---

[31] Or, approximately, whether the present value of the additional consumer surplus on Road II:

$$350 \times \tfrac{1}{2} \text{ (congestion levy } HB \text{ with Road I)}$$

exceeds the difference between the cost of Road II and that of Road I.

[32] For geometry, see Annex Note ii.

[33] Alternatively one may express the argument in terms of the total curves; then the slope of the consumer surplus chord and the slope of the cost curves at the capacity points are compared (see Annex Note ii).

50

Road II was constructed and is just as valuable now as it was then; when Road II is in operation a smaller congestion levy is extracted from these journeys. To summarize, the important practical point is that, again, we do not have to measure the whole area under a demand curve; we have to concentrate on measuring only the additional value. The more numerous the potential and actual roads, the more likely it is that the consumer surplus element will be small.

Deficits or Surpluses on Urban Roads

86. One of the most persistent features of road finance is the allegation that deficits will arise. As we have seen, deficits are likely on roads which have light traffic flows. The question remains whether or not roads which have high traffic volumes will also incur deficits. Would it be efficient to build large urban highways so that there was little congestion and so that such low prices were levied that the highways would not recover their costs? Let us examine the conditions under which we obtain a result of this kind.

87. It is clear that the presence of increasing or decreasing long-run cost will play a critical role. If there are *no* discontinuities in investment, then, when investment and price are optimal, whether there is or is not a deficit will depend only on the shape of the long-run cost function. If the long-run average cost increases, the roads should earn a surplus in excess of costs.[34] The roads which were constructed some time ago become more valuable as the demand for them increases. And since new roads can be constructed only at increased cost, the existing roads earn a surplus because the price to road users will be levied so high that they will cover the cost of constructing the new roads. As the road network of urban areas is expanded one would expect them to earn larger and larger surpluses over cost.

88. Now when we introduce discontinuities into this argument, the simple result disappears. One can no longer be certain that the proposition of increasing long-run cost is sufficient (or even necessary) to result in a surplus. We shall continue to assume, however, that there are increasing long-run costs associated with the discontinuous increases in the size of the urban highway network: this will isolate the effects of the discontinuities. Consider then the case where there are *two* roads which one may possibly construct as shown, in Figure 10, by I and II. Let us suppose that P_1 and P_2 are the "break-even" prices for Roads I and II.

[34] This is a standard theorem of price theory (see, for example, George J. Stigler, *The Theory of Price*, 3rd ed., (Macmillan, New York, 1966). Unfortunately, the proof requires a little mathematics; but the rationalization of the text may make the implications fairly clear.

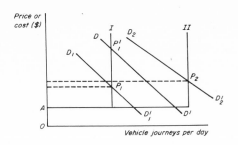

Figure 10.

89. With Road I already constructed any demand curve in excess of D_1D_1' will produce a surplus. Let us suppose that for a demand greater than DD' the consumer surplus exceeds the cost of constructing Road II, so that it becomes desirable to build II. The price then falls from P_1' to OA (the variable maintenance cost and operating cost). The road will incur a deficit. Eventually, as demand expands further, the road will earn a surplus—when the demand is in excess of D_2D_2'.

90. In principle, therefore, the urban road system will go through periods of surplus, deficit and surplus again.[35] But one may reasonably ask what is the likelihood of this sort of pattern—in particular would one expect to incur sizable deficits? Obviously much depends on (a) the elasticity of demand, and (b) the size of the discontinuities as well as (c) the extent of the increasing long-run cost.

91. It seems to be a reasonable conjecture that for a *particular* urban road the demand will be very elastic. Many alternative routes will normally be available and so the demand will approach perfect elasticity. The addition of even a large amount of road space in the form of a particular road in a city adds a relatively small amount to the total number of feasible ways of traveling economically between two points in a city. The conjecture of an almost infinitely elastic demand for a particular road is supported by the common complaint that new urban highways quickly become as congested as the old facilities.

92. Of the other two factors—(b) is perhaps the most difficult to determine. One suspects that the extent of discontinuities is much exaggerated in practice—but as we shall see there is no reliable statistical evidence to support the allegation that discontinuities are of little importance. As to the last effect (c), a rising long-run cost curve, one may conjecture that it would

---

[35] It is obvious that with decreasing or constant costs a similar pattern may emerge.

occur in urban areas because of the increased density, higher rents, greater interference of traffic with land use and access, etc. These would be offset to some extent by the economies of scale of large machines used in constructing the large amount of road space. As we shall see, there is some evidence of quite sharply increasing long-run cost.

93.   To summarize, the existence of multiple discontinuities in urban situations is unlikely to result in overall deficits, partly because of the sharply increasing costs and partly because of the relatively high elasticity of demand for particular urban highways. Efficient pricing of roads and efficient investment programs will tend to give rise to surpluses.

Stage Construction, Probabilities and Uncertainties

94.   Thus far we have assumed that the growth of future traffic demand was known. But, of course, in practice there are many uncertainties. We do not know the level of future traffic; we have to predict on the basis of existing evidence.

95.   Let us now examine how *probabilities and uncertainties* affect our previous conclusions. To begin with, suppose, most unrealistically, that each demand curve has a probability attached to it—and that that probability does not change over time. This is the classic case of actuarial probability.[36] Now we cannot assign periods to the demand curves; instead we postulate that each of the, say, two curves may be applicable in any period with, let us say, a probability of $\frac{1}{2}$. (One can imagine a fair coin being tossed each year to see which demand condition is realized.) The calculation of the best investment program is then quite straightforward. We weigh each outcome with the associated probability and find the average or expected outcome for each possible investment program, calculated again in terms of surplus above costs—not, as in the usual case revenue above costs. The investment program that maximizes the expected or average surplus above costs is the optimum plan.[37]

96.   Such a model, whatever its importance in price policy, has very little relevance for investment programming over time. The problem of choosing a road investment plan is that one simply does not know what the future development of traffic is going to be. In year 0 one may make a best guess as to the future course of demand in year 1, 2, etc. For year 1, one will be reasonably sure of the outcome, for year 2, less sure, and so on—until for

---

[36] It will be developed at some length in connection with marginal cost concepts in the last section of this chapter.

[37] We are assuming that the road authority believes that it should have no aversion to risk.

year 10 the likely demand conditions will be quite obscure; these are the views as seen *from* year 0. If, however, we move forward in time to year 9, then, taking a view from that period, we should be reasonably certain of the demand conditions in the next year, i.e. year 10, but we should be just as hazy as before about the outcome in ten years' time.

97.   The importance of stage construction is that by delaying the investment in Road II, in our earlier example, we can "buy" information about the future pattern of demand. Instead of building Road II in year 0, we build Road I with the option of building, at greater expense, Road II in year 10. The formal analysis of such an option theory is very complex. But one may get some insight by considering a highly stylized version.

98.   Let us characterize demand conditions as "high" or "low" from year 10 onwards, and let us suppose that our belief in year 0 is *polarized* about these values. The beliefs and associated outcomes may then be set out in a table as follows:

Belief about demand in year 10	*Action: building Road I (low capacity) or Road II (high capacity)*	*Outcome*	*Valuation*
High	II (i.e. normal)	High	Good
		Low	Bad
High	I (i.e. perverse)	High	Bad
		Low	Good
Low	I (i.e. normal)	High	Bad
		Low	Good
Low	II (i.e. perverse)	High	Good
		Low	Bad

The "normal" actions need little by way of explanation. But the "perverse" actions do. Why would one choose to build I in spite of the fact that it was believed that the demand in year 10 would be high? Two factors enter into this decision. First, although we may believe that the demand will be high rather than low, the degree of confidence in this prediction may be quite small. The present belief is then of little importance and should be accorded only a small weight in the decision process. Furthermore, by delaying building II we can increase greatly the degree of confidence in the prediction made in year 9, when indeed the weight of evidence may favor the low demand for year 10. Secondly, it may not cost very much to delay building II. That is to say, the two "bad" outcomes associated with building I (see the above table) may involve only small losses compared with the two "bad" outcomes associated with building II in year 0. These two factors may indeed lead us to prefer the "perverse" decision to build I now; thus we buy the option of avoiding overbuilding.[38]

99. Even this simple example is quite complicated in its structure and solution, and there are no obvious shortcuts. But the general precepts accord with common sense: one should purchase an option if one is very hazy about the future and if the option does not cost much—and if the haze is likely to diminish considerably over time and if *all* costs are reckoned, i.e. all alternatives foregone are duly weighted with their degree of belief. Theory serves merely to work out these common sense ideas.

Savings in Operating Costs[39]

100. The foregoing discussion of multiple discontinuities and stage construction showed that, in practical terms, the availability of alternative sizes and types of road reduces the role to be played by consumer surplus calculations. However, the irreversibility characteristic does tend to increase the number of choices that must be made "in-the-large" and so increases the role of the consumer surplus criterion. Any course of action involves hostages for the future.

101. This is equally relevant for an investment criterion, of much practical importance in developing countries, which, for short, we shall call the *operating cost criterion*. Broadly speaking the vast majority of non-urban road improvements in developing countries are justified on the grounds that it costs less in terms of total costs to carry the existing volume of traffic on an improved road than it does on the existing highway. Since the road is not congested—or congestion costs are so low that they can be ignored—the extension of capacity is irrelevant. The only effect that matters is the reduction in the operating costs of motor vehicles, the change in the maintenance costs—both variable and invariate—and the change in the fixed costs. These conditions correspond to the joint-product model which we developed above. The essential conclusion there was that at low levels of traffic, we would never operate roads at capacity because we would always find it efficient to build a higher capacity road to reduce operating costs (including maintenance and fixed costs) well before the traffic built up to capacity.

102. The criterion as formulated here only takes account of cost savings on so-called "normal" traffic, i.e. traffic that would have existed even

---

[38] The reverse argument holds for preferring building "large" in spite of "low" demand expectations.

[39] See Annex Note iii for the geometrical presentation.

without the road improvement. What about the traffic induced by the reduction in costs? If there are indivisibilities in road improvements the expansion of traffic will be non-marginal and will give rise to consumer surplus that, in principle, should not be ignored in the investment decision.[40] Those consumer surpluses will tend to be larger, the greater are the indivisibilities in road improvements, and the higher is the elasticity of demand for transport.[41] In many practical cases the consumer surplus element is likely to be small in relation to the cost savings on normal traffic; the operating cost criterion is then a perfectly acceptable approximation.

103. This concludes our survey of the investment criteria for uncongested roads. We again end up with the importance of a largely unknown factor— the elasticity of demand for transport. We shall try to sharpen the elasticity concept in Chapter IV. In the final section of this chapter we shall look more closely at the relevant cost concepts. But first we need to consider some difficulties with the consumer-surplus criterion.

5. *The Consumer Surplus Criterion and Its Limitations*

104. The consumer surplus criterion is a tool of analysis that must be handled with care and circumspection. In the foregoing discussion we talked about comparing the sum of the congestion (and variable maintenance) levy and consumer surplus with the total investment and maintenance costs of the road. This is, of course, easier said than done. (In fact, even our Figures 9 and 10 did not permit the actual comparison, since fixed and variable maintenance costs were not shown. However, this could easily be remedied.) Even in the "simpliste" case with constant cost and demand conditions, estimating the demand curve for transport on a particular road with some degree of precision is no simple matter.

105. Quite apart from these direct problems of measurement, the consumer surplus criterion needs to be treated delicately and watched carefully to see that the conditions are auspicious. It is necessary that the resources for the road construction should not be abstracted from one particular industry but should be taken in small amounts from a large number of industries. Consider, for example, the case where the road is financed so that only one industry, say, the housing industry, suffers contraction and contributes all the resources needed for constructing and maintaining the road; all other industries produce the same outputs as before.[42] The

---

[40] It is a frequent practice to allow, on induced traffic, one-half the unit savings on normal traffic.

[41] For geometry see Annex Notes ii and iii.

[42] We ignore the resources used up in collecting the taxes, and we ignore the fact that such specific resources may be imported at constant prices.

simplest case is where the authority taxes the housing industry so that the quantity of new housing produced annually diminishes just sufficiently to supply enough resources for the road. The output of the housing industry declines because of higher after-tax prices and consumers lose the "housing" consumer surplus which they once enjoyed. Clearly one must debit the surplus lost as well as credit the surplus gained by the construction of the road. There is indeed no reason why the surplus lost should not exceed the surplus gained! Then the road would have to earn a *profit* to be worth building: the revenue from congestion levies would have to exceed the fixed and invariate maintenance costs by a margin sufficient to offset the net loss in consumer surplus.

106. Specificity of the resources employed in road building and maintenance may also modify the consumer surplus criterion. If road building resources were specific, say, to the building and construction industrial group which had as its only other branch the housing industry, then all resources for the road building industry *must* be taken from housing. Then, the only way to expand the road building industry would be by contraction of the housing industry. The specific character of the means of production results in non-marginal adjustments—and loss of consumer surplus—in other industries affected by the shift in resources. However, consider the case where the only alternative use of the resources of the road building industry is iron ore mining. The resources are specific, but if the iron ore is sold at a constant price on the world market, then only foreign currency earnings, not consumer surpluses, are reduced.[43]

107. Complete specificity models are extreme but useful examples. In most cases there is greater flexibility in resource use and particularly in the employment of relatively unskilled labor. Much depends on the structure of the economy and on the alternatives available. But clearly, in actual cases it will be much more difficult to trace the non-marginal supply adjustments—and the resulting changes in consumer surplus—than in the simple (extreme) examples above. It should be noted also that if, in spite of the taxes raised to finance the roads, consumers continue to buy relatively large quantities of goods which use intensively the specific factors employed in road building, their prices will rise and these factors will earn surpluses or rents.[44] Although high rents *ex post* reflect true scarcities in this situation, the lumpiness of road investment does involve difficulties

---

[43] Obviously the value of foreign currency may exceed its nominal value so the loss may have to be revalued.

[44] Note also that some other rents of specific factors, employed by industries which have suffered a decline in demand, will be reduced.

in pricing resources, and consequently in determining net consumer surpluses. We will return to the series of problems associated with estimating costs in the final section of this chapter.

108.   Using the consumer surplus criterion when the road user charge is "wrong" causes no problems, however, provided that price is equal to marginal cost in the rest of the economy. These incorrect road charges may be the result of a policy which differs from the optimum pricing policy in aims and objectives, or they may be a consequence of the bluntness of the administrative instruments used to carry out an optimum policy. Whatever the cause of the "wrong" pricing, it is easy to see that the consumer surplus criterion carries over to this case. The only difference is that in each situation one must take the price, and its consequences for demand and output, as *given* by the policy of the authorities. On this basis one can calculate the consumer surpluses and apply the criterion as before. With the prices as given one might call this the conditional consumer surplus criterion.[45]

109.   Since the consumer surplus criterion is used for all-or-nothing propositions, one might ask how one can be sure that the best list of projects is chosen. Unfortunately the consumer surplus criterion itself gives no assurance that the government's investible funds are optimally distributed. The consumer surplus calculation shows whether we would be better off with a particular road than without it. It does not tell us if it would be *best* to have the road; it may, for example, be best to have another kind of road instead. In order to achieve the ideal solution, one should in principle survey all possible constellations of investment and output. For a project to be worthwhile it must pass a consumer surplus test; this test is a *necessary* condition. But such a test is not a *sufficient* condition for the project to be included in the best constellation of investment and output. The *maximum maximorum* can be found only by scanning all possible investment-output mixes and deciding among them.

110.   By using the consumer surplus criterion we improve the distribution of resources. People are better off with the investment than they were before. By itself, the criterion will not ensure that the Elysian fields of the ideal are achieved. But in our existing state of knowledge and uncertainty it surely seems worthwhile just to try to improve matters. This is a tough enough job.

---

[45] The conditional criterion and its implications have been examined in A. A. Walters, "The Consumer Surplus Criterion for Investment in Roads," *Discussion Paper B2*, University of Birmingham, (1959).

111. There is no doubt that one of the main objections of the practical administrator to the consumer surplus criterion, apart from difficulties of measurement, is that it is thought necessarily to involve budgetary deficits. And for a particular project for which the consumer surplus criterion needs to be used, this view is correct. There would indeed be no need to use the criterion if there were no deficit. Furthermore, the deficit will tend to be the larger, the greater the *in*elasticity of demand; for then the consumer surplus will be higher. This is obvious from the geometry—but the economic argument is that *in*elasticity of demand implies that some persons would be willing to pay very high prices indeed for journeys along the road. People would suffer greatly if they were denied the services of the road and they would be willing to pay a very large sum for the building of the road. This will usually be the case where there are no close substitutes—such as railways, waterways, and airfields.[46] In these circumstances it would be efficient for the road authority to incur large deficits—given that these inelastic demands encounter roads of the all-or-nothing type. Conversely, if the demand were very elastic, the deficits would be smaller—since people would not place such a high value on the provision of the highway.

112. But the deficits incurred on some investments undertaken under the auspices of the consumer surplus criterion are, of course, only one side of the coin. With the all-or-nothing roads, others will earn profits from their congestion levies (over and above recovery of investment costs). Deficits and surpluses will also occur if consumer surplus criteria are applied in more realistic conditions with multiple discontinuities and stage construction. Decreasing costs prevail at low traffic levels, as on many intercity and rural roads, and increasing costs at high traffic levels in urban areas. This tends to result in surpluses in congested urban areas, and deficits on low-volume intercity roads.[47]

113. Whether the surpluses collected from the urban highways will counterbalance the deficits (or, strictly, negative surpluses or rents) on the intercity and rural highways is an arithmetical matter of considerable administrative and political importance. Whether the state raises taxes to finance the net deficit or whether it enjoys a surplus so that it may remit other taxes—these are matters of much economic interest. We shall examine

---

[46] In Chapter V, however, we shall show that this is not as obvious as it sounds—and that there are good reasons for believing that the elasticities are much higher than usually supposed even when there are no close substitutes. The "development effect" is not insignificant.

[47] For geometry, see Annex Note ii.

the consequences in detail in the next chapter. What must be emphasized here is that there is no economic rationalization for "balancing the road budget"—although, as we shall see, a case may be argued in terms of the consequences of alternative policies. Each policy must stand or fall by the *consequences* and not by any abstract *obiter dicta*. If it be thought that the roads should bear higher taxes than those which emerge from our economic analysis—then let the case be argued in terms of the alternatives, such as running a budget deficit, or reducing government expenditure or increasing running a budget deficit, reducing government expenditure or increasing other taxes. The balanced road budget is, to the economist, merely a graven image.[48]

6. *Concepts of Cost and Their Difficulties*

The Unit of Cost Analysis

114.   Some exponents of the theory of road pricing have argued that the *long-run* marginal cost is the appropriate value for fixing prices. In this study, however, we have stressed that the short-run marginal cost and not the long-run marginal cost is always the appropriate concept for pricing purposes. It is easy to show that the long-run marginal cost is efficient only when three conditions are met. The first requirement is that traffic be growing and expected to grow, so that there is no question of simply making the best use of a road that is too big; all roads must be enlarged. The second condition is that there be no indivisibilities and joint-product relationships in the supply of roads. In other words, the highways should be described appropriately by a putty model. The third condition is that the government always carries out the efficient investment program; it never lags behind in building new roads when they are desirable and it never makes mistakes by overbuilding.

115.   If these three conditions are present, the long-run marginal cost will provide an appropriate measure of the efficient user charge. It is important to see why under these conditions the long-run marginal cost pricing policy

---

[48] Since there is a complete theoretical symmetry between the deficits arising from the use of the consumer surplus criterion and the profits that may arise from congestion levies, they should be treated symmetrically. Both are rents—the former are negative rents and the latter positive rents. Administrators are much more concerned about negative rents than about positive rents. Yet if one is concerned about too little money being extracted from private persons for government schemes in the first case, should one not, in the positive rent case, be equally concerned about *too much* resources being siphoned off to the public sector? Administrators rarely evince any concern of the second kind—largely because they are under pressure to provide a tax base for government schemes. Whether governmental expenditure is "better" than the private expenditure it displaces is another, rather large matter.

is correct. For it is *only* when these three requirements are met that the long-run and short-run marginal costs are equal. In other circumstances they will generally be different. Thus the long-run marginal cost is useful as a criterion for user charges *only* when it is equal to short-run marginal cost. When the long-run differs from the short-run cost, the long-run concept is the wrong basis for pricing policy. The short-run marginal cost is *always* the appropriate value at which to fix the user charge.

116.   Any concept of cost must be associated with the decision to which it is related. The concept of cost used throughout the whole of this study comprehends solely the escapable cost as one course of action is selected rather than another.[49] In any well specified situation there are a number of feasible alternative courses of action; and also a set of circumstances which one cannot change. Taking the latter as given, we calculate the value of the resources used up if we adopt different courses of action. There is therefore an infinity of concepts of cost—but each one is uniquely related to the decision specified in each situation.

117.   Which concept of cost is relevant for the user charge policy of the road authority? For this purpose we must inquire into the role of price in the budgets of consumers and firms that use the highways. Clearly each user takes the price (user charge) as given and "buys" highway services so that the additional satisfaction derived from the last unit of highway service just equals the price he has to pay. Since the consumer of highway services can buy units of highway services as small as he likes, the relevant unit for pricing purposes is the "small" increment in road service which the consumer may buy. The appropriate cost concept is therefore uniquely defined as the marginal cost of supplying an additional (small) unit of the road service—and the marginal cost is "the value of the resources which would be saved by not supplying a (small) unit of road service."

118.   It is quite wrong to imagine that this concept is arbitrary. It is not. It is determined by the nature of the "commodity"—it is possible to use a road in very small units at a time[50]—and by the fact that the decisions of

---

[49] It will also be recalled that, in the extreme simplified model of Figure 3 marginal cost was defined to *include rent*. We return to this problem below.

[50] It is easy to sketch (but perhaps hard to imagine) the conditions under which the relevant pricing unit would be much larger. Suppose, for example, that the road authority decided to sell road journeys in "blocks" of 1,000 vehicle-miles, and that subcontracting (or retailing road services to third parties or trading in any units smaller than 1,000 vehicle-miles) was declared to be illegal with very high (prohibitive) penalties. Then the only possible unit of contract is the 1,000 vehicle-miles of road service, and this is the relevant unit for the analysis of cost. But it is misleading to talk about the marginal cost of these large units. We shall analyze all cases with "sticky" prices in the next subsection.

consumers in allocating expenditure between road services and other goods take this divisibility into account. The road user decides on the little more or the little less, and so it is the cost of the little more or the little less that is relevant for determining the price.

119.　One of the greatest sources of confusion in the analysis of road costs is the confounding of discontinuities on the *supply* side with those divisible and marginal decisions on the consumption side. The decisions of the road authority encompass both the supply of the road and of road services. What about the additional cost of *supplying the road*? Clearly, if we lumped all the road users together and treated the *collective* as a contracting party there would be a correct criterion for investment by asking whether it would pay a sum of money greater than or equal to the cost of the road. (This is, of course, simply a version of the consumer surplus criterion, but we leave this aside for the moment.) This is no basis for determining the price of *road services* however. The collective does not buy road services; individuals do. Thus, as we argued above, the consequence of the decision of the consumer, in buying a little more or a little less, is the relevant concept for the calculation of cost, and thus the price of road services. The road authority makes investment decisions in accordance with the evaluation of the collective; but it sells road services to individuals, not to the collective. Again we conclude that the marginal cost of a small unit is the relevant concept for pricing.

The Definition of the Short Run

120.　Characteristically we think of price as the value that moves to "clear the market." Price adjusts to the level where supply equals demand. Movements of price, we assume, do not involve any real costs; there is no cost involved in "relabelling" the price tag. This picture of frictionless price adjustments corresponds closely to reality in markets for certain kinds of road haulage, taxis and buses in some countries of the developing world. Under competitive conditions no seat would be vacant and no capacity unoccupied unless the price dropped to zero; then it would be a free good.[51] Price will move costlessly and swiftly to the value that clears the market.

121.　In the instantaneous run (or the very very short run) the price of road services is determined by the demand in conjunction with the existing capacity.[52] Since capacity at any instant of time is given, and since bar-

---

[51] I am assuming here that the cost of filling a seat is zero.

[52] What we have elsewhere called variable maintenance costs are committed and fixed in the instantaneous run.

gains can be concluded costlessly, no resources can be saved by supplying one less unit of the service (for example, by not filling a seat on the bus), nor is it possible to supply any more (no standing passengers permitted by law). The maximum volume of services is given in the instant—and price must perform the task of allocating the services among the users who are prepared to pay.

122. This model is the same as the simplified model of a road which we developed earlier; the only difference is that the instantaneous operating cost may be taken to be almost zero. The solution there was to charge a price of marginal cost including the rent necessary to equate demand and supply. The marginal cost used for pricing purposes was carefully defined to include the rent (para. 16). In the instantaneous run, it seems that the rent will comprise virtually the whole of the marginal cost, as we have defined it. Price, duly fixed at every instant at marginal cost, will move immediately to clear the market if there is excess demand or excess supply. The appropriate concept of cost for pricing purposes is, therefore, the instantaneous marginal cost (including rent), or, to use the usual terminology, the very short-run marginal cost.

123. With this model of a frictionless price, we might now consider a longer period where some obligations are escapable; the vehicle owner can decide whether or not to take the vehicle journey. Of course price is still determined by the instantaneous market conditions. The vehicle owner, however, now takes into account the alternative use of the resources which he may commit to road transport for the period. If it seems profitable to put more of his resources into road services, the vehicle owner will run more vehicles, and the increased service capacity will depress the price.

124. Of course this frictionless price model is of limited use for *practical* application in road pricing. Frictions *do* exist. But it is important to see that the "pure" frictionless case *does* require that price be fixed each instant at the very short-run (instantaneous) marginal cost (including rent). The instantaneous "period" is defined automatically by the frictionless character of price; there is then no problem of defining appropriate periods for pricing purposes. It is also worth stressing that the completely flexible frictionless price, moving effortlessly and costlessly to the value that "clears the market," is the peak of efficient pricing. It represents a standard of aspiration which is useful to keep in mind when developing more mundane and workable schemes. It is, indeed, important to get as much "built-in" flexibility as one can into administrative schemes of prices.

125. The main *frictions* in road pricing arise from the political and institutional processes that determine user charges. To discuss their impact

would require a survey of the political institutions of each country. Instead we shall briefly discuss some of the principles of pricing under conditions of friction. Obviously the most straightforward approach is to include a "cost-of-changing-the-price" term in the model.[53] The formal conclusions of the model are easy to predict; it would sometimes pay to waste some road services rather than change the price, and, up to certain levels, it would pay to tolerate queueing and congestion rather than increase the user charge. It would be worthwhile to vary the price only if a large change were to be made. Small changes would be too costly and would be ruled out. Prices (or user charges) must then be moved only in steps; the property of infinitesimal adjustments disappears. Price is "sticky."

126. With this model it *is* necessary to deal with "blocks" of services. If the price is reduced then, since it must be reduced by a "large" amount, the expansion of services must also be more than infinitesimal. The cost of changing the price must be introduced into the cost calculations for the purpose of fixing a new price. The discontinuity introduced by the "cost-of-changing-the-price" term is analogous to the "all-or-nothing" investment decision. This implies that we must analyze the cost of a *lump* of output, that is a *block* of road services.[54] In principle, this also involves the calculation of consumer surpluses—just like the lumpy investment decision. The gain from reducing the price, when there has been a fall in demand, will be reckoned in terms of the amount which users would be willing to pay for the additional services; against this gain is to be set the cost of changing the price and the cost of supplying the additional services.

127. A diagrammatic illustration (Figure 11) might help clarify this point. Let us begin with the demand curve D_o, the marginal cost curve MC, and the price P_o. Suppose that demand falls to D_1. If the price were frictionless it would fall to P_1. But suppose there is a "cost-of-price-change" involved; then there is a choice between holding the price at P_o and reducing output to q_1, or lowering the price to P_1 and expanding output to q_2. Consumers therefore are better off if the road price is reduced by an amount represented by the triangle ABD. The producer surplus is given by the triangle BCD.[55] But against these two gains from the price move

---

[53] Formally this could be done by using a dummy variable z, which takes a value 0 if there is no change and 1 if changed; so the cost of the price movement (if any) would be represented by zx where x is the cost if the movement is actually made.

[54] Some exponents of cost analysis talk about the marginal cost of a *block* of road services. This is, however, misleading since marginal analysis applies only to infinitesimals and the solution of "all-or-nothing" pricing proposals involves much more complex analysis and calculation.

[55] The consumer gain of $P_oP_1 BA$ is, of course, offset by the same producer loss.

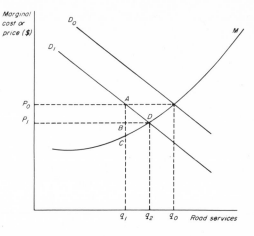

Figure 11.

we must set the cost of changing the price. If the cost of reducing the price is sufficiently large it may offset the gains to be obtained.

128.   We might at this stage ask whether the "costs-of-price-changes" can be reckoned to be important enough to dominate the analysis of user charges. No definitive answer can be given until there has been an adequate study of the facts, but some points seem clear. There is a great difference between a change in the structure of prices, including changes in the relative prices of different types of roads, etc., and changes that involve simply predetermined variations in user charges. The former cost a lot, the latter are almost free. Really major changes in user charge policy are almost once-and-for-all changes and one would not expect them to be repeated frequently. But it does not seem difficult or expensive to introduce some "built-in" flexibility into user charges.[56] They might well be varied at trivial cost under rules of procedure; for example, the price on an urban tollway could be raised for the rush hours and reduced for off-peak periods. Thus it seems likely that, for normal price changes, the cost of variation will not be so high that it dominates the analysis. But it is important to check these conjectures against the facts.

Expected Costs and Variable Demand

129.   There is, of course, an infinite number of other models by which we can introduce friction into the pricing process. For a model that prob-

---

[56] We examine some of the practical problems in Chapter VII.

ably corresponds to some essential aspects of reality, it might be suggested that the user charge cannot be varied except every year at budget time.[57] But variation at that time is to be considered costless. Clearly the user charge would be fixed at budget time so as to make the best use of the roads available during the year. Associated with a given road there is a cost curve. What must be taken into account is the variation in traffic and cost over the year in response to a fixed price.

130. The most obvious variability arises from seasonal and time-of-day effects. This "peak" problem has received much attention in the literature. In this study we shall be concerned only with the relationship of diurnal and seasonal variation to the main framework of the analysis. No attempt will be made to complicate the formal models to include these influences.

131. The main feature of diurnal and seasonal variation is its *predictability*. We know that the peak traffic in London will occur from 5 P.M. to 6:30 P.M. and no one is surprised when the streets get jammed. Statisticians normally define the diurnal or seasonal component of the time series of traffic as that variation which has no random component.

132. In terms of our simple demand and supply model, the effects of peaks and troughs may be recorded by describing a different demand curve for each time of day or season. Thus the demand curve for a road service at 5 P.M. will be quite different from the demand at 12 midnight. It is indeed quite sensible to regard them as different services since they are required at different times. Road services are *time specific*, both on the demand and on the supply side. However, the demand curves of road users for different times of the day are not entirely independent of one another: many users would regard a journey at 5 P.M. as a fairly close substitute for a journey at 5:10 P.M.—but a journey at midnight would not be even a remote substitute. More important, these services are in joint supply, since the road is there both night and day. Supplying the commuter at 5 P.M. inevitably implies that some "spare" capacity will be available during the night.

133. The combination of these various demand curves with the one cost curve suggests that there should be a different price for each time of day. The user charge should be high for the high demand period, and low for the periods when there are few users. The technical and practical problems of this kind of road pricing are formidable but may not be insoluble.[58] We shall return to them later in this study.

---

[57] Plausible though this assumption may be, the British Government frequently introduces interim budgets—and has in fact increased gasoline and diesel oil duties in the process!

[58] See the Smeed Report.

134.   There is another component of the time series of traffic flow, the *random component*. The essence of the random component is that it is un-predictable—one day up, another day down. On the other hand, we may know quite a lot about the *general* pattern of random components—from past evidence, and perhaps also from *a priori* knowledge. (Just as we know that over the history of tossing a coin roughly half will be heads—but we do not know whether it will be heads or tails on a particular throw.)

135.   The price of road or rail service is fixed by a transport firm or au-thority and users buy the services at that price. Thus the authority will not be able to foretell exactly the number of users, whose demand will vary from one period to another. The rail or road authority will find it adminis-tratively impossible, or too costly, to vary the price according to the num-ber of users that actually turn up. Essentially, price is fixed and the number of "takers" is a random function. The administrator must plan his price and investment policy with this random variation in mind.

136.   In setting the price, therefore, the authority will take into account the *"expected cost,"* i.e. the cost averaged over all of the chance outcomes. A simple example will help to illuminate some of the concepts involved. Suppose that the authority thought that, when charging a given price, there was an equal chance of having 80 vehicles an hour and 120 vehicles an hour. For a certain size of road, therefore, there will then be two costs—

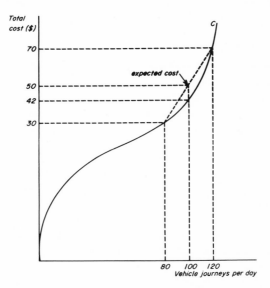

Figure 12.   A Cost Curve with Random Variations in Traffic.

let us say $30 for 80 vehicles, and $70 for 120 vehicles. Thus the *expected* costs are $0.5 \times \$30$ *plus* $0.5 \times \$70$, i.e. $50. This is the cost which the authority will take into account in setting the price. We note that the cost of the average (expected) output of 100 journeys is not necessarily the same as the expected cost. In Figure 12, we have supposed that over the 80 to 120 range of vehicle journeys the marginal cost is increasing. Thus we see that the cost of a steady vehicle stream of 100, without any random variations, is only $42. The $18 difference is the cost of the random variations. Analogously we observe that if marginal costs are *de*creasing the expected cost (with random variations) will be less than the cost of the equivalent steady stream of traffic.

137.   The important qualitative result is that taking expectations and averaging over the random variation of output smooths out the discontinuous jumps in cost occurring as the number of vehicles an hour increases. The absurdities attendant on not taking probabilities into account are illustrated by Gabriel Dessus' cautionary tale of the traveler from Calais to Paris.[59] If there is an extra empty seat on the train then the marginal cost of filling it will be nearly zero, but if the coaches are full another coach must be put on for him so the marginal cost is the cost of providing the coach. But if the train cannot pull another coach we must put on another train for him and the marginal cost shoots up, and so on. Of course, common sense revolts against this account. Rail authorities (and road authorities for that matter) do not plan and react in this way. An administrator will clearly be planning for a number of passengers and road users; he will not be supplying a personalized service! If there is a large gulf between theory and practice—so much the worse for the theory.

138.   In the example of the passenger traveling from Calais to Paris, the railway authority would consider one passenger more or less a mere random event—a chance variation over which it has no control and for which it can plan only in a general way. One individual passenger more or less means virtually nothing to the railway administrator; but a general increase in the level of traffic is important.

139.   In Figure 13 (p. 69) we have plotted the "expected" cost curve on the same "certain" cost curve for a given size of highway. The general result is that the expected cost curve is much flatter and less "kinky" than the ordinary cost curve. The analogous concept to marginal cost is now *margi-*

---

[59] Gabriel Dessus, "The General Principles of Rate-fixing in Public Utilities," *International Economic Papers*, No. 1, (London, 1951).

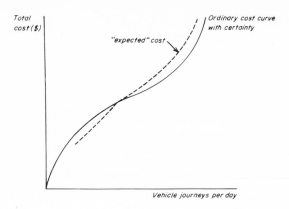

Figure 13. The Expected Cost Curve.

nal expected cost.[60] This tells the administrator by how much he should reckon that costs would increase if there were a small increase in the expected traffic level. It will be observed that the marginal expected cost will be much closer to average cost (short-run) than the ordinary marginal cost will. Indeed it is possible for marginal expected cost and average expected cost to be approximately the same over wide ranges of traffic in spite of the fact that the ordinary marginal and average costs differ widely for these same traffic levels. The expectations approach thus rationalizes the concern of practical administrators with concepts which approximate more closely to average costs than to marginal cost as conventionally defined.

140.   This concept of a random distribution of traffic rationalizes the existence of some spare capacity. This term "spare capacity" may conveniently be used to distinguish it from "excess capacity" which does not arise from probability considerations. With cost curves that rapidly increase in the region of "capacity" one would indeed find that on most days the road would be operating with spare capacity. This would be economically justified to cater for the occasions when there was, by chance, a high demand, which could otherwise only be met at exorbitant costs.

141.   The remaining component of the time series of traffic is the *trend*. This long-term movement in the series is predictable to some extent, but current projection techniques leave large uncertainties which cannot neatly be comprehended in a probability sum. As we have seen earlier in paras. 94–99, one must devise strategies to deal with the future by hedging

---

[60] Note that this is not expected marginal cost; the averaging over probabilities is done *before* we differentiate to get the marginal concept. See Walters, "The Allocation of Joint Costs with Demands as Probability Distributions," *American Economic Review*, June, 1960.

against the unexpected but possible outcome. No simple transformation of cost relationships provides any analytical shortcut—such as we have found with the random variations discussed above.

Prices and Shadow Prices

142.   Rather different problems arise in the valuation of costs. What prices should be used in the calculation of costs (and benefits)? Market prices, the obvious answer, may differ from opportunity cost because of (a) taxes and subsidies levied on commodities and services (e.g. gasoline tax, license duties), (b) alternative uses of resources in a non-competitive industry where their productivity exceeds their price, and (c) the fact that certain prices are determined partly by administrative action or by convention so that they do not fall when there is an excess supply, (the classic case is that of wages in underdeveloped countries). We shall call these three well-known reasons (a) the tax, (b) the monopoly, and (c) the "shadow price" reasons for the deviation between price and cost.

143.   It is usually claimed that public road schemes should be evaluated at prices which exclude *taxes* and subsidies. It seems wrong, for example, for the government to value fuel saving at a market price which includes a tax per gallon; government investment should not be justified on the basis of reducing tax receipts! However, appearances may be deceptive where roads are concerned. Suppose for example the fuel tax represented a rough approximation to a congestion levy plus the variable maintenance cost; then clearly the objective of investment is to expand capacity and *reduce* the congestion levy. In the standard road model of this chapter (Figure 2, p. 24) the congestion levy at the margin measured the real marginal costs; consequently, the reduction in the congestion levy is then a sensible measure of the real gain from the investment in highways.

144.   One cannot pretend, of course, that all, or even most, duties on road use measure the difference between private and social cost. The exigencies of raising revenue usually lead to the imposition of discriminatory taxes which do not nicely measure any deviation of this kind. Then the case for eliminating taxes from both costs and benefits seems much more clear-cut. But even here it is not crystal clear. Suppose there is a swingeing gasoline tax. This will lead people to devise and use technologies and products that save gasoline. If the road authority deducts the gasoline tax from its benefit calculations it will build fewer gasoline-saving roads than people as a whole desire. This will lead to more private investments to reduce gasoline consumption, accentuating the original bias in the technology. The re-

sources saved from road investment will at least partly be wasted in the inefficiencies of individuals trying to save gasoline.

145. The general conclusion is that whether or not one deducts discriminatory taxes from prices (or how much one deducts) depends very much on the technological possibilities of distortion and on the users' evaluation of these alternatives. As a general rule one might conjecture that it is sensible to deduct discriminatory taxes from benefit calculations on the argument it is not wise to try to put one distortion right with another. But this is a working rule in which one should have only a low degree of confidence, and which should be used with caution.

146. The *monopoly* effect is essentially similar, except in one respect. The monopolist imposes a "private tax" on the consumers of his product—and this is analogous to the discriminatory tax imposed by government. The main difference is in the motive and strategy of a monopolist's behavior. Suppose, for example, that the railways are run by a private unregulated monopolist. Any road user pricing policy pursued by the road authority will affect the price policy of the rail monopolist—and so it is natural for the road authority to take this into account in fixing its road prices. But we cannot stop here—for clearly the monopolist will take into account the reaction of the road authority to its pricing policy, and so on. We cannot assume one pricing policy is given for the purpose of calculating the other's reaction. One cannot predict what the outcome will be, although it would clearly help if one knew the sanctions each could impose against the other. The essential problem is one of *strategy*, of bluff, and of political bargaining and maneuver. The bewildering varieties of strategy are quite beyond the reach of the formal framework of economics, and we must give up the chase at this point.

147. Fortunately, in most practical cases, legislation or government regulation of the monopoly—usually in the form of nationalization—prevents the self-interested development of strategic bargaining.[61] Often the prices of regulated monopolies may be conveniently taken as given. The political

---

[61] It would be naive to suppose that nationalization *per se* avoids strategic bargaining of the sort outlined in the above paragraph. It merely takes a different form. Furthermore, it is not at all clear that the agreements which emerge from the conflict between nationalized railways and the national road authority would be superior, as far as the public are concerned, to the result of leaving them to the private monopolist. The "cat-and-mouse" game of public corporation and public authority—with its tactics of threat and counter threat—usually goes on behind closed doors; but occasionally the outsider catches glimpses of the tactics—as, for example, in the Geddes Committee, *Carriers' Licensing*, (London, 1965) which heard evidence by British Rail, on the one hand, and by the road interests on the other. See: Transport Holding Co., *Road Revenues and Costs*, (London, 1964).

process of changing prices is usually either lengthy or impossible. In many cases prices appear essentially as constants and we may treat the difference between marginal cost and price as a tax (or subsidy).[62] As a general rule one would therefore tend to deduct the tax (or add the subsidy) in making calculations about costs and benefits. But this rule must be used with caution.

148. The *shadow price reason* for deviations between price and cost is usually thought to be of great importance in developing communities. For example, many developing countries have an excess supply of labor—too few jobs and too many people anxious to acquire them. In a competitive market the wage would be reduced until the number of persons who wished employment at that wage had jobs. Often, however, wages are fixed by custom, or in modern states by minimum wage legislation, or by a variety of other institutional factors. There will then be involuntary unemployment of labor—which may be disguised as *under*employment in agriculture. Employing more labor on road building will then not mean that the flows of any other goods are reduced. Since the cost of employment is only the leisure foregone, the wage used in calculating costs and benefits should reflect only the valuation of leisure given up. It is not easy, however, to obtain suitable measures of the value of leisure foregone—especially since leisure almost always involves some "productive" work. In short there is often a good case for valuing labor at some price less than the wage rate, but it is much more difficult to determine the precise amount.[63]

149. Other important cases for "shadow pricing" are foreign exchange and interest rates. The price paid for foreign currency may be fixed by the government well below the price which would rule in a free market. To maintain this exchange rate the government resorts to quota controls, rationing and similar administrative exclusions. Similarly, interest rates on foreign loans are often administered rates applicable to rationed quantities only; and local capital markets are notoriously "imperfect" with rates of interest reflecting mainly institutional idiosyncrasies. These problems are

---

[62] This constancy of price may simply result in a reversal of the normal roles of price and investment policy. If price is given, and investment is variable in the long run, we shall adjust the capital stock to the output determined by the given price confronting the demand conditions. This topsy-turvy economics is the *result*, not the cause of fixing prices rigidly for all time.

[63] It is important to stress that in some countries the wage rate is fixed *below* the value that would rule under free market conditions—and so the shadow price should exceed the money wage. This was found to be the case in Liberia, where various "recruitment" practices were used to ensure that labor moved from nonwage (tribal) employment to wage employment. See: R. W. Clower, G. Dalton, M. Harwitz, and A. A. Walters, *Growth without Development: An Economic Survey of Liberia*, (Northwestern University, Evanston, Illinois, 1965).

common to all forms of planning and are not a special aspect of road investment. We shall not pursue them further here.[64]

The Interaction Effect

150. A further conceptual problem in the valuation of costs is the "interaction effect," which is most easily explained by means of an example. Suppose one builds a road in an otherwise completely inaccessible area; thus (ignoring speculation, etc.) the land had no value without the road. Now when the road is built the land becomes worth $1,000 an acre. The increment in the value of the land is therefore entirely due to the road. The question is: should one value the land used in road construction as nothing, or $1,000 an acre, or some value between these extremes?

151. In order to answer this question one must specify whether there are or are not discontinuities in the supply of roads. If there are, and the minimum scale of road is built, the appropriate price for the land used for the road is zero. This is the opportunity cost of the road in the all-or-nothing case provided there is no possibility of substituting other factors—such as more elaborate engineering works—for the land input into the highway. It may be possible, however, to build the equivalent road with a *different* land input. For *this* choice between input combinations to provide the same road service, the cost of land must be reckoned at $1,000 an acre, as this is the value of the alternative foregone.

152. Finally, suppose that there is no minimum scale of highway and that roads may be built of continuously varying quality.[65] If the optimum price is always charged for the road, the appropriate price for the land used up by the road is, of course, the land rent level associated with that particular quality of road. The price of land will then be a function of the size of the road investment; there is an "interaction effect." In its investment planning, the road authority should take account of the changes in land prices associated with different types of roads.[66,67] This will ensure the best distri-

---

[64] A theoretical solution to the interest rate problem where there are extensive markets in government paper is easily derived. Such a solution seems irrelevant for most developing countries. The practical problems have been explored by Jochen K. Schmedtje in *On Estimating the Economic Cost of Capital*, IBRD, EC-138, (1965).

[65] This implies that there will be a schedule relating the reduction of transport costs and the increase in rents.

[66] It should never behave like a monopsonist, however; for small variations in the input of land into the road it should take the price (or the rental value) of land as given.

[67] Strictly speaking we should include in the valuation only the *rental* value of the land. The purchase price of land will reflect a myriad of expectations about future road development, as speculation takes place on estimates of the probabilities of the various outcomes. The current rent indicates the land's current productivity in its currently most profitable use.

bution of land between highway and other uses, and construction of the road in the most efficient manner.

153. Although we have couched the above argument in terms of that classic fixed factor land, the same line of reasoning may be applied to other factors in similar situations—according to the degree of "fixity" involved. For certain regions where roads are built it may well be a sensible approximation to regard the quantity of labor as fixed. During the construction period of the road labor would then earn "rents" (assuming there was full employment before the road constructors arrived). Exactly the same conclusions apply as discussed above—except that of course we must make allowances for the special features of labor (such as the possible relevancy of the leisure margin).

154. The relative "fixity" of inputs into road construction is the main reason for the rising costs of road construction. In our first example, the *stock* of roads affects the relative scarcity of land and drives up rents—a feature particularly important in urban areas. In our second example, it is the *rate of investment* that affects the price of labor. This is an important distinction—but in a growing economy both will give rise to increasing costs.

ANNEX

Microeconomic Decisions on Pricing and Investment

155. In this note we examine first a diagrammatic treatment of the decision about price and investment when there is no problem of indivisibility of road investment (Note *i*). Secondly, we examine the problem when there is lumpiness in road building (Note *ii*). Thirdly, (Note *iii*) we examine the "operating cost" valuation of benefits. The treatment of the consumer surplus criterion requires a small innovation in diagrammatic techniques. The discussion in *i*, *ii* and *iii* is merely to expand the treatment in the text of Chapter III. Strictly the diagrammatic treatment is not necessary to "prove" or even in order to understand the points appearing in the body of the chapter. But a statement in different terms, in the language of geometry, may help some readers sharply to appreciate and criticize the approach.

(i) *Pricing and Investment with Divisibility*

156. We now set out the model with divisible investment in diagrammatic form. Using the simplified cost model of Figure 3, let us record the *total*

cost of road transport (including track costs) with different amounts of road. For example, the total cost curve labeled C_2 shows the total cost of carrying vehicles along the road when fixed costs are F_2 and the capacity of the road is represented by B_2. The curve C_1 shows the total cost when the road is a little larger. Suppose by some accident we had a road represented by cost curve C_2. Let us also stipulate the demand conditions represented by the total revenue curve OR. With these two sets of conditions the price, which is measured by the slope of the line from O to P_2, will be set such that the road is fully employed. When the price is set at the slope of OP_2 the number of journeys will be B_2. The operating and variable maintenance cost is represented by the line F_2B_2—the slope of which is less than the slope of the price line OP_2. The difference is the optimum congestion levy. The (invariate) maintenance costs which are independent of traffic volume should be included in fixed costs. Thus the difference P_2B_2 represents the "rent" which the road authority earns on highway C_2; and since fixed costs have been excluded this "rent" is a *net* surplus of the asset.

157.   Now let us ask whether it is worth while for the road authority to expand road investment so that we have cost conditions represented by C_1 instead of those of C_2. The costs of expansion (the long-run marginal cost if they are close enough together) is given by the slope of the line through B_2 and B_1. A high slope of the B_2B_1 line would indicate high marginal costs of adding to the road network. In our figure, however, the slope

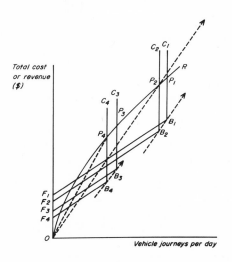

Figure 14.

of B_2B_1 is approximately equal to the slope of the price line through P_2. Thus the price is just about equal to the long-run marginal cost. There is no incentive to expand or contract the road; C_2 is just about the right size. In this long-run equilibrium, short-run marginal cost (and rent) is equal to long-run marginal cost.

158.   Suppose that we had accidentally started with road C_4 rather than C_2. Then the price line OP_4 has a steeper slope than the expansion cost from C_4 to C_3. The slope of the ray from the origin through P_4 is greater than the slope B_4B_3—so the price which people are willing to pay for an additional vehicle journey exceeds the cost of expanding capacity to cater for it. Long-run marginal cost is less than price and the road should be expanded. It is however worth emphasizing again that the price should always be equal to *short-run* marginal cost (including rent); if one fixed the price at long-run marginal cost one would simply price too low and too many people would try to use the road with the consequence of queues and undue congestion.[68]

(ii) *Consumer Surplus Criteria in the Discontinuous Case*

159.   Consider the situation pictured in Figure 9, p. 49. With that apparatus it was easy to see the optimum price policy and the optimum number of vehicle journeys; but whether the investment is or is not justified remains quite obscure—at least as far as the figure is concerned. Consumer surplus appears as an area while total cost does not appear at all.

160.   For applying the consumer surplus criterion we plot the total cost curve as shown by the lines FCN in Figure 15. As before OF represents the fixed costs including invariate maintenance costs, and the slope FC measures variable maintenance and operating costs. Capacity is q and this is the maximum number of vehicle journeys per day.[69] Demand conditions are represented by the total revenue curve $OPRD$. Revenue at first rises as the price falls indicating that there is an elastic demand at low traffic levels. But the demand eventually becomes inelastic and the revenue curve turns down, until at zero price there will be OD journeys per day. If this road exists the price charged should equal the slope of the line OP. This

---

[68] It will be observed that, as the figure has been drawn, there is no difference in the variable cost as we increase the scale of the road. This simplification does no harm for congested roads—but it is not correct for uncongested highways. The essential point is, however, that with perfect divisibility *there would be no uncongested highways* except by accident and in the transitory state of adjusting from one demand to another.

[69] In the simplified model, feasible and maximum capacity are the same.

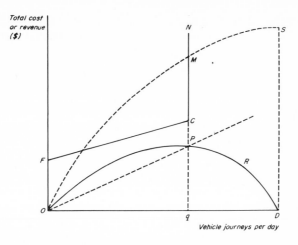

Figure 15.

price is in excess of the variable cost (the slope of *FC*) and is just sufficient to induce the users to use the road to capacity—and no more. It is less than the total cost; the resulting deficit is *PC*.

161. To see whether it is worth building the road we must construct the consumer surplus curve *OMS*.[70] This records for each number of vehicle journeys the total value which users place on them, i.e. the consumer surplus. The consumer surplus curve rises monotonically from zero for no journeys to a maximum *S* when there are *OD* journeys. It will always lie above the total revenue curve since the consumer surplus (including revenue) will always be larger than the revenue collected.

162. One very useful property of the consumer surplus curve is that the slope of the surplus curve is equal to the price. Thus, for example, the slope of the curve *OMS* at *M* is the same as the slope *OP*. It follows that the greater the degree of concavity of the total revenue curve (the greater the *in*elasticity) the higher the consumer surplus curve will be above the revenue curve.

163. One can easily see that with the total cost and revenue conditions in the figure the building of the road is justified. The consumer surplus curve rises above the total cost curve and this implies that people would be better off with the road than without it. It may also be observed that the road will run a deficit of *$CP* per day. The deficit *could* be reduced by charging a higher price—but this would result in a waste of road capacity.

---

[70] Strictly this curve is a consumer surplus *plus* revenue curve—a total value curve—but we prefer to call it a consumer surplus curve partly to distinguish it from the revenue curves.

164. It may be efficient to have excess capacity on the road—provided that the revenue curve is sufficiently "humped" and falls rapidly before the capacity of the road is achieved. This will provide a consumer surplus curve that may "overtake" the total cost curve. But the price falls to variable cost before capacity is reached. These conditions are illustrated in Figure 16. It will be observed that the price line OP is parallel to the

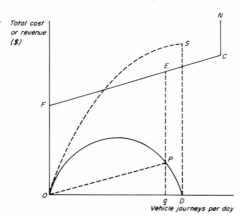

Figure 16.

variable cost line *before* the road carries capacity traffic flow. This result is exactly the same as that which we expressed in terms of ordinary demand and marginal cost curves; but now one can see that the investment criterion is also satisfied.[71]

165. The symmetry between the use of the consumer surplus curve and the total revenue curve of a monopolist is exact. The monopolist maximizes the difference between revenue and cost, the road authority should maximize the difference between consumer surplus and cost. The monopolist expands his plant if the additional revenue exceeds the additional cost. The road authority should build bigger roads if the addition to consumer surplus (and revenue) is in excess of the costs of expansion. Of course the *marginal* consumer surplus is simply the price. But since the consumer surplus criterion is designed for dealing with the lumpy or discontinuous case, such a "small-change" concept is rarely of any use. With large jumps in output, one has to measure the slope of the *chord* of the consumer surplus curve. This tells one the increase in surplus from the low to the high

[71] It can also be proved that if the OS curve just touches the FC line (i.e. the investment is just worth while), the point of contact will be at the optimum output when the slope of the price line is just equal to the slope of the variable cost line FC.

output; this can then be compared with the costs involved in making such a jump.

166. This completes the diagrammatic development of the simple consumer surplus criterion. Now we may use the basic model to examine problems of road investment. But instead of an all-or-nothing road, we shall suppose that there are *two* roads which may be chosen. (And, of course, this can easily be generalized to many roads.)

167. The total cost and total revenue and surplus curves are represented in Figure 17. Demand conditions appear in the form of the total revenue

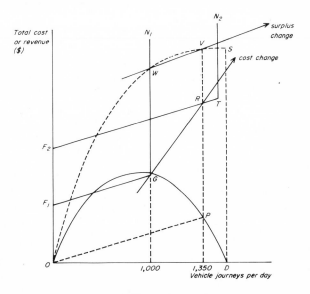

Figure 17.

curve OPD and in the consumer surplus curve OS. Total costs curves of the two roads are illustrated by F_1GN_1 and F_2TN_2. Since the revenue curve overtakes the road 1 cost curve at capacity it may be concluded that road 1 will earn a profit. Now consider the expansion to road 2. Price would fall to the slope OP, which is equal to the slope of F_2T and the tangent at V. The gain in consumer surplus is indicated by the slope of the chord through WV. The increase in total costs is shown by the slope of the line through GR. Clearly the conclusion to be drawn from the figure is that the costs increase by more than the surplus—so investment in road 2 is not worthwhile. Better to stick with road 1.

79

(iii) *The Use of the Operating Cost Criterion*

168.   In many practical cases transport authorities believe that it is desirable to use the reduction in vehicle operating cost for the existing vehicle flow as a measure of the benefits of improving a road. In order to examine this criterion, let us imagine a road in existence whose cost conditions are represented by the fixed cost F_1 in Figure 18 and the capacity line N_1.

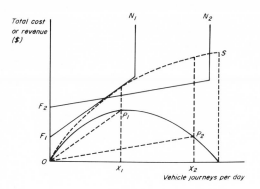

Figure 18.

With the total revenue curve OP_1P_2, we can imagine that the road is just worthwhile in the sense that the consumer surplus curve just touches the total cost curve when price is equal to variable cost, i.e. price is represented by the slope OP_1, and the number of vehicle journeys per day is X_1. The operating cost criterion applied to *existing* traffic would clearly call for investment to improve the road to give conditions represented by the total cost curve F_2N_2. At the optimum traffic flow X_1 the improved road would effect savings. And the consumer surplus criterion also indicates that the improvement is desirable. When the improvement is effected, the price should fall to the slope of P_2 and the vehicle traffic expand to X_2.

169.   The agreement of the consumer surplus criterion and the operating costs criterion for *existing* traffic is however merely an accident due to the fact that the cost curve with the improvement was, at the existing level of traffic, below the original cost curve. In Figure 19 the total cost of carrying X_1 on the improved road is *greater* than on the old road. Nevertheless, the improvement is clearly worthwhile since the consumer surplus curve OS rises well above the improved road's total cost curve.

170.   Furthermore, Figure 19 shows us that even if for some reason we cannot charge the optimum price on the improved road, i.e. OP_2, there is

80

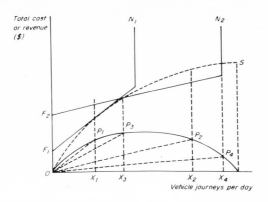

Figure 19.

a range of prices and vehicle journeys where we would be better off with the improved road. These are indicated in the figure as OP_3 to OP_4 and X_3 to X_4.

171. The net results of these arguments is to suggest that the operating cost criterion is too conservative if it is applied only to *existing* traffic. But this conservatism will matter only insofar as the demand is relatively elastic. As one can see in the figure if the revenue curve is very humped and is the same as the existing one up to P_1—but then falls to zero before the number of vehicle journeys reaches X_3, then the operating cost criterion and the consumer surplus criterion will give rise to the *same* conclusions. As common sense suggests, if the demand is sufficiently *in*elastic the operating cost criterion may be perfectly good enough for all practical purposes. We can now see exactly what is meant by "sufficiently inelastic."

IV

COVERING THE COSTS

1. *Introduction*

1.   Since the earliest days of motor highways, the opinion that road users should pay for the costs of the road system has been influential. It was recognized that roads would be required for access and social and administrative reasons, even in the absence of the motor vehicle. But the provision of highways suitable for the internal combustion engine has obviously given rise to very large expenditures. The responsibility for these costs can be defined on two counts. First, there would have been no need for such large expenditures in the absence of motor vehicles. Secondly, the user of the highway benefits from the expenditure. These two reasons have given rise to the "incremental cost" method and the "differential benefit" method of highway finance. The essential rationale of both these methods is that the costs of the highways used for vehicular traffic should be paid by the users; the difference arises only with the *distribution* of this cost between one user and another.

2.   One might reasonably ask, however, whether there is any justification for covering the costs by user taxes? Is it sensible to aim at levying user taxes that are just sufficient to repay the costs of the roads? What are the definitions of "user taxes" and "costs" that must be incorporated in any such rule?

3. There are at least two basic ways in which we can approach this problem. First we can ask whether the economic theory of road pricing in any form will ever give rise to a rule of this general "cost-covering" type? If it does not, we might ask whether the principles of administration or of political science support such a rule. If the rule fails on all these grounds, then it is at least not a self-evident basis for determining practical policy. A second approach is to take the definitions and rules which have been suggested in practice and to examine them critically. This again can be done at various levels. We can examine whether the concepts can be clearly defined in *principle*, and whether any practical measure is possible. But with this approach it is sometimes more fruitful to examine the *consequences* of the actual systems proposed. In this chapter we shall use both approaches but shall rely primarily on the first.

2. *Optimum Charges and "Covering the Costs"*

4. Earlier in this study we showed that, in principle, the motorist should pay for each journey an amount representing the value of the resources used up and including the rents of scarce facilities. The general result was that for intercity and rural roads the charge will be low whereas for urban roads, where congestion is common, the charge will be high. These prices reflect the real cost of the journeys concerned. If these optimum prices are levied, the question of whether and where there is a deficit or surplus turns primarily on the technological conditions and investment policy pursued.

5. As discussed at length in Chapter III, if we assume, unrealistically, that the roads are "putty," then the price for vehicle journeys reflects the maintenance and congestion costs on the existing road which will equal the cost of adding another yard of putty. And, in this highly abstract model, the question whether total charges cover total costs hinges on whether or not there are economies of scale in the production of putty roads. If there are diseconomies (e.g. if the locations from which putty must be brought become more distant), then new roads will cost more than old ones. The price used to ration the existing stock of roads will represent the cost of supplying new roads, so old roads will earn a profit or surplus or rent. Conversely, if the roads were produced under increasing returns, the optimum price-investment behavior would give rise to a deficit. Only if putty roads were reproducible at constant cost would the costs just be covered by revenues. Thus whether the road accounts are balanced, depends on the conditions of production in the road building industry. The requirement of "covering costs" then implies that returns to scale in road

83

building are judged to be constant. This may well be correct, but it seems hasty to prejudge the issue before the facts have been examined.

6. Roads, of course, are not like putty. They are more like baked clay. Mistakes cannot be easily and quickly put right; one must live with them for a long time. Furthermore, there are discontinuities, irreversibilities, geographic specificity and joint-product effects which are clearly ignored in our "putty" roads. All roads and road services cannot be treated as though they are identical stuff. One must take into account the special circumstances existing on each road. However, to save repetition we shall only talk of *typical* roads, and to sharpen the argument further, we shall suppose that the discontinuities (lumpiness) in the system are such that only two types of road can be constructed—small-capacity and large-capacity.

7. The small-capacity road is constructed for "rural" traffic and the large-capacity for "urban" traffic. We have seen that the rural roads will normally have a capacity in excess of the traffic flow even when the user charge consists only of variable maintenance cost and even when road investments are optimally adjusted to the traffic flow. Consequently there will be an accounting deficit on rural roads if user charges reflect the real cost of each journey. On the other hand, urban roads will typically be congested. The user charge levied for urban journeys must therefore be high—reflecting the marginal social costs of highway congestion. This may well produce an accounting surplus over and above the costs of urban highways. As we have seen, this depends primarily on the extent of diseconomies of scale in urban road building, and the level and growth of demands in relation to the discontinuities. The general expectation is therefore that the rural highways will be in accounting deficit, while the urban streets will earn an accounting surplus. Will there be an overall deficit or surplus on all highways? To some extent this depends on the precise accounting rules adopted, and the definition of costs and revenues for this purpose (see section 8). Surpluses are, of course, more likely if investments lag behind so that congestion becomes more widespread; and deficits will be ubiquitous if uneconomic operations are not abandoned in time or if there is overbuilding. More important, however, than accidents of accounting and sub-optimal investment policies, is the specific mixture of traffic conditions prevailing in a country at a given time.

8. There is no good and convincing reason why economies in different stages of growth should have overall deficits or surpluses—the critical factor is the proportion of traffic concentrated in the towns. This may be

very great at low stages of development.[1] On the other hand, even in countries as advanced as New Zealand, the relative concentration may be low. Thus there are no general rules that determine whether a country should or should not have a balanced road account according to its stage of development. Each case must be argued on its merits.

9. One further conclusion should be stressed: *there is no argument for balancing the account of the rural highways separately*. It is clear that, if optimum charges are levied, the (uncongested) interurban and rural roads will certainly be in deficit (on any of the numerous accounting conventions customarily used). This is as desirable a state of affairs as it is that the urban streets should earn an accounting surplus when proper prices are charged. This implies that the ultimate aim of most "cost-covering" studies is a misplaced one. The vast majority of practical studies of user charges are concerned with raising sufficient revenue to cover the costs of the interurban (or rural) system.[2] To balance the budget of the interurban system alone, the authority would have to raise charges on rural roads above, and probably far above, economic levels. This requirement is therefore a prescription for waste.

10. How large a waste will be engendered by a balanced-budget requirement depends partly on the elasticities of demand (as well as the extent of the discontinuities). The smaller the elasticity of demand, the greater the incentive to build more roads with excess capacity (because the consumer surplus is larger for a given volume of traffic) and, if we charge on a marginal cost basis, the larger the deficit tends to be. But also, the smaller the elasticity of demand for road services, the less important it is that they be properly priced. The amount of motoring done will not be cut back much by the high user charges. In other words, with a highly inelastic demand, although the deficit is likely to be large, it does not greatly matter if we try to cover it by raising user taxes since the quantity of traffic is not very sensitive to such charges. This argument cannot be pushed very far: first, it is clear that one can never recover all the consumer surplus by raising

---

[1] There are examples in Liberia, Thailand, Singapore, and Central America.

[2] To quote from one of the most recent:

"*Objectives of Study*
1. To revise the level and structure of road-use taxes and other special charges in order that they may approximately cover the cost of providing and maintaining the country's interurban highway facilities."

Wilbur Smith and Associates, *Memorandum of Methodology: The Study of Road Use Charges; National System of Highways, Republic of Peru*, (processed, Columbia, South Carolina, undated), pp. 1–2.

charges; and secondly, there are grounds for believing that in developing areas the demand for transport is not inelastic. Nevertheless, this model may be useful in cases with little or no development (generated) traffic, and without water or rail substitutes, where the main problem is merely to cater for existing traffic streams.

11. With high density demands, traffic volumes will tend to be larger and the deficits smaller; and rates need to be raised less above their optimum values in order to "cover costs." Where demand elasticity is high, however, small deviations from optimum user charges are important because they reduce substantially the volume of traffic. This will be important where much development traffic is expected, or where close substitutes to road transport exist. A casual review of the facts suggests that there is no *prima facie* argument for ignoring such cases.

12. The general conclusion is that the requirement of "covering the costs" cannot be deduced by economic reasoning. If, however, a balanced road budget is desired for administrative, political or social reasons, then it is best to require that it apply to areas that include both congested and uncongested roads. It would invite inefficient pricing if the rule were applied separately to congested and uncongested areas. Indeed, the more homogeneous the subset of roads for which a balanced budget is required, the greater the likelihood of inefficient pricing. It is easy to show that *a fortiori*, insistence on a budgetary equilibrium for a particular road may lead to quite appalling results. Attempts to "cover costs" may lead to progressively increased user charges and reduced traffic. It may be impossible to cover costs by charging a single user charge.

3. *Balancing the Road Budget and the Railways*

13. Although there is no general economic reason for balancing the road budget, particular justification may be sought in the peculiar conditions of regulated competition in the transport industries. In the literature of transport economics, one of the most persuasive reasons for requiring roads to cover their costs is that railways are required to cover theirs. To permit the road user to escape without paying the total cost would be to give roads an unfair competitive advantage. The proper procedure, it is alleged, is to put roads on the same basis as railways.[3] Then the two main modes of transport can be left to fight for traffic under similar rules and handicaps.

---

[3] The reader will find the classic account of this argument in the Salter Report.

14. What precisely is implied by "putting them on the same basis" varies according to the political power of the railroad and its affiliated unions. It may include imposing on the roads regulations and controls "similar" to those enforced on the railways. In some cases, for example New Zealand and South Africa, the railways' traffic and their money investment are protected by regulations so strict that they constitute nearly a complete ban on competitive traffic. In the shadow of such restrictive legislation the requirement of a conventionally defined balanced budget for the roads hardly seems to matter.

15. Many countries, however, still have a more or less freely competitive trucking and road passenger industry, and so it is instructive to ask whether there is any general presumption that, if the railways are required to balance their budget, the roads should also. One preliminary point of some importance is that even though railroad corporations or authorities may be *required* by law to aim to cover their costs "taking one year with another," only a very small fraction of them actually avoid accounting losses. Indeed, some of the losses are astronomically large—for example, the railways of Argentina in 1966 were losing US $1 million equivalent a *day*. Even in the developed countries of the world it is rather rare to encounter a railroad that is not suffering a loss on normal accounting criteria, even though the roads are saddled with heavy taxes.

16. A second consideration is that in developing countries the railway network may well be small and have only a small amount of traffic that is competitive with the highways. Even when the railway system is reasonably well developed, competitive traffic may be less than one-tenth of total road traffic. Thus competitive traffic often does not seem to matter very much as far as the roads are concerned. For the railways, however, road competition is usually considered vital. Roads are alleged to take away the cream of the railways' traffic—that high-rated traffic which is thought to provide much of the railways' profit.[4] The effect on the accounts of the railways, it is thought, is proportionately very large and it is the genesis of much of the recorded loss. It seems a bad policy, however, to impose special charges on all road traffic merely for the sake of the small fraction of road haulage and passenger traffic which competes with rail in order to produce a black figure in the books of the railways.

---

[4] In fact, it seems that the profit is to be found in the low-rated goods, which can be transported at even lower costs. In Gilbert Walker's famous aphorism "The cream is at the bottom of the railways' bottle." See "Transport Policy Before and After 1953," *Oxford Economic Papers*, Vol. 5, (London, March, 1953).

17. Furthermore, the theory of "charging what the traffic will bear" suggests that high-valued commodities should be charged high rates, that is, rates in excess of marginal transport cost. These levies are a form of taxation of high-valued commodities, imposed by the railroad board or Ministry of Transport and not by the ordinary internal revenue departments of the Treasury. Road competition would seem a welcome stimulus to keep down high railway rates and to encourage the railways instead to balance their accounts, so cutting out some of the subsidy which they give to other traffic. Thus the (implicit) user subsidies usually given to short-distance stopping-train traffic, to congested traffic and to certain branch-line traffic would be eliminated. The interest groups that enjoy these subsidies are reluctant to give them up and can bring into play considerable political pressure to defend their prepared positions.

18. To try to protect these inefficiencies by creating parallel ones on the roads involves the tricky arithmetic of two wrongs making a right. It is obviously not a good policy to impose a balanced budget requirement for all road traffic, whether or not it is competitive with the railways' "cream." For non-competitive traffic, this simply adds inefficiencies by levying uneconomic charges. For competitive traffic alone, the outcome depends on the extent to which any reduced distortion in the supply of transport services is or is not offset by the greater distortion in the use of transport. There is perhaps a presumption that distortions in supply will tend to be greater than in use. This is the more likely, the greater the elasticity of substitution between rail and road services, and the smaller the elasticity of demand for transport generally. Alternatively, it might be better to compensate by direct subvention to the railways for any subsidies to users that are considered unavoidable for political or social reasons. It would be logical in that case to subsidize not only the railways, but also competitive forms of transport; that would provide the subsidy to the transport *user* in the most efficient manner.[5]

19. In practice, railway deficits are due mainly to technological developments on the roads. Railways were usually built before the great rise of the internal combustion engine; rail is now outmoded and inefficient in a wide variety of transits. Yet the book value of the railways continues to reflect their value when they were transferred to their present owners. The burden of stale debt is upon them. Part of the accounting deficit—and perhaps the whole of it in some cases—could be eliminated by simply writing down the value of the railways' assets to something like their present value. Then the

---

[5] Realistically however, it is often the local railway labor that is subsidized; thus a *rail* subsidy is thought to be the least bad solution.

accounts would tell us the modest truth of the present rather than the past history of greatness. To try to protect the "true" historical value of the railways is like trying to retain the "inherent skills" of the hand-loom weavers. Only the traditionalist opposed to growth and progress would support such policies.

20.   Whether or not the railways would incur a deficit if they did not give subsidies and did not charge discriminatorily high rates is a good question. The presumption is that they would tend to be in the red—at least until they managed to get rid of historical excess capacities. Then the outcome depends on much the same constellation of factors (of demand, capacities, and cost) that we have discussed with regard to roads in the previous chapter. Provided that suitably high charges are levied on congested transits, there does seem to be a chance that there will be a zero deficit or even a modest profit—when the assets are properly valued. But this is pure conjecture!

21.   Whatever the "best" or "natural" deficit or profit however, we should always judge taxes and subsidies on their *effects* and not on any *a priori* notions of "fairness," "propriety," or "moral values." The case for the railways being required to "break even" may be argued in terms of the effects. Eminent railway authorities have contended that the accounting discipline of the balanced budget is one of the strongest incentives for efficiency in management. To strive to make a profit, or at least to avoid a loss, is one of the main aims of management in ordinary commercial undertakings. The most persuasive measure of the success of management is contained in the accounts; if profits have increased, or the loss has been reduced, then management may receive an accolade; if the deficit is larger, then excuses and scapegoats must be sought.[6] If, on the other hand, the consequences of managerial performance are buried inextricably in a general government budget, and if it is recognized that the government will simply levy taxes to make good any deficits incurred by railways, management will have little incentive to cut costs, to seek more efficient methods, to eliminate unprofitable traffic, to close redundant lines and to improve services.[7]

22.   There are, of course, also other reasons for requiring the railways to cover their costs. If the railways did receive a subsidy from the general

---

[6] The best statements of the "efficiency" reason for requiring balanced budgets for railways are to be found in the various writings of Sir Reginald Wilson, sometime Comptroller of the British Transport Commission.

[7] The great efficiency drive on British Railways during the era of Lord Beeching was largely spurred by the desire to eliminate the deficit.

budget there would surely be strings attached. A subsidy is very likely to involve political interference in running the railways, in fixing freight rates and in the day-to-day administration of railway operation. The requirement, and even more the achievement, of a balanced budget will help insulate the railways from political pressures. The railways are less likely to be a pawn, or perhaps a bishop, in the political struggles for power.[8]

23. It seems therefore that there are good reasons for requiring the railways to "cover their costs, taking one year with another." As we have seen, however, there are many definitions of "cost" that may be used, and the definition chosen must depend entirely on the purpose to be served. For each administratively feasible definition of "costs" one should examine the expected gain in managerial efficiency and compare it with the loss incurred because of the constraints imposed on pricing by the requirement to balance budgets and to adjust taxes accordingly. Unfortunately it is very difficult to make such calculations in practice—because little is known about the reaction of railway administrations to different types of budget constraints. One generalization can be risked in this state of ignorance; it is clearly better not to require the railways to attempt to cover their historical costs.

24. Suppose that, with whatever definition is used, the railways are required to balance their budget (and let us assume that they always succeed!) and let us suppose, for the sake of highlighting the problem, that *all* rail and road traffic are closely competitive; then what are the implications for road pricing? In particular, does it imply that a balanced road budget would be a good thing? The short answer is no.[9] A requirement of a balanced rail budget may give rise to rail fares and rates above costs for traffic where the railways have some relative advantage, but *ceteris paribus* some traffic would be lost to the roads which could be more cheaply carried by rail. It may be desirable therefore to increase the price of road haulage in order to improve the allocation of traffic between road and rail even at the expense of foregoing some road traffic altogether because of the higher price.

---

[8] It should be observed that all subsidies do not have deleterious effects on efficiency. For example, subsidies which are paid as a specified sum of money per unit of output, such as those frequently used in agriculture, leave the producer free to make as much profit as he can. There need be no interference in the operation of the firm—and in agriculture, for example, there is in fact very little. The most depressing effects on efficiency are where the subsidy takes the form of the government underwriting the deficit of the organization, however large the loss may be. Unfortunately this sort of "featherbed" subsidy is typical of those in the transport sector.

[9] For a formal statement and proof of the theorems used in the text the reader is referred to the mathematical note at the end of this chapter.

In other words, given the balanced budget requirement on the railways, it may be a good idea to raise road taxes above the marginal cost charges on the highway.[10] But a balanced road budget would not give the amount of adjustment required, except by the most fortunate of accidents. True, it seems superficially that the requirement of a balanced road budget would result in an adjustment in the right direction; a tax would be levied above the marginal cost. But even this is not certain, for it is conceivable that the marginal cost charges themselves will be sufficient to balance the road budget. And it is conceivable that the requirement of a balanced budget may result in taxes which are *lower* than the marginal cost charges (for example, on congested highways in densely populated areas).

25. We conclude therefore that a balanced budget on the railways may well be a useful stimulus to efficiency. The bad effects of such a restraint may be more than offset by the good. But it does not follow that a balanced road budget would ameliorate the bad effects of a balanced rail budget. As we saw in the discussion of the railways' regulated rate structure above, a balanced road budget may do more harm than good. It is certainly no general panacea.[11] In order to protect the railways' traffic it may be better to require the trucker to buy a special license if he wishes to carry traffic that is considered to be efficiently carried by rail. By setting the price of the license at an appropriate level, one could ensure that the railways were not inefficiently denied this traffic. But such methods, although better than simple administrative exclusions, have a detrimental effect on development traffic. This also should be weighed.

4. *User Charges in a Monopolistic Environment*

26. One of the important limitations of the theory of user charges presented in this study is that it presupposes that the remainder of the economy consists of competitive firms and industries. The conclusion that the marginal cost is the appropriate levy is derived from the postulate that the prices of other goods and services measure the marginal cost of their production. We have just discussed the consequences of departures from the marginal cost rule when an onerous "cover-the-costs" rule is imposed

---

[10] This is a "weak" conclusion however. It is also possible to argue that a balanced rail budget condition may imply that a subsidy to road users would be desirable! Much depends on the interrelation of demands, the extent to which rail and road interact, and the extent of substitution possibilities. See the note at the end of this chapter.

[11] The argument for balancing the road budget on the grounds of "managerial efficiency" of the road authority is very weak. The efficiency with which roads are constructed and maintained, depends on the contractual arrangements made with an "open bid" system. A budget constraint on the authority will have little or no effect on efficiency.

on the railways. This is probably the most important general form of restraint that is imposed on (but rarely achieved by) the railways. There may be significant differences, however, between cost and price in other industries due to the existence of monopoly or government regulation or both. How do these elements of monopoly affect the general marginal cost rule? And, in particular, can they be held to justify the roads covering their costs?

27. The first point to be emphasized here is that there is no simple theory that can provide any general rules of pricing in general conditions of imperfect competition. Indeed, since the departures from competitive conditions can be so complicated, it is easy to see that any general rule of wide applicability will be rough and ready. And it also follows that any precise solution that could be derived from any given set of specified monopolistic and competitive conditions would be of such bewildering complexity as to be useless.

28. Simplicity is the hallmark of useful theory. And so, faced with such a problem, one naturally grasps for some simple assumption that will, at least, give rise to tractable results. A simple approach is to suppose that there is an *equal* amount of monopoly in all other industries in the economy. All firms charge a price that is a constant fraction of value added above their marginal costs. Then it seems to be an appropriate policy to levy user charges at the same fraction above the marginal cost. However, this only follows if the rate of transformation throughout the whole economy—including the leisure-income margin—is twisted to the same proportionate extent. There are also distortions due to the existence of a subsistence economy which will be concentrated in those activities where there is close substitution between market and non-market organizations. And in developing countries it is clear that there are dominant activities such as agriculture and retail trade that are very competitive; a few industries— and probably the least important (excepting perhaps the railways)—are monopolistically organized.[12] But even if one did think that this was an appropriate model for levying user charges, it would make little practical difference to the result. The main problem of the road deficit arises from the fact that interurban and rural highways are used much below capacity. On such paved roads therefore the marginal cost is almost zero. Consequently if we increase the charge by some constant fraction above marginal cost, the result would still be near enough zero. On the other hand, the

---

[12] And many of the monopolies are state owned and perhaps even controlled by government; clearly there are many more degrees of freedom in the situation than the one we are dealing with.

congestion levies raised for urban traffic would have to be increased to reflect the margin of price above marginal cost, and clearly this would be a significant sum. If however, it were thought that the simplified model of Chapter III were appropriate—with constant costs up to capacity—then the proportionality rule would be irrelevant for roads operating at capacity. The price charged on these roads is simply that which "clears the market"—and this price is not changed at all. If, however, the appropriate model is the one with increasing costs as we approach capacity, then the price should be raised above marginal cost. Thus the proportionality rule would have little effect on the deficit of the rural and interurban roads, but it would increase or decrease the profit (or rent) of the roads—depending on the elasticities of demand and on the slopes of the cost curves.[13]

29. Of much more interest are realistic models where some industries are monopolized and some are suffering competitive conditions. It is likely, for example, that the steel industry is a nationalized monopoly, whereas retail distribution, fishing, and agriculture are essentially competitive industries. The difficulties that arise here are mainly because of the interrelations among industries in different competitive situations. To illustrate this point we might consider an extreme example. Let us suppose that there are a number of competitive industries in the economy and an iron and steel industry that is effectively a monopoly. The iron and steel industry is completely integrated—buying only factors of production in a competitive environment and road services. It is also convenient to assume that the iron and steel industry sells only to consumers. Let us also suppose that the competitive industries make no use of the road (we can imagine them using water transport instead). It is clear that the price of iron and steel would be above the marginal cost, whereas in competitive industry price and marginal cost would be equal. Thus people would be better off if the price of iron and steel were reduced and resources transferred from the competitive industries to iron and steel production. Accepting that nothing can be done about the monopoly pricing in iron and steel and that prices are set above marginal cost, one may then try to find the optimum road user charge policy in this environment. Since consumers would be better off if the iron and steel industry expanded, it should be the policy of the road authority to stimulate the production of iron and steel. This can be achieved by lowering the road user charges *below* the marginal cost (in-

---

[13] It must be emphasized that there is more to the "proportionality model" than appears in this account. One must, for example, exclude strategic behavior on the part of the participating monopolists. Thus there must be a sufficient number of competitors so that each firm, although in some sort of monopolistic position, will not take account of its behavior on others and their reaction back on its own behavior, and so on. Each must react to events passively.

cluding rent of scarce road space); in principle it may be best to subsidize the road transport of the iron and steel industry! The fall in the marginal cost of the iron and steel industry will (*ceteris paribus*) induce it to expand output at the expense of competitive industries.[14]

30. The conclusion that one should subsidize a monopoly is, of course, offensive to one's ethics and one's common sense. Even if the subsidy per unit of output, to increase production of iron and steel, were combined with a tax on the monopoly's rents to siphon off the profits, it is clear that many more direct ways might be used to control or ameliorate monopolistic restrictions on output. Why not simply control the price at which the monopoly sells its output? This would surely be better than indirectly influencing the costs by lowering the price (road user charges) on one of the monopoly's inputs.

31. Nevertheless, the argument has been put in this form because it is necessary to demonstrate that the existence of monopoly in other industries does *not* imply that the best charge to levy on the highways is above the marginal costs. Formally, it might be better to levy charges which are below the marginal cost. It all depends on the structure of industry (who takes in whose washing), on whether the road service is competitive or complementary to the product of the industry, and the degree of competition within that industry. No general results are available.[15]

32. It seems that, in our present state of knowledge, it may be best to approach the problem pragmatically in each particular case. The basis, however, should be the marginal cost (including, as always, rents), since it is clear that the general environment must be competitive. Then we should examine the closeness of competition between rail, water and road, and the extent to which road transport is used in different industries. If, for example, roads are used almost exclusively by the highly competitive industries—such as agriculture and retail trade—and to a very small extent by the iron and steel and mining monopolies, then there may be a good case (*ceteris paribus*) for raising user charges above the marginal cost. Sup-

---

[14] In the interests of brevity I have omitted from the text many other assumptions that ought to be made: for example, the decrease in the charge for the roads may give rise to inefficient substitution of roads for other factors of production in the production of iron and steel; a sufficient condition then is the existence of rigid proportions between the input of road services and the output of iron and steel.

[15] The reader might think that the so-called "theory of the second best" might provide an answer to these questions. Unfortunately it does not. The "second best" approach is simply to reduce n Pareto conditions to $n - 1$ Pareto conditions by writing the nth condition as a constant. No reaction functions are involved. It simply reduces the degrees of freedom in the system and so reduces the number of independent equations. So it really amounts to "Pareto with constants."

pose that charges above marginal costs are levied on the rural roads used almost exclusively by agriculturalists. Then we must ask what resources would be freed by such an increase of the user charge; would those resources be specific or would they be freely transferable to the other (monopolistic) industries? If, for example, it merely results in a reduction in the amount of land cultivated and, because of immobilities, no transfer of labor, then it would clearly be better to levy only the marginal cost charge.

33. Obviously such conjectures take one far afield. And it is clear that one needs to know much more about the reaction of industry and agriculture to varying user charges. To a very small extent we shall try to fill this gap during the course of this study. But no one should pretend that there will ever be sufficient information to apply the pragmatic approach at all extensively. Information is expensive and one must grasp the nettle and make recommendations without the aid of suitable data. It seems that, in view of the above arguments, the best single recommendation is that the authority levy the marginal cost. And if a case can be made on "monopolistic" grounds for deviating from the marginal cost (and on the many other grounds discussed in this study) then it should be amended accordingly.

34. Although there are few positive results to be derived from these monopolistic considerations there is one negative result of some consequence. The presence of monopoly in the rest of the economy provides no inkling of an argument for balancing the road budget.

5. User Charges, Location of Economic Activity, and "Full Costs"

35. It has been alleged that user charges which are determined by the marginal cost rule will give rise to inefficiency in the location of industry and agriculture. The argument runs roughly as follows:

> In deciding where he will locate his factory (or farm) the businessman will take into account only the costs that appear in his private accounts. These costs will include the marginal cost of using the road. But when there is no congestion, the amount of money collected by the road charge will be less than the total cost of providing and servicing the road (suitably discounted). Consequently, the full cost of providing the road (as distinct from the cost of providing road services once the road is built) will not be reflected in the accounts of the businessman. Consequently a business will be induced to locate its plants inefficiently because it does not take into account the total costs of its decision. Furthermore, (and this is strictly an additional point), the fact that the businessman chooses inefficient locations that require too much road transport will imply that too many roads are built and too great a fraction of resources is used by road transport. The solutions are various versions of full-cost pricing. With these there would be no deficit; each tub would stand on its own bottom.

36.   In order to deal with this argument we shall assume that there is no congestion at all on any of the roads, that appropriate marginal cost prices are always levied, and that the appropriate "cost-reduction plus consumer surplus" investment rule is always used. Furthermore, we shall suppose that the pattern of cost curves is the same as that outlined in Chapter III—with both indivisibilities and joint-cost characteristics over the relevant range of traffic flow; therefore levying the marginal cost as a user charge will be insufficient to cover the total costs of the road.

37.   Consider first a very *simple model* where there is just *one firm* that will use the road (yet to be built). Imagine that there is just one type of road that may be built but that it may be of any length. The variables in the situation are therefore the length of road to be built and the location of the firm. (We might, for simplicity, think of the firm always locating itself at the end of the road; then the problem is even easier.) Suppose that the business firm *knows* the investment criterion of the road building authority (which in this simplified case is the decision about the length of the road), and that the authority knows all about the profits of the firm with different locations. Thus the road authority can draw up an account showing the profits related to the ton-miles (or vehicle-miles) for different lengths of road. The difference in the firm's profits when there is two miles of road and when the road is three miles long represents the amount which the businessman would be *willing* to pay for the extra mile of road. And this is precisely the amount which enters into the calculation of the surplus, i.e. the amount which users would be willing to pay rather than do without the additional mile of highway.

38.   Thus the entrepreneur, in choosing his location, knowing very well the investment criterion of the road authority, will take into account the fact that the road authority will only build another mile of road if the additional profit in the accounts of the firm is sufficient to *cover* the road building costs. If the profits would not increase by more than the cost of the road, then the road extension is not worthwhile; the firm would know that the road authority would not extend the road and would locate accordingly.[16]

39.   This decision about the location of the firm and the length of the road is exactly the same as that which one would obtain if the road authority and the firm were one organization. Naturally, if the firm were building the road itself, it would construct an extra mile of highway if the

---

[16] We may think here of a simultaneous decision by entrepreneur and road authority. The complications of induced investment after some time lag are considered below.

additional profits were in excess of the additional costs. This is exactly the same as the solution we have suggested above.[17] The main conclusion therefore is that the combined policy of charging marginal cost and of investing according to the consumer surplus criterion will in this case result in the optimum location of the firm and the optimum amount of road building.

40. It does not matter at all, as far as the location and road building are concerned, whether the profits which are generated by the road are distributed to the shareholders of the firm or whether they are taxed away by the government. This would be simply a transfer arrangement and would not affect the decisions on the allocation of resources, the location of industry and the amount of road building which should and would be done.[18] Whether the profits generated by the road are taxed away (by a levy on rents for example) or whether they are left in the hands of the lucky recipients in no way affects the investment and location solution. This conclusion is of crucial importance for all the analysis that follows. It may be considered "equitable" to tax away the receipts generated by road construction; but it is *not* required for the correct allocation of resources and the efficient location of economic activity. It may be thought to be a good idea to set up an investment test by trying to collect the increment in profit that justifies the road construction; but it is *not* required for efficiency in road investment and in the location of industry.

41. Efficiency in the allocation of resources and economic activity requires that the road authority levy charges at marginal cost. If it is administratively feasible to collect the benefit generated by the road (by means of two-part tariffs or land rent taxation), then it is possible to levy duties which may make the distribution of income more consistent with concepts of equity and which may generate information from which more accurate investment decisions can be formulated. So much the better. But suppose that it is not possible to levy the fixed charges of a two-part tariff or to tax away any substantial fraction of the increment of land rent. Is it then desirable to increase the *user charge* above the level of marginal cost so that "full costs are covered"? Would not this give rise to a more efficient system of allocation and location? The answer is an unequivocal

---

[17] It will also be obvious that for internal costing procedures the firm would cost actual vehicle *journeys* at marginal cost—the same policy as we proposed for the road authority.

[18] It is necessary to add that it matters considerably as far as the distribution of income is concerned. In a micro-context the firm may not *exist* if it is required to pay the total road costs, and it may well be that in a macro-context the distribution of income will greatly affect the mobilization of savings and the characteristics of investment. But this is another aspect of the problem which will be taken up in Chapter VIII.

"no." If user charges are raised above the marginal cost, resources will be thrown away, roads will be underutilized and land will go uncultivated even though it could earn a surplus above true cost. Of course a government may well decide that it can afford to waste some of its resources in order to achieve what it may regard as a better distribution of income, etc., but this decision should be taken with its eyes open. It is a delusion to imagine that charges above marginal cost can achieve both efficiency and equity.[19]

42. Although the model we have developed involves only one firm, it is easily extended to encompass *a number of firms*. Again the road authority will build the additional mile of highway only if the additional rents so generated are sufficient to offset the highway costs involved. It is worth noting that the marginal firm will of course earn zero rents; but this does not mean that such a marginal firm is inefficiently located because it does not pay its "share" of the full costs of building the road. Since it pays the marginal cost for all its traffic it covers all the real costs associated with its location. The intra-marginal firms earn rents (or pure profits) from their locational advantages; they would be willing to pay more than marginal cost in order to transport the vast majority of their goods. The difference between the amount they actually pay and the amount they would be willing to pay constitutes the surplus on the road. As before, a comparison of this surplus with the costs of constructing the highway gives a criterion for investment. But again efficiency in pricing requires that the charge be levied at marginal cost. No fixed charge (of a two-part tariff) or land tax is required for economic efficiency. It may be desirable to tax away the surplus created by the construction of the road; but granted the feasibility, this decision must be made according to the canons of equity, on the one hand, and in the light of the amount of information which may be gathered and used in the investment decision, on the other. No rent tax or fixed charge is required to "correct" the allocation of resources.

43. There is however one difficulty, which has received much attention in the literature,[20] when there are a number of firms, as distinct from one firm. An individual firm will not find incentives to move from a consideration of the current prices facing him in the market. If an individual firm moved, its action would not justify building the road; only if many firms moved would the road authority extend the road by the extra

---

[19] It is only a slightly smaller delusion to suppose that the normal forms of user charges are equitable. See Chapter V.

[20] Tibor Scitovsky, "Two Concepts of External Economies," *The Journal of Political Economy*, Vol. LXII, No. 2, (Chicago, April, 1954), pp. 143–151.

mile. Two subcases can now be distinguished. The first is when the road authority acts in a promotional sense, rather than simultaneously as assumed above. The road authority does its calculations and finds that it would be profitable to have a road since the surpluses generated by the firms that would newly locate there would be more than sufficient to offset the costs of the investment. The authority therefore announces that it *will* build the highway. Then there are no improper locational decisions taken provided that each firm reacts passively to current prices and current intentions of the authority. If the government "leads" and the firms follow, there will be no wrong locational decisions provided that the authority only builds roads when the traffic generated will justify them. This is, after all, no more and no less than the policy which we suggested as efficient in Chapter III.

44. More problems are raised by the second subcase, where the firms "lead" and the government follows. The policy of the road building authority is now to construct the road *after* there exists a sufficient amount of traffic to justify it rather than in anticipation of generated traffic. It is clear that there is now the danger that individual firms will not move because they as individuals would not profit by such a move— unless many other firms also moved and created an amount of traffic sufficient to induce the authority to build the road. All or nothing. It seems likely, however, that firms do not behave in this passive manner; each firm would calculate the strategy and reaction of other firms in this situation—as the first to move would get the favored location, there might in fact be a scramble onto the bandwagon. Nevertheless, in this case there is indeed doubt about the efficacy of the price system in supplying the appropriate signals for location—there may well be too little movement rather than too much.

45. Let us further consider the problems raised by leads and lags, and the proper signals given for road investment and location. Take the problem of locating a plant to supply the market in Calcutta, and suppose that the plant might be built in *either* Bangalore *or* Calcutta.[21] If the plant is located in Bangalore, the road transport of goods from Bangalore to Calcutta will entail improvement of the road earlier than would otherwise have occurred. Should one therefore not consider the costs of an earlier improvement of the road as part of the costs of locating in Bangalore, and so should not the firm be debited with these costs if it locates in Bangalore?

---

[21] This example was suggested by Benjamin B. King.

At first sight it seems as though in this example there may be too great an incentive to move to Bangalore unless the true total costs of the decision are reflected in the private accounts of the firm.

46.   In many respects the problem is similar to the one discussed above. Suppose location in Bangalore *is* justified from the point of view of the economy, i.e. the additional profits of locating in Bangalore offset the costs of (earlier) improvement of the road. Then again, if the government leads, i.e. announces its intention to improve the road, say, three years from now, and if the firm or firms believe the government and act accordingly, location and road investment will be efficient. This is essentially the same case as above except that the "lead" given by the government anticipates its actual investment in the road by several years. Without improvement of the roads, in due course, the firm may be better off in Calcutta. The problem is therefore to convince the firm that the government will really improve the road. A location subsidy may be necessary to carry conviction. Otherwise, there may be too little movement of firms to Bangalore.

47.   Suppose now, however, that firms should *not* move to Bangalore and that the road should not be improved, because the additional road investment costs outweigh the advantage of location in Bangalore. If the government makes its decision known, and firms follow the "lead" given, they will locate in Calcutta as they should. However, what happens if the firms do *not* follow the lead and locate in Bangalore, in the belief that the government will after all not stick to its announced intention not to improve the road? In fact, although before the decision to locate in Bangalore was made, location in Calcutta without road improvement would have been better; now that the plant has actually located in Bangalore, the road improvement has become worthwhile. If bygones are considered bygones, and the government does improve the road, the firm will have succeeded in being better off, but the economy will be worse off than if the firm had been located in Calcutta. It appears then the firm can "force" the government to follow this wrong location lead. Not charging for the cost of improving the road has resulted in too much movement of firms to Bangalore.

48.   Should the government consider the location decision as a bygone and in a sense, bail out the firm that made the wrong decision? Whether it is a good idea for the government to improve the road depends on whether such action creates a precedent. Suppose that such a road-building operation were a once-and-for-all event which would create no precedent for future government investment. Then it is sensible for the government to construct the Bangalore road. But suppose, *per contra*, that this is merely one project in a long series of similar projects; clearly the

Bangalore construction may be taken as a precedent. This will mean that on future occasions firms will be able to count on the government building a road, once a firm has shown that its location is a bygone, for the government will then find that the road passes its investment test. The danger is clearly that the government, by passively reacting to the decisions of firms, will change the criteria on the location decision. The firm will know that it can *lead* the road investment of the government. Consequently there will be a misallocation of resources.

49.   There are many policies which might be used to deal with this problem. First, it might be suggested that the best policy is for the government not to invest *ex post* even though, considered as an individual investment, it would be worthwhile. The government may well conclude that the advantages of following *ex post* a rational investment rule are offset by the fact that future decisions by firms will be inefficient. One policy is then for the government to stick to its announced policy of investing only if the surplus exceeds investment cost before the firm locates its plants. The disadvantage of this policy is that it does not enable the government to make investments that become worthwhile only after firms *have* made wrong location decisions. The advantage is that firms will know clearly the investment criteria used by government—and they will know that, if they make a mistake, the government will not bail them out; they will sink. Consequently there will be a great incentive for the firm to make the correct decision.

50.   An alternative policy is for the government to devise "location taxes" (and perhaps also "location subsidies" though we shall ignore this alternative). In order to give additional discouragement to the firm to locate in Bangalore, a large lump-sum, once-and-for-all tax would have to be paid if the firm located in Bangalore.[22] Thus firms can be guided to their most efficient location.[23] The advantage of such location taxes is that, in principle, the government can now take advantage of the road investments that be-

---

[22] It is important to note that the location tax should *never* be added to user charges. If location is a once-and-for-all decision the charge should not even be an annual levy. It should be a once-and-for-all tax—like the classic capital levy of the textbooks.

[23] A particular form of this policy is for the government to announce its policy that it will not build roads unless the surplus exceeds the cost. Suppose that for Bangalore the surplus does not exceed cost so the road should not be built—but nevertheless firms move to Bangalore. The government announces that it will indeed build the road if the firms will pay the total once-and-for-all cost. With their location costs a bygone, firms may then find it profitable to pay for the costs of the road. But *ex ante* the total costs to firms (including the road costs) exceed the cost—so they will be induced to locate in Calcutta. So in fact one would rarely observe the case where the firms actually paid for the costs of the road—for that would be only when a "mistake" was made.

come worthwhile because of mistakes of firms, without fear of the consequences for future decisions.[24] The disadvantage is that such a system of
taxes must involve detailed estimates, calculations, and, inevitably, mistakes. The attempt by government to correct for the "mistakes" of business
may generate even more costs in terms of incorrect investment decisions
due to the wrong location taxes. There is no way in which one can theoretically weigh these effects; the facts only can decide. And such a survey is
beyond the scope of this study.

51.   To sum up, in general the pattern of the location of industry will be
optimum if the marginal cost is levied and if the road authority follows
the surplus criteria for investment. For efficiency no other prices or taxes
are required. However, once-and-for-all location taxes (or subsidies) may
be useful in discouraging firms from taking the wrong location "lead" (or
inducing them to follow the intentions of the government). If it is feasible,
and if thought desirable for equity reasons, one may tax away the surplus
created by the road improvement. But such taxes should not be permitted
to infringe on the *use* of the road, or on any other marginal conditions.
Such taxes should be levied on the rents and profits so that they do not
result in resources (and particularly road space) being wasted.[25] Efficiency
always requires the *user* charge to be priced at marginal cost. Under no
circumstances would "full-cost" pricing be consistent with efficiency.

52.   Thus there is no argument which can be deduced from the theory of
the location of industry to show that the roads should cover their costs.
We do not require that the surpluses be collected; the surpluses must
simply exist in order to justify the investment and location patterns.

6. *Political and Administrative Reasons for Covering the Costs*

53.   The main political reason for a balanced budget is that it provides
an automatic discipline on the general road lobby. Road investment is a
decision taken by the public authority. In principle, investment should
take place if the benefits exceed the costs; but, in practice, governments
decide according to other criteria which may be vote-catching, graft or
more statesmanlike reasons. The ability to influence these decisions by

---

[24] Again one would find that, if the taxes did their allotted task and actually resulted in the
firms being discouraged from locating wrongly, then one would not collect any revenue from
the tax!

[25] If, on the other hand, the government decides that it is willing to throw away resources
(such as road space) in order to achieve some given equitable distribution of benefits and
burdens, then one should devise a system of taxes that will minimize the waste. This is the
burden of Chapter V.

various means exists in all governmental systems. If road pressure groups do not have to pay for the roads, they are unrestrained in promoting their joint interests in better highways.[26] A constitutional requirement that users must pay for the total cost of the road would prevent the worst excesses of logrolling. In an ideal case it is possible to imagine that the pressure groups would then have an incentive only to press for investment if the benefits exceeded the costs which their members would incur.

54.   But one must not exaggerate the efficiency of an overall restraint on aggregate road expenditure. First, it is well known that pressure groups are political organizations with internal conflicts. Procedures for arriving at agreed policies are likely to be inefficient and to produce one out of a class of less desired outcomes.[27] It would be naive to imagine that a pressure group reflects the properly weighted interests of its members. Secondly the pressures are likely to be local and particular, rather than nationwide and general. A national balanced budget for the roads would not dissuade a road user from politically pursuing local schemes that benefit him. He would put pressure on his political representative to secure a larger share of the national cake, which, since there is a *nationally* balanced road budget, will be paid for by all other taxpayers. All other representatives will be under the same sort of pressure, and thus we have the ingredients of a classic "logrolling" decision. The outcome may well be that we would end up with *too much* investment in roads.

55.   The best political answer to such criticism is to decentralize budgetary responsibility. This suggests that in each local area there should be a fiscal discipline of balancing the road budget. The more particular the discipline is, the more effective it is in constraining "logrolling." But, as we have seen, the smaller the area for which the budget is balanced, the greater the likelihood of inefficiencies due to charging prices that differ substantially from the economic price in order to cover the costs.[28] The practical problem is to choose a compromise between the disadvantages of misinvestment and those of under- or over-utilization of existing facilities. Fortunately, however, we shall find much room for maneuver in devising various kinds of taxes that both permit a balanced road budget and, at the same time, do not restrict inefficiently the use of the highways, or give rise to undue congestion.

---

[26] In principle the pressure groups would spend money on lobbying until their expected marginal gains from expenditure on roads, etc., just balanced their marginal costs of lobbying.

[27] On the analysis of such processes see Buchanan and Tullock, *op. cit.*

[28] To avoid misunderstandings, it may well be that the prices are too low in some cases, as well as too high in others. Balancing the budget may be bad for urban areas because the city streets *should* make a profit!

56.   The objective is to produce a system of taxes that minimizes the harm of departing from optimum pricing and, at the same time, provides a discipline for investment and spending on roads. Certain general principles emerge from the framework of political economy. First, the taxes levied to give a balanced budget should be extracted as far as possible from those who benefit from the investment. This is a sensible principle of social justice; insofar as it is possible to allocate benefits to individuals, the beneficiaries should pay taxes to finance expenditures for such benefits. This provides an investment check as well as an equitable distribution of the burden of new works and their maintenance. Second, these taxes should be distributed so as to interfere as little as possible with the optimum charge for *using* the road. The main practical problem is to design taxes that have these two desirable effects, and, second, to find administratively feasible ways of arranging taxes so that they automatically fall on the beneficiaries. In some cases these are a small easily identified group, whereas in other cases, perhaps the majority, the benefits are spread widely throughout the economy.

57.   The case for a balanced national road budget is relatively weak on political grounds, because it does not provide an effective check to local and particular pressure groups. The argument for a balanced budget for a local or particular group of roads is much stronger—but correspondingly the economic harm, in terms of under- or over-utilization of existing roads, is likely to be larger. The problem becomes a practical one of discovering administrative arrangements that minimize the harm in each direction.

7. Definitions of User Charges, Taxes, and Subsidies

58.   So far we have shirked the problem of defining the concepts, such as user charges, taxes and subsidies, which have been used liberally throughout the foregoing pages. Now is the time to say what we mean. There is little help to be obtained from practical studies in defining user charges or user taxes. Transport experts use the terms indifferently to cover any charge which is thought to be somehow related specifically to road users. Widely different interpretations occur. Some include import duties on vehicles; some do not; some estimate what the special import duty on vehicles is, over and above the "normal" import tax. (This latter is presumably the conjectural value which would be levied if vehicles did not require roads!) There is clearly a need to define terms more carefully.

59.   The essential quality of any definition is that it be useful for analysis and policy. Definitions are made relative to a theory of the policy we are

examining; they are a consequence of postulates of behavior patterns. The behavioral standards adopted here are the usual ones of economic thought—that people try to get as much satisfaction as they can from their given resources. Similarly, the government, as the agent of society as a whole, is concerned with meeting desires for public goods so that it maximizes the satisfaction of the individuals of society. True, there is then the complication of weighing one individual's satisfaction against another—but the essence of the calculus of the welfare from public goods is the same as that from private goods; we try to maximize satisfaction and minimize costs. The mechanism of maximizing or minimizing is through marginal adjustments. Small changes are made, and then we ask whether the lot of a person or a group is improved or worsened. If small adjustments cannot be made—for various technical reasons—but large changes are necessary, the same aim applies, but we have to be more careful in measuring the changes since the "distance" is larger. User charges and costs must fit into this pattern if they are to be interpreted in the framework of economic analysis.

60.   We have discussed at length the optimum price for a highway journey—and this price measures the value of resources (including rents of fixed "plant" or roadway) used up in providing that journey. It measures the resources saved if that journey had not been undertaken—or the satisfaction of other goods foregone. This optimum charge is the linch pin of all economic analysis of roads. We shall henceforth refer to it, as we did in Chapter II, as the *Economic User Charge*, or *EUC* for short. This represents the normal price which would be levied by a competitive industry supplying road services—were it possible to organize this industry in a competitive form.

61.   We must now distinguish between taxes and subsidies, on the one hand, and the *EUC* on the other. If the payment for a journey is less than the *EUC*, the difference may be described as a *discriminatory user subsidy* (or *DUZ* for short). If the price exceeds the *EUC* the difference is a *DUT* or *discriminatory user tax*. "Taxes" and "subsidies" therefore disturb the ideal marginal relationships.[29] They differ from the *EUC* by being discriminatory. A proper and useful definition of *discrimination* is that there is discrimination when the money extracted for a service differs from the relative cost of supplying it, or when differences in price are not explained by differences in cost.

---

[29] This is the logical and natural use of these terms. See Abba P. Lerner, "Conflicting Principles of Public Utility Price Regulation," *Journal of Law and Economics*, Vol. VII, (Chicago, October, 1964), pp. 61–70.

62. It is easy then, in principle, to determine which duties imposed by the state give rise to *DUT*'s on vehicle journeys; but it may be more difficult in practice. Consider, for example, a license duty on the annual ownership of the vehicle. This is not obviously a *DUT*, since it does not directly influence the decision about a vehicle journey. But it does so indirectly. The vehicle duty results in a smaller number of vehicles for a given number of standard vehicle journeys—and in rather fewer vehicle journeys than in the absence of such a duty. An additional journey will involve utilizing more intensively an already overutilized stock of vehicles. Thus the monetary costs are higher than they would be in the absence of the duty. Such a difference is part and parcel of the *DUT*, even though it looks as though it is a real cost.

63. Import duties on new motor vehicles and parts combined with excise duties on locally manufactured vehicles obviously give rise to effects similar to those of license duties. The difference is that this import duty falls directly only on the new vehicles—but of course it is passed down to all second-hand vehicles. Vehicles are maintained for a longer life than in the absence of such a duty. The cost of an additional vehicle journey is thus higher than it would be without the duty. This *DUT* is exactly analogous to the annual license duty case discussed above.

64. One important practical difficulty occurs because import duties and excise duties (or sales levies) may be exacted from *all* products. Clearly if the import duty on motor vehicles is the same as that on all goods including the excise duty on domestic products, there is no *DUT* involved. It is important to note that the import duty should be the same as the excise duty on domestic goods; if they differ there is discrimination. Indeed there is very little if any difference between a proportional income tax and a proportional *ad valorem* levy on all imports and home sales. If, however, the tariff on motor vehicles is higher than the general import levy and domestic excise tax, this will be reflected in a *DUT* for a vehicle journey.

65. In many countries import duties are used as a substitute for a progressive income tax. The import duty levied on cars may be much larger than that on trucks, and the tariff on large cars may be much higher than that on small vehicles. This still gives rise to a *DUT* through the full amount of the import duty. The intention of the tariff does not matter; the *effect* is to discriminate against vehicle journeys. It also discriminates against the rich—but *only* insofar as the rich buy large cars and the poor do not. The rich man who does not buy a large car will escape the duty. Logically therefore it is a *DUT*.

66. Again in many countries the governments have built up complicated and elaborate systems of controls, regulations and exclusions which substantially affect the choice of individuals and corporations in allocating their resources. For example, there may be an absolute ban on the import of motor vehicles or their parts. A typical case is when a country bans the import of tires in order to develop, by brute force, a domestic tire industry. Can one distil from this a *DUT*? In principle, an absolute ban is equivalent to a tariff high enough to exclude all imports (excepting smuggled goods). Thus there is an implied *DUT* which is equal to the exclusive tariff *minus* the general tariff (which is the same as the excise tax) on all goods both domestic and imported. This implied *DUT* is "paid" over to the tire producing industry as an implied subsidy, so that, at the high internal price, the domestic tire manufacturers satisfy the home market.[30]

67. But, one may consider that this ignores the fact that the price of tires measures the high domestic cost of marginal tire production. The expansion of tire consumption from additional road use will come from this high-cost domestic industry, for the road user has no access to tires on the international market. Thus it is tempting to conclude that there is no *DUT* on tires since the price measures real marginal (domestic) production costs. But such a definition merely confuses the issue. The main objective of our definitions of *DUZ*, *DUT*, and *EUC* is to measure the opportunity costs. Since importation of tires was the alternative foregone it is that value, the import cost, that is the relevant comparison. If the government wishes, or feels compelled, to arrange tariffs or quotas so that domestic production is expanded, that is a policy decision with its own costs, taxes and subsidies.

68. Our concern in this section is with useful definitions, not with policies *per se*. But it is interesting to pursue this line of argument a little further. Given that the government will arrange matters so that the high cost domestic tire industry expands (and imports remain constant) is it not sensible to charge a *higher* tax than implied by the calculation of the *EUC*? For if the *DUT* in tires were very high it might mean that the *EUC* is less than the existing *DUT*—thus levying only the *EUC* would result in an increased use of tires and in an *expansion* of the inefficient domestic tire industry. But of course this is an argument about the desirability of levying *EUC*'s when other price-cost relationships are out of joint. It is analogous to the "monopolistic environment" case discussed in section 4 of this

---

[30] An extreme case is when the ban on imports is considered immutable—like a fact of nature—and unchangeable by government. Then indeed the marginal cost of tires is the high domestic cost, not the import price.

chapter. It may well be a good idea to charge road prices above the *EUC*, if the government is determined to expand domestic tire production to meet the market demand, just as it may be a good policy to charge road prices above *EUC* if there is a monopolistic (rail) competitor. This is a question of *policy*, whether or not to increase the price above the *EUC*, and it must be argued on the grounds which we discussed in section 4 above. The definitions of *EUC*, *DUT*, and *DUZ* are best left as we have defined them to reflect the opportunity costs.

69.   Obviously it is possible to deal with other restrictions—such as limited quotas—in the same way. It is instructive to take the extreme case, however, and ask what would be the *DUT* if *all* imports were banned. Would this not mean that there was zero discrimination against road users? The answer is obviously no. The impact of a total import ban will not be the same over all commodities and services and persons. A ban on the import of cassava into a West African forest belt country will affect no one; a ban on the import of motor vehicles will discriminate against those who consume these services. The differential effect depends on what would have happened if there had been no such ban; from these differentials we can impute the implied *DUT*'s.

70.   The most difficult imputations occur where there are complex regulations governing the ownership and operation of motor vehicles. Whatever the reasons given for regulating the road haulage industry, (be it to protect the investment in railroads, to protect the hauler from himself, etc.) the effect is to change the amount of road use from that which would emerge in a free market where only *EUC*'s were levied. Consider an archetype where the government simply imposes an effective limit on the number of vehicles by a certain rationing device. (Such rationing may be effected through the bureaucracy or the courts determining "public need," "social welfare" or some other alleged desideratum.) To discover the equivalent tax we must find the duty on vehicle ownership that, in a free market, would reduce the number of vehicles to that determined by the regulating authority. This vehicle tax can then be translated into a *DUT* for vehicle journeys, when the *EUC* has been subtracted. Those truck owners who get on the approved list receive an implied subsidy as their reward. In effect the truck owners levy a tax on the traders who use (or would use) road transport for their goods—and this is of course usually passed on to the consumer.[31] This is therefore a *DUT* on road "consumers" and a *DUZ* for the happy truckers on the approved list.

---

[31] We are not here discussing the other wastes of such a regulation arrangement—in particular the costs of regulation itself are the wastes due to truckers investing in litigation and bribes in order to get themselves on the approved list.

71. Let us now consider a common complication of this model. Suppose that the truck limitations are introduced because the authority knows that the rail competitor cannot levy charges that reflect the additional cost of carriage but is forced to fix rates which exceed marginal cost because of some institutional or legislative constraint. Then it might well be argued that the two DUT's have countervailing effects and cancel each other out. This is, however, an incorrect conclusion; the point is that *both* rail and road are suffering discriminatory taxes compared with other goods and services.

72. In some countries the reliance on administrative control and regulation is so ubiquitous and the departures from free choice and marginal-cost prices are so great that it is difficult or impossible to trace the DUT's and DUZ's through the system. The cost-price relationships are buried so deep it is impossible to disinter their remains. In these circumstances it makes little sense to talk about user taxes or user charges or costs. The point of reference has disappeared and the analysis cannot proceed until some other standard unit is discovered. I conjecture, however, that such cases are rather rare; even the East European countries are turning more and more to reliance on a cost-based price system.

73. This concludes our discussion of the meaning of road user charges and taxation. The definitions are primarily useful if we wish to pursue a policy of maximizing the welfare of individuals. They are of little direct use if the state evokes some moral principle (such as, for example, "fair play" or "social justice") which supersedes welfare maximization. But even then the definitions given here can be used indirectly to compare the effects of using some moral precept instead of economic maximizing. For example, if it were decided that all traffic should pay the same sum per ton-mile under whatever cost conditions emerged, we could examine the DUT's and DUZ's with respect to our standard EUC's. This is, as we have defined it, economic discrimination; but according to the moral principle—which indeed may also be enacted as a *legal* rule—there is no moral discrimination involved. Moral principles of this kind lie behind popular conceptions of "fair and reasonable" road pricing. In our framework of analysis these are DUT's and DUZ's which have more or less moral sanction.

8. *Definitions of "Costs" of the Road System*

74. A review of the literature shows that practicing transport economists are not at all agreed on what precisely constitute the "costs of the road

system." Indeed, disagreement even extends to the definition of "the road system"—what roads or facilities should or should not be included. However, before discussing the actual valuations, we might reasonably pose the following questions. For what purpose are cost data necessary? In particular, do we require to know "the costs of the road system" for any practical economic policy?

75.   If we are to pursue the maximizing policy outlined in the first chapters of this study, it is obvious that only certain specific concepts of costs are relevant. We need to know the *EUC*—that cost which measures the resources used up by an additional journey.[32] This is the marginal cost of a journey when the road network is "held fixed." This concept is the center-piece of the whole analysis and policy. Correspondingly, when we examine whether it is worthwhile to change the road system, we need to consider the cost of improving an existing road—or perhaps building a new road. Additional resources are to be sunk now and in the future, in return for a future stream of services. Some of the problems of determining the cost of the resources have been discussed in Chapter III—such as the familiar issues of market prices which may not reflect the real resource costs, the effect of the investment itself on prices, and the impact of uncertainty on the relevant marginal cost concept. Other problems relate to the need to reduce all future costs (and benefits) to present values by discounting them at appropriate interest rates. All future costs should, of course, be valued at relative prices (indicating relative scarcities) as they are expected to occur in the future. For example, it is widely believed that vehicle prices will fall relative to the prices of other goods. This should clearly be taken into account in assessing the merits of the investment.

76.   The important point here is that these problems concern the costs of expanding or improving the road network—they are problems of the *future* commitments of resources in terms of their present values. One of the main aims, however, of most policies of "balancing-budgets" is that the user should pay the "costs" of *existing* roads. They are not concerned with future expenditures, their intention is to recover the money that was sunk in the roads in the past, and to charge a reasonable rate of interest on such investments.

Historical Costs

77.   "Costs," in this sense, emerge from mists of history. With an assumed amortization rule and a postulated interest rate, accounting responsibility

---

[32] Note that in the case of the simple fixed-capacity road the EUC includes the rent.

for those costs can be distributed over time to the various generations of users. Many accountants would tend to use the actual historical spending as the basis of "cost"; this is at least a clear and unequivocal money value in a certain year. Many transport economists (and some accountants), however, would revalue the existing stock of roads at *current* prices; they would find how much it would cost to construct the existing roads at *present*. Such a revaluation is necessary in some circumstances, so as to prevent the exercise from being patently silly (for example, in Chile or Brazil where there has been a high inflation). Often this involves asking the question whether or not the road would (or should?) be built today. The more sophisticated balanced-budget studies exclude roads which would not be built again and add up the costs only of the roads that are still thought to be worth while.

78. A wide variety of arbitrary decisions is needed for estimating the total costs of the roads and the distribution of these costs over the years. Each investigator, since he will be a reasonable man, will have his own reasonable solution to these problems. There are no objective criteria to which one can appeal; for there is no maximizing or minimizing purpose for which the calculation is required. The purpose of balancing budgets is to conform to political, administrative or moral precepts ("that road users should pay the accounting costs of the road"). There is no unique definition of costs that can be derived from the theory of politics or administration or moral philosophy.

79. In terms of ordinary common sense or economic theory it is impossible to see any relevant place for either the historical cost or the replacement cost concept. We cannot rewrite history, and the question of replacement should be decided on its own merits. The historical cost is not relevant for any decision to be made now or in the future. Whatever was or was not paid for the construction of highways, the only reality that matters now is the existing stock of roads and how best to use them, adapt them and expand them in the future.[33] The fact that an Inca highway cost some sum in a strange currency of antiquity, or that it would cost so many dollars to replace it by the same (!) or "equivalent" modern road, is clearly of interest only to the historian or the curious.

80. We are usually interested in the cost of an asset because it gives a good idea of the exchange *value* on the market. With roads, however, there

---

[33] This does not mean that the present situation is independent of how the roads were financed. If the roads were financed by a loan the burden of present and future taxes will be greater than if they had been financed by contemporaneous taxation.

is no secondhand market and no amortization rules can be adduced from the market.[34] Furthermore, many roads are built whose value is less than their cost; for there is no competitive discipline on the public authority that supplies and finances the highways. Lastly, demands do change over the lives of the roads; even the 14th century builders could not have anticipated that their English bridges would be used by buses, trucks and cars.

81.   Consequently, cost has no relevance for the *value* of roads. However, the *value* of the whole road system has a relatively clear economic definition; it is the amount which people would be willing to pay rather than do without the road system. But such a value is impossible to measure. It is, indeed, not at all clear what purpose would be served by such a measure—unless one were thinking of letting the whole road system rot (opportunity cost). This is never a practical question, therefore even a measure of the *value* of the road system as a whole seems irrelevant. After all, no one is proposing to sell or buy the road system as a whole; one's concern is with expanding, improving or contracting it.

82.   The reader may well ask why all this fuss over historical costs? Are not these calculations simply an excuse (and not even a rationalization) for raising taxes against road users? It may or may not be a good idea to tax road users differently from their present levels. But the only rational way to deal with this is to ask what are likely to be the *consequences* of higher and lower taxes, or of different tax structures. All policy proposals should be judged in terms of their future effects and not in terms of the past. It may be a good idea, in trying to show that an increase in road taxes is "just" or "proper," to carry out some calculations of historical cost (duly revised at current prices). But this is a matter of propaganda not principle. The essential point is that the consequences, and only the consequences, are the criteria by which any policy is to be judged; the philosophical or rational basis of the policy is irrelevant.

Development Costs

83.   These criticisms of the "historical cost" method suggest that there are other techniques that get around these difficulties. These are the variants of the so-called "development cost" methods. (There is no standard terminology in this field, so the same animal or species of animal may be known under several different names.) The total costs of maintaining, expanding and renewing the road system must be covered by the charges on

---

[34] Amortization rules depend on a given schedule of expected prices. To use amortization to determine prices is to lift oneself up by one's own bootstraps.

users. Two alternatives are then open: either we prepare amortization accounts and, at the rate of interest, distribute investment costs over future users. Or we can regard investment as a current expense to be recovered along with the maintenance expenditure—a "pay-as-we-go" system. To distinguish between the two we shall call the former the *Development or Long-run Marginal Cost Method* and the pay-as-you-go system the *Incremental Method.*

84.   In the Development and Long-run Marginal Cost Methods the cost of providing an additional road is divided by the expected quantity of services to be derived from that road in the future. The difficulty is, of course, how to distribute the capital costs over time: amortization rules are essentially arbitrary from an economic point of view. The Development Method "solves" the dilemma by postulating that road charges per vehicle-mile are to be kept constant over the life of the road. For a given flow of traffic over time, this determines, of course, the level of charges needed to amortize the road. The Long-run Marginal Cost Method has no such conventional rule to make the year-by-year allocation of amortization charges determinate. This method should, in principle, take into account the movements in demand expected in the future and the price determined by the intersection of the demand curve and the long-run marginal cost.

85.   It may be appropriate, of course, in some cases, to run down the road; the cost of running it down is then defined as the escapable cost divided by the services which the road is still to supply. Let us call this the "running-down-cost." Obviously it will often be much lower than the "development cost." Now the development cost methods assert that when the roads need to be expanded in the foreseeable future we should use the development cost to charge for the road, whereas if roads are not be to replaced we should use the running-down-costs. It is important to observe that these are actual projected costs of feasible alternatives, rather than notional costs of programs no longer being considered.

86.   This approach avoids many of the great difficulties of calculating costs inherent in the historical cost approach. It deals with the present and the future and is not preoccupied with the past. Furthermore, if the roads were expandable like putty, with no joint-product aspects of disproportionalities, and if putty could be produced at constant costs per unit, the development cost (and running-down cost) would be exactly the same as the *EUC.* The Development Cost Method would give us a practical way of measuring the *EUC.* But as we have argued above, the roads are obviously not putty. Joint-products and lumpiness are typical of road investment. Furthermore, the stock of roads is not always easily adjusted to the

113

ideal level—partly because of institutional lags, and partly because of the real lags of planning and execution. The Development Cost Method must also be arbitrary in its choice of the size of road considered appropriate for investment and user charge calculations.[35]

87. The Development Cost Method will not necessarily result in a total amount of taxes and user charges that will cover the total road budget as defined in the accounts of the public authority. For example, traffic would normally be increasing over time, so that a newly constructed lumpy road would have light traffic in early years and so earn a low revenue. In later years, as traffic increased, the revenue would grow larger. Where there is much new construction a deficit may be incurred for extended periods on the road account as conventionally defined.

88. The Incremental Method is broadly the same as the development cost approach except that it incorporates a pay-as-you-go principle. Investment expenditures are counted as current costs in the year in which they are undertaken. No amortization and depreciation accounts are used; all expenditure is treated as used up in the year it is spent.[36] The big difference between the Incremental Method and the development method is that the former is concerned only with *actual* expenditures as they occur, whereas the latter measures *notional* expenditures—what would be the cost if the road system were increased. The Incremental Method charges the actual expenditure incurred in successive road development schemes.[37] (As we shall see, the incremental costs can be easily allocated to different types of vehicles.) The incremental cost concept is the most unambiguous of all the conceivable measures of total cost. It ignores interest and amortization—those twin tenuous values—and concentrates on the current drain on the government budget. For these reasons, incremental cost has the best claim to be the most suitable concept for defining the balanced budget requirement. It is directly and immediately related to the values that appear in the government's accounts.

89. The disadvantages of the Incremental Method, however, are equally obvious. All the cost burden is borne by the present users, notwithstanding that future users benefit from the valuable assets so created. Only with zero net investment over time will the incremental cost measure the value of the roads; if net investment is growing linearly over time then the capi-

---

[35] The size of the "lump" of road we should measure depends on future traffic which depends on the charge which, in turn, depends on the size of the "lump."

[36] This is the treatment of road investment adopted by national income statisticians. They recognize that any amortization rule would be so arbitrary as to be useless.

[37] This concept of cost—the pay-as-you-go concept—is the one that was adopted for the financing of the Interstate Highway System in the United States.

tal stock of roads will be growing quadratically. All the oscillations in net investment are fully reflected in this measure of costs, whereas a figure reflecting the true value of resources used would be much smoother.[38] If there were no oscillations in investment, and if investment increased at the same steady rate for a very long time, then the incremental cost would grow at the same rate as the development and long-run marginal cost. For any given year, however, the incremental cost would be higher than either the development cost or the long-run marginal cost. With steady growth the incremental method has the effect of shifting the responsibility for cost to an earlier period in time.

90. This is analogous to calculating the cost *as if* the roads were all used up in the year in which they were built. Thus in years where investment is a large fraction of the capital stock of roads, the convention of the incremental method will overestimate the cost of the roads used up, whereas in periods when the investment in roads is a relatively small fraction of the capital stock, the Incremental Method will underestimate the value of the roads used up. Thus the Incremental Method is a particularly misleading measure of costs when investment varies considerably over time and when the ratio of investment to the capital stock of highways changes greatly from one period to another. This is a serious disadvantage of the incremental concept.

91. If one accepts the political and administrative reasons for "covering the costs" however, the incremental cost does seem to be the least bad definition available. It has the additional advantage that the increased taxes may stimulate saving to match the increase in road investment. There is, as it were, a built-in stabilizer. This has a great appeal to development economists faced with the problem of mobilizing resources for development.

92. The main purpose of this chapter was to examine the case for departing from the *EUC* principle and to decide whether road charges should cover the costs of the highway system. The main conclusion is that, although one may justify some departure from *EUC*'s in certain practical cases, there is no *economic* argument for balancing the road budget.

ANNEX: MATHEMATICAL NOTE*

93. We can show that if a budget constraint is imposed on the roads the formal solution is for the road authority to recoup its costs where the

---

[38] Note that if the investment follows a *sine* curve the capital stock will follow a *cosine* curve—i.e. the oscillations will have the *opposite* movements over time.

* I am very grateful to Professor William Vickrey who found an error in a draft of this note.

elasticities are lowest, i.e. to charge in proportion to what the traffic will bear.

Let benefits be B and the costs C for n road services, the quantities of which are denoted by $x_1, x_2, \ldots x_i \ldots x_n$. Each of the services is sold at a price $p_1, p_2, \ldots p_i, \ldots p_n$. The condition that the budget be balanced is then

$$C = \sum_i p_i x_i$$

To find the best price system we maximize the *net* benefits $\underline{B} = B - C$, subject to the condition that total costs are recovered. With Ψ as a Lagrangean multiplier, we have:

$$\underline{B} = B - C - \Psi(\Sigma p_i x_i - C)$$

Stationarity conditions are given by finding:

$$\frac{\partial \underline{B}}{\partial x_i} = \frac{\partial B}{\partial x_i} - \frac{\partial C}{\partial x_i} - \Psi\left(p_i + \sum_j \frac{\partial p_j}{\partial x_i} \cdot x_j - \frac{\partial C}{\partial x_i}\right)$$

and equating to zero, i.e.

$$0 = p_i - \frac{\partial C}{\partial x_i} - \Psi\left(p_i + \sum_j \frac{\partial p_j}{\partial x_i} \cdot x_j - \frac{\partial C}{\partial x_i}\right)$$

or we might write it as:

$$p_i - \frac{\partial C}{\partial x_i}(1 - \Psi) = \Psi\left(p_i + \sum_j \frac{\partial p_j}{\partial x_i} \cdot x_j\right)$$

Now the bracket on the right-hand side of this equation measures the marginal revenue which the authority obtains by expanding its service x_i by a small amount and maintaining constant all other services. (Prices must adjust so that the same x_k, $(k \neq i)$, are bought.) The natural interpretation is therefore to define the right hand bracket as follows:

$$p_i + \sum_j \frac{\partial p_j}{\partial x_i} \cdot x_j = p_i\left(1 + \frac{1}{\epsilon_i^*}\right),$$

where ϵ_i^* is defined as the *total* elasticity of demand for the ith service. This *total* elasticity takes into account the indirect effects, on the prices of other services, of expanding the ith service on the revenue of the authority. Thus we obtain the simple result:

$$\frac{p_i - \dfrac{\partial C}{\partial x_i}}{p_i} = \left(\frac{\Psi}{1 - \Psi}\right)\left(\frac{1}{\epsilon_i^*}\right)$$

116

Thus the "mark-up" of price above marginal cost should not be constant but should vary in inverse proportion to the *total* elasticity of demand for the service.

A particularly simple case of this rule is where:

$$\sum_{j \neq i} \frac{\partial p_j}{\partial x_i} \cdot x_j = 0$$

and so the cross-effects on demand cancel out. Roughly interpreted, substitute road services are as important as complementary road services. Then the rule becomes:

$$\frac{p_i - \dfrac{\partial C}{\partial x_i}}{p_i} = \left(\frac{\Psi}{1 - \Psi} \right) \left(\frac{1}{\epsilon_i} \right)$$

where ϵ_i is the *partial* elasticity of demand for the ith service.[39] The proportional "mark-up" of price above marginal cost is inversely proportional to the partial elasticity of demand for each service.[40]

94.   In examining the road/rail problem the same approach can be used. The first practical question is, supposing that the railway is constrained by the requirement of a balanced budget, would it be a good idea also to so constrain the road authority? Clearly no such general presumption can be deduced. Indeed it is always true that one can find an optimum policy for roads, given the rail budget constraint; and that policy will only accidentally give rise to a balanced road budget. Thus when the balanced road budget is imposed it is either unnecessary or harmful.

95.   Given the fact that the railways are required to break even, a balanced road budget *may* be better than the simple EUC on the roads. But one can always achieve at least as good a solution, and in the vast majority of cases a better one, by adjusting the EUC's in some other way—for example one would adjust only those road prices that were competitive or complementary to rail, leaving the others at the EUC.

---

[39] A sub-case is the much more restrictive case where:

$$\frac{\partial p_j}{\partial x_i} = 0 \text{ for all } j \neq i \text{ cases}$$

This is where demands are independent.

[40] It would perhaps be more relevant if we took the prices of the services, other than the ith, as *fixed* and considered the net benefits as the p_i is varied with consequential variations in the x_j to maintain the same prices $p_j(j = i)$. Such an approach however causes complications in the analysis of costs and has not been pursued here.

V

BENEFITS AND TAXES ON AN UNCONGESTED ROAD

1. *Introduction*

1. In the first three chapters of this study we have examined the general principles of road pricing. The policy that emerged was the simple proposition that road user charges should be determined by marginal costs and the requirement that demand be equal to supply. These principles were quite general—indeed in some respects they were too general. We did not specify the form of the demand curve for the road transport or anything about its elasticity, and the theory thus far provided no obvious limitation which we could impose on the demand curve. Nevertheless, the shape of the demand curve turned out to have a considerable effect on the investment calculation and the importance of optimum pricing. On the other hand, the theory was much more specific about the form of the road cost curve. We conjectured that the cost curve was approximately constant for most rural roads—the pure public goods case. The cost curve for most (congested) urban roads could also be predicted with a fair degree of accuracy. There is indeed considerable empirical evidence to be reviewed in Chapter VI that the cost curves are of the form predicted by theory.

2. We know a fair amount about how road improvements affect the track maintenance costs and the operating cost of vehicles. But much less is

118

known about how the reduction in operating cost affects the transport rates which in turn influence the development of natural resources and the location of economic activity; that is, we know little about the demand for transport. In urban transport, the problem is mainly that of the passenger, his intermodal choice, and the division between public and private transport. In rural transport, the main concern is freight haulage, the extension of the margin of cultivation and the transformation from traditional pursuits to producing for the market. This is the main focus of this study and particularly of this chapter.

3.   A simple model of a new road in a rural area is helpful for this discussion. What would be the consequences on the volume and character of traffic, on the area of cultivation for the market and on the increase in marketed produce? Certain restrictive assumptions must be made in order that the model give useful results. The main assumption is that there is free entry to the road haulage industry and that it enjoys constant costs. Thus when a road is improved the reduction in operating costs are *wholly* passed on to the users in the form of lower rates. No part is kept by any ring or monopoly of the truckers. Secondly, we suppose that the marketing arrangements are organized under highly competitive conditions—so that a fall in wholesale prices will be passed on immediately in the form of lower retail prices. No fraction of the reduction in transport cost is soaked up by the higher margins of distributors. These assumptions—and they are crucial—enable us to isolate the effects of road improvement in terms of changes in production and rents of location.[1] Other assumptions may be relaxed, as shown in several variants of the basic model, without basically altering our results.

4.   One of the first uses of the model is to examine who benefits from the road. Given the assumptions of the model one can show exactly how the benefits will be allocated between one farmer and another, or strictly between the various landowners. One may identify "iso-benefit" contours as those locations of farms that enjoy the same benefit from the road. We also show the form of the rent "surface" both before the road and after the construction. Lastly, we examine the effects of some inelasticity in demand. In that case the benefits appear partly as "rents" of location to consumers.

5.   Although the theory of user charges suggests that for a congestion-free rural road no price (other than for variable maintenance cost) should

---

[1] It is, of course, perfectly possible that with a monopolized distribution industry, the reduction in transport cost merely increases the profits of retailers and wholesalers. This appeared to be the case in one area in Iran. See H. G. van der Tak and J. de Weille, *Reappraisal of a Road Project in Iran*, World Bank Staff Occasional Paper No. 7 (1968).

be levied for the use of the highway, one knows that in fact user taxes will often be imposed on such highways. The pressure towards balancing the road budget will often result in levying DUT's on road users. A wide variety of taxes are available in practice—and one must choose between them. The main purpose of the model is to examine the effects of different types of taxes. The main types of taxes which we examine are the land levy, the income tax and its variants, ton-mile taxes, and tonnage (export) levies. We are interested in how these duties affect traffic, the area of cultivation and the benefits and rents accruing to individuals.

6. In terms of the strict theoretical model, one may easily show that the ideal tax is the levy on rents. This does not affect the area of cultivation and nicely siphons off the benefits brought by the road. In principle it is possible to collect all the additional rents generated by the new highway, and to appropriate them for the Treasury. In the case of the perfectly elastic demand for the product at the port, to be discussed below, these additional rents are a measure of the benefit from the road, and hence in principle if the road is justified it can be fully financed from taxes on these rent increments, though where the road is just barely justified the tax may have to approach 100 percent, with consequent accentuation of the administrative difficulties and inequities resulting from errors in assessment. If the demand for the products transported is less than perfectly elastic, only a part of the benefit from the road will be reflected in increased rental values of the land served by the road, the other part of the benefit will be reflected in the lower consumer prices (the "rents of consumer location"). Full financing out of land value taxes may not even be theoretically possible. And whatever the theoretical attractions and possibilities of land value taxes may be, the practical problems of administration and valuation are often so severe, particularly in developing countries, that complete financing of road improvements out of land taxes is rarely feasible— except for certain minor rural developments. (Essentially, we shall also reach the same conclusion for the income tax.)

7. The practical problem is likely to be one of choosing between taxes on ton-miles (such as the fuel tax) and taxes on tonnages (such as the export tax). One of the important tasks is to examine the relative efficiency and the "equity" of these levies. Broadly two approaches are adopted. First, we examine the effects of the two levies when they both raise the same amount of revenue. The question is then: which levy gives the largest amount of development (area of cultivation)? The answer is always the tonnage tax; and we show that the area is substantially larger. Secondly, and, I believe critically, we examine the relative efficiency of the two

taxes in raising revenue when the areas of cultivation are the same. The most striking result there is that the tonnage tax will raise at least 50 percent more revenue than the ton-mile tax—given the same cultivated area. The tonnage tax is always a much better revenue-raising tax than the ton-mile levy.

8.   We also use the model to derive a number of subsidiary results about tax rates. The first is to find the rate of the ton-mile tax that gives rise to the maximum revenue for the Treasury. This is shown to be 100 percent of cost—or even higher if the road is very short. Then we also examine the problems of policies concerned with covering the costs rather than maximizing revenue. Unfortunately there is no unique solution—but we show that it is likely that, if the road authority chooses the "high-traffic" solution, there will be little difference between the revenue-maximizing solution and the cost-covering solution—provided that costs are not *very low* relative to the benefits of the road. Many of these results can be most usefully cast in the form of traditional demand and supply analysis—and we can show exactly the position and shape of the demand and supply curves for road services.

9.   During the course of this chapter we shall occasionally drop one or more of the restrictive assumptions. In particular, we shall often assume that there is a demand that is less than perfectly elastic. We shall see that it is easy to take into account the numerical consequences of a sloping demand curve. No attempt has been made to develop the theory taxonomically to include all conceivable variations. But it is clear that the basic pattern of the theory does not change—and it should be judged not by the plausibility of its assumptions but in terms of the veracity of its predictions. We shall return to this aspect later in this study.

2. *The Basic Ellet Model*[2]

10.   Consider a country where the land is homogeneous with the same rainfall and soil conditions. We can imagine that before the road construction the land was only used for subsistence agriculture—the growth of cassava or hill rice, for example, which have no commercial market. With access to the market, however, the inhabitants could produce one commercial crop, say, rubber, at a constant productivity of one ton per acre per annum. (We imagine that the additional work involves no disutility—that

---

[2] This name of the model pays tribute to an early version put forward in 1836 by Charles Ellet. My attention was drawn to this by Dr. Hugo Sonnenschein.

is to say, we assume that the shadow price of additional labor from the existing work force is zero. Later we drop this assumption.)

11. Let us also suppose that the country has a coastline with a port at P (see Figure 20). All rubber is exported through the port at P. We assume that this area provides only a small part to the world market so that any amount of rubber can be sold at a constant price, which we therefore supposed fixed at $\$k$ per ton at the port P.

12. Rubber can be transported by two modes. It can be carried by porters on their heads, which we call *headloading*. The costs of headloading are constant at $\$b$ a ton-mile. Along the road goods are carried by motor vehicle at $\$a$ a ton-mile—a cost which is also assumed constant. Transport can only take place in a north-south or east-west direction. We can imagine that the paths run only in this grid-like pattern. No one can walk diagonally in a NE-SW or SW-NE direction. (This restrictive assumption will later be dropped.) Consider now a road of uniform quality, constructed from the port at P due east into the interior. Suppose also that the length of the road is not nicely adjusted to its productivity—it just continues eastwards at least until the agricultural development runs out. We shall often call this the "endless road case," to distinguish it from the "truncated road case" when the length of the road is determined by the rule that the cost of the last foot of road should be just equal to the additional net product so generated.

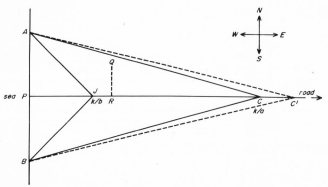

Figure 20. A Plan of the Cultivated Area with an Endless Road.

13. With these assumptions consider the farmer at $\mathcal{Q}$ in Figure 20. The transport cost of his ton of rubber to the market is given by:

$$a(PR) + b(\mathcal{Q}R)$$

122

A farm can be represented by its coordinates on the map, with the port at P as the origin and the east-west road as the x-axis and the coast as the y-axis. For any farm, therefore, y can be positive or negative, i.e. north or south, whereas x can only be positive—there are no farms in the sea. For any farm, the condition that describes whether or not it will produce for the market is, in our simple model, whether the transport costs are less than the market price.

14.   This determines the area of cultivation for a farm that is north of the road, for example, the farmer will produce for the market if:

$$ax + by \leq k$$

Similarly, for a farm south of the road the condition is:

$$ax + b(-y) \leq k$$

Thus the area of cultivation is represented by the triangle ABC, where the line AC, the northern limit of cultivation, is:

$$ax + by = k$$

Similarly, the southern limit of cultivation, BC, is given by:

$$ax + b(-y) = k$$

Determination of the corner points A, B, and C is simple. From the points A and B the rubber is headloaded all the way to the port at P. The distance AP (or BP) is thus given by:

$$y = \frac{k}{b}$$

From the point C the produce is carried all the way by road to the port. Thus the distance PC is given by:

$$x = \frac{k}{a}$$

15.   With this framework we can ask various questions. The first obvious question is what would be the area of cultivation in the absence of a motor road, i.e. when all produce has to be headloaded to the port at P? What difference does the road make? Clearly, if all produce was headloaded to P the conditions of cultivation would be:

$$b(x + y) \leq k \qquad \text{for } y \geq 0, x \geq 0$$

$$\text{and } b(x - y) \leq k \qquad \text{for } y < 0, x \geq 0$$

These conditions describe the triangle AJB where J is the same distance

k/b from the port P as points A and B. The difference between areas ACB and AJB can be attributed, on our assumptions, entirely to the existence of the highway.

16. A second problem to which we can address ourselves is to find the *elasticity of demand* for transport along the road. If the road is improved, operating costs fall and the area of cultivation will expand. Let us suppose that the operating cost on the road falls from $\$a$ a ton-mile to $\$a(1 - \lambda)$ a ton-mile, where $1 > \lambda > 0$. Thus λ represents the proportional reduction in operating costs of motor transport which, on our assumptions of a competitive trucking industry, is reflected completely in the price of motor transport. The effect of this fall in the price per ton-mile of motor transport is to extend cultivation along the road to the point C'. By analogy with the foregoing discussion, the distance of C' from the port at P is now:

$$\frac{k}{a(1 - \lambda)} \text{ miles}$$

and the new area of cultivation is described by the triangle $AC'B$ and by the inequalities:

$$a(1 - \lambda) x + by \leq k \qquad y \geq 0, x \geq 0$$
$$a(1 - \lambda) x - by \leq k \qquad y < 0, x \geq 0$$

17. There are any number of concepts of the elasticity of demand for transport according to the difference in acceptable definitions of the *quantity* of transport services. One of the simplest definitions is the number of *tons* carried; that is to say, we ignore the variation in the mileage over which commodities are carried and merely measure the weight carried some distance along the highway. Using this definition, one notes[3] that the proportionate expansion in tonnage (area) is:

$$\frac{\lambda}{1 - \lambda}$$

---

[3] The original area of cultivation (in tons as well as in acres) is:

$$\frac{k^2}{ab}$$

and the new area is:

$$\frac{k^2}{(1 - \lambda)ab}.$$

Note also that one may find the elasticity by differentiating:

$$\frac{d \log(k^2/ab)}{d \log a} = -1$$

The advantage of using first principles, however, is that one can *see* the result.

Since the proportionate change in price is $-\lambda$, the elasticity of demand for transport in terms of *tons*, which we call ϵ_{tons}, is given by:

$$\epsilon_{\text{tons}} = \underset{\lambda \to 0}{\text{Limit}} \ \frac{-1}{1 - \lambda} = -1$$

Thus in this model, the elasticity of demand for *tons* transported is minus unity. A 10 percent reduction in the price per ton-mile of transport will lead to an expansion of 10 percent in the *tonnage* carried.

18. For many purposes a more appropriate measure of the quantity of transport is the *ton-mile*. This takes into account the distance over which the weight of goods is transported. We can now measure the elasticity of demand for transport, measured in ton-miles, with respect to the price of transport per ton-mile. In one sense, this is the natural measure of elasticity since both the quantity and the unit in which price is expressed are the same—the ton-mile. The proportionate increase in the ton-mileage can easily be shown to be:[4]

$$\frac{1}{(1 - \lambda)^2} - 1$$

As before, the proportionate change in the transport price per ton-mile is $-\lambda$. Thus, the elasticity of demand in terms of *ton-miles* is given by:

$$\epsilon_{\text{ton-miles}} = \frac{1}{-\lambda}\left[\frac{1}{(1 - \lambda)^2} - 1 \right] = \frac{-1}{\lambda}\left[\frac{+2\lambda - \lambda^2}{(1 - \lambda)^2} \right]$$

$$= -1\left[\frac{2 - \lambda}{(1 - \lambda)^2} \right] = -2 \text{ as } \lambda \to 0$$

This shows that, in this model, the elasticity of demand for transport in terms of *ton-miles* is -2. A 10 percent fall in motor transport costs will generate a 20 percent increase in ton-miles. This is, again, an exceedingly simple and sharp result.

19. Whether these two elasticity results can be considered as at all fundamental and useful depends on their robustness. Since we shall be using

---

[4] The number of ton-miles by motor vehicle is measured by the integral

$$\int_0^{\frac{k}{a}} 2x\left(\frac{-ax}{b} + \frac{k}{b} \right)dx \quad = \frac{k^3}{3a^2b}$$

With a fall in motor transport cost per ton-mile to $\$a(1 - \lambda)$, the new quantity of ton-miles will be:

$$\int_0^{\frac{k}{a(1-\lambda)}} 2x\left(\frac{-a(1 - \lambda)}{b}\, x + \frac{k}{b} \right)dx \quad = \frac{k^3}{3b[a(1 - \lambda)]^2}$$

the basic model for many of the investigations of the effects of different types of road taxes, it is worth examining some of the possible complications and their impact on our simple results.

3. *Variants of the Basic Model**

20.   As a preliminary we should consider whether the results are at all affected by the assumption that only transport costs are considered. What about wage and equipment costs? How do they affect the elasticities? Suppose that factor payments for a ton of the commodity amount to, say, f, and are not affected by the level of output. Then the condition of production is simply:

$$ax + by + f \leq k \qquad y \geq 0, x \geq 0$$
$$ax + b(-y) + f \leq k \qquad y < 0, x \geq 0$$

i.e. total cost is less than or equal to the price.

21.   These basic equations give exactly the same sort of results as those of the simple model. The only difference is that k is replaced by $(k - f)$, the price per ton less the factor costs (other than transport) per ton. The distance along the road of the cultivated area is $(k - f)/a$, and the distance on either side of the road at the coast is $(k - f)/b$. The area of cultivation is then $(k - f)^2/ab$.

22.   It is obvious that the elasticities of demand for transport are exactly the same as those in the simple model—minus one for tons transported and minus two for ton-miles of transport. Thus it does not matter that factor inputs, other than transport, are required. The results are the same. This is a fortunate conclusion since our model would have minute application if it could not encompass other factor inputs. For most purposes, we can simply ignore other factor inputs provided we may assume that the price of factors does not increase as the demand for them increases. At this stage this seems to be a reasonable presumption of the analysis.[5]

A Truncated Road

23.   The next assumption which we might relax is the supposition that the road is endless. If agricultural development were the only reason for

---

* The reader interested only in the broad outline of the argument may proceed directly to Section 4.

[5] Note that when we consider the case when the elasticity of demand for the product is less than infinite, the fraction of factor inputs does matter.

the highway, it would be wasteful to continue building the road if the additional income (rent) generated by an additional mile of road were not greater than the extra cost of extending the highway a mile. The authority should stop the road development when the increment of rent income falls to the annual cost of an additional mile of road.

24. Consider the road that ends at C'' in Figure 21 instead of continuing endlessly into the interior. Now the area of cultivation is represented by the figure $AA'C'''B'B$. If the road ends at C'' the "end-of-the-road" area of cultivation is the triangle $A'B'C'''$, where $A'C'' = C''C''' = B'C''$. It is just worthwhile headloading from the farm at A'; therefore, it is clearly also just worthwhile headloading from the same distance from any farm along the boundaries $A'C'''$ and $C'''B'$. (Again we remind the reader that headloading is assumed to be restricted to a north-south or an east-west direction.)

25. If the road were improved, the motor costs of transport would fall. It is clear, however, that an extension of the road beyond C'' is then desirable in principle since there will be more demand for traffic at and beyond C'' than there was before. Let us ignore this possibility of new investment— with the plausible excuse that it is inefficient to extend the road by such a small amount. The new area of cultivation, with this assumption, is illustrated in the following figure by the polygon $AA''DB''B$.

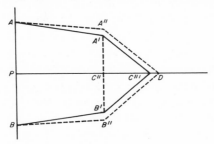

Figure 21.   A Plan of the Cultivated Area with a Truncated Road.

Note that the lines $B'C'''$ and $B''D$ are parallel, and the lines $A''D$ and $A'C'''$ are also parallel. Up to the end of the road C'' the expansion in the area is exactly the same as that in the endless road case. From the end of the road onwards, however, the "end-of-the-road" triangle expands in each dimension proportionately to the reduction in motor transport costs for the whole distance of the road.

26. The main question to which we seek an answer is what are the elasticities of demand with the truncated road. Unfortunately, the neat simple

results which were obtained for the endless road do not carry over to the truncated case. If the length of the road from P is d, the elasticity of transport demand in *tons* is given by:

$$\epsilon_{\text{tons}} = \frac{-ad[db + 2(k - ad)]}{db(2k - ad) - (k - ad)^2} \qquad \left(\frac{k}{a}\right) > d > 0$$

This is far different from the result of minus unity in the endless road case.[6] The question arises whether the elasticity for the truncated road is lower that that for the endless road. By calculating suitable values one can easily see that the absolute value of the elasticity will always be less than if there were an endless highway.[7] Indeed, when the road is very short, i.e. (ad/k) is very small, the absolute value of the elasticity is very much less than unity.

27.   There is, however, a commonsense interpretation of this result. It will be recalled that we have assumed that the length of the road remained constant. When there is only a very short road, i.e. when (ad/k) is, say, less than $\frac{1}{2}$, the improvement of the existing length of road will generate only a small increase in traffic. One may therefore conjecture that it is best to increase the length of the road rather than improve the existing highway. We continue a detailed discussion of the problem below. But here one may conclude that it will normally be a better policy to lengthen the road if (ad/k) is small. In practice what is meant by "small" will depend on the extent of discontinuities in road construction and the relative costs of improving the existing road and of constructing new extensions. To feed such assumptions into the model would unduly complicate matters, so, instead, we shall arbitrarily suppose that if (ad/k) is less than 0.75 it is worth lengthening the road, whereas if the road is longer than this we shall suppose that improvement of the existing surface is the best thing to do.

28.   This suggests that the elasticities will therefore be somewhat less than unity for the truncated road of fixed length. One may use values between -0.7 and minus unity as indicative measures of the elasticity in

---

[6] One can check, however, that when $d = k/a$, the elasticity becomes minus unity.

[7] For $a = 1$, $b = 10$, we find that:

If $(ad/k) = 0.95$	$\epsilon_{\text{tons}} = -0.92$
$= 0.90$	$= -0.85$
$= 0.80$	$= -0.71$
$= 0.50$	$= -0.42$
$= 0.10$	$= -0.27$

And it is obvious that as (ad/k) approaches zero, elasticity also approaches zero. For high values of (ad/k) we can use the approximation: elasticity $= -(ad/k)[2 - (ad/k)]$.

terms of tons. As one might expect the formulation with the ton-mile as the unit of measurement is rather more complicated; but the results turn out to be broadly similar to those which we obtained for tons. For roads longer than d, where $(ad/k) > 0.75$, we find elasticities between about -1.4 and -2.0.

29. The complications of the truncated road calculations are great and we shall pursue them further in this chapter. But first we shall briefly examine some related complications.

Road Sections Differ in Quality

30. The first of these complications is that the road may well be designed so that it is of lower quality the further one gets away from the port at P. This implies that the further one gets away from P the higher are the motor ton-mile costs. We might express this cost relationship by means of a quadratic, i.e.:

$$\begin{aligned}&\text{average cost per ton-mile for}\\&\text{distance } x \text{ from the port} \quad = c + ax \quad\quad c > 0\\&\hspace{20em} a > 0\end{aligned}$$

Then the area of cultivation is described by the inequalities:

$$(c + ax)\, x + by \quad\ \leq k \quad y \geq 0$$
$$(c + ax)\, x + b(-y) \leq k \quad y < 0$$

This area may be described graphically as in Figure 22, by the bullet shaped convex area AMB, where M is at a distance of

$$\frac{(\sqrt{c^2 + 4ak}) - c}{2a}$$

from the port at P.[8] And, of course, this distance must exceed k/b (i.e. M must lie east of J).

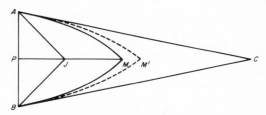

Figure 22. A Plan of the Cultivated Area with a Road of Declining Quality.

---

[8] Only the positive root of the solution of the quadratic is required.

31.   With this non-linear model the concept of a "road improvement" needs careful definition. Probably the simplest improvement is a proportional reduction in costs on the whole length of the road. Such an improvement will give us a pattern of new cultivation essentially similar to that which we examined in the linear case. The new area of cultivation will then be $AM'B$. But the equations for elasticity do not have the simple values of those in the linear model. One suspects, however, that they will be smaller.

32.   The supposition that the quality of the road declines as we go inland appears more realistic. But we also know that the cost per ton-mile of freight *declines* with longer distances. Since the assumption of our model is that all produce is exported through P it implies that the produce that comes over the bad road in the interior is carried for a longer haul than that which travels over only the better quality roads. So it seems that one effect will at least partially cancel the other.[9] In spite of the simplicity of the linear model it may well be a reasonable caricature of true situations.

Two-way Traffic

33.   In our model we have supposed that goods only flow out; none come back. But imports will in fact enter port P and both goods and people will flow back into the hinterland. There are some back loads. It is, however, surely a reasonable presumption that the tonnage and cubic footage of goods transported to the coast will exceed that imported and carried into the interior. Consequently, there will be full trucks traveling to the port— and partially empty vehicles driving from the port into the interior. Thus

---

[9] It is unlikely that the two effects will exactly counterbalance one another, however, except over a certain limited range. Some statistics may illustrate this point. Cost per ton-mile on good paved roads may be approximated by:

$$\text{US\$ cost per ton-mile} = \frac{2.80}{m} + 0.056 \qquad m \geq 50$$

where m is the mileage and costs have been increased to 1966 values. [Source: A. A. Walters and C. H. Sharp, *A Report on Traffic, Costs and Charges in Britain*, Ministry of Transport, (processed, 1958)]. If we suppose that the road steadily declines in quality after 50 miles so that ton-mile costs are increased by 0.1 US cent for every mile over 50, we obtain:

$$\text{US\$ cost per ton-mile} = \frac{2.80}{m} + 0.056 + 0.001(m - 50)$$

or approximately $$a = \frac{2.80}{m} + 0.001m \qquad m > 50$$

In terms of the standard paved, gravel, earth classification this would imply that the road became "gravel" at about 80 miles and "earth" at about 120–130 miles. (Note that we treat the last term only as the "operating cost"—the first term is the "fixed" terminal cost.) It is easy to see that a is not constant—it reaches its minimum value at about 53 miles.

the marginal cost of traffic carried back from the port is very low. Transport costs are almost wholly determined by the amount of the product shipped outwards. The basic model is therefore not seriously affected by ignoring traffic inwards. Furthermore, an improvement in the quality of the road will expand the area of cultivation and that is likely to increase the imports by the same fraction that it increases exports. Thus, the elasticities of demand for transport *as a whole* will be the same.[10]

34. The general upshot of this discussion is that the existence of transport inwards does not much affect the implications of the basic model. For the vast majority of uses to which we put the model the back haul can be ignored.

Inelastic Demand for Output

35. The basic model assumed that demand for the output is perfectly elastic. Let us make the other extreme assumption that the elasticity of demand is zero. Only one quantity of output can be sold at P, and the price will settle at the level just sufficient to induce that quantity to be supplied. Thus, k will now be a variable in the analysis.

36. The situation may be easily illustrated in Figure 23. The area of cultivation without the road is again ABJ. When the road is built, cultivation clusters along the road in the usual triangular form $A'NB'$, but the new triangle has the same area as that of ABJ. And since the relative cost of motor transport and headloading is the same as in the basic model and is

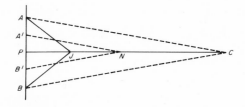

Figure 23.   A Plan of the Cultivated Area When Demand is Rigidly Inelastic.

not affected by the elasticity—$A'N$ is parallel to AC and $B'N$ to BC. The result is simply a redistribution of cultivated area along the new highway. We can usefully represent the reduction in the area of cultivation (as compared to the perfectly elastic demand for output case) by measuring the factor Ψ by which the distance AP is reduced to $A'P$. That is to say, we

---

[10] If the price of transport inwards is near zero, there are problems of indeterminacy.

can write: $A'P = \Psi(AP)$. In the case where the elasticity is zero, the areas $A'B'N$ and ABJ are equal, so that

$$\frac{\Psi^2 k^2}{ab} = \frac{k^2}{b^2} \text{ i.e. } \Psi = \sqrt{\frac{a}{b}}$$

Thus, the "squeeze" of the area is measured by the relative transport cost.

37.   It is obvious that the elasticity of demand for road transport in terms of tons is zero. Any reduction in transport cost is transmitted entirely to the consumers and no expansion of the area of cultivation takes place. What is perhaps not so obvious is that the elasticity of demand for road transport in terms of *ton-miles* is (minus) unity.[11] It will be quickly seen, however, that such a result is sensible; the given area of cultivation becomes concentrated around the road and strung further along it. Thus the ton-miles will increase as the road is improved.

38.   So much for the case of rigid inelasticity of demand; now we must deal with the case where the elasticity of demand for the product is between zero and infinity. The obvious conjecture is that the elasticity of demand for transport in terms of tons will lie between zero and minus unity, and the elasticity in terms of ton-miles will be between -1 and -2. This is, in fact, the correct result; the closer the elasticities of demand for the commodity approach the two limits, zero and infinity, the closer (monotonically) the two elasticities of transport demand approach their respective limits.[12]

---

[11] *Proof:* Let $a = (1 - \lambda)b$, then $\psi = \sqrt{1 - \lambda}$

Ton-miles with the road built $= \dfrac{k^3}{3(1 - \lambda)^3 a^3}$

Ton-miles without the road built $= \dfrac{k^3}{3(1 - \lambda)^2 a^3}$

Thus: $\epsilon_{\text{tons}} = \left(\dfrac{1 + \lambda - 1}{1 - \lambda}\right) \div (-\lambda) \qquad \text{as } \lambda \to 0$

$\qquad\qquad = -1$

[12] One can easily work out the appropriate values by substitution, first by finding the "shrinkage" factor ψ from the elasticity of demand for the commodity η, then by substituting ψ in the formula for calculating the area and ton-miles.

$$\text{Elasticity of demand} = \frac{\text{proportionate change in tons}}{\text{proportionate change in selling price}}$$

$$= \frac{(a^{-1}b\psi^2 - 1)}{\psi - 1}$$

This formula shows the relationship between the elasticity of demand for the commodity and the "shrinkage" factor. Now we proceed to calculate the elasticities of demand for trans-

39.   The results so far suggest that the model can be easily adjusted to fit conditions where there are different elasticities of demand for the commodity. But we must now take into account that there are factors, other than transport, that are required in order to produce the commodity. If, as before, we suppose that the costs of factor inputs, other than transport, are constant amounts per unit of output, we can write the area of cultivation in the usual way:

$$ax + by \quad\ \le k - f \quad\ y \ge 0$$
$$ax + b(-y) \le k - f \quad\ y < 0$$

The only difference between this case and the case where there are no non-transport inputs is the smaller effect of a given percentage fall in transport cost on the final price and thus on the area of cultivation and the quantity of goods transported.

40.   First, let us state the results in the limiting cases. If the demand is perfectly inelastic, then it is easy to see that the elasticity of demand for transport in terms of tons is zero. The area of cultivation does not change, but it does get stretched out along the road. Therefore, the elasticity of demand for transport in terms of ton-miles will not be zero; and in fact it is easy to see that it is -1 by using the argument of footnote 11 above. Now let us consider the other limit, when the demand for the commodity is perfectly elastic. Then it does not matter how large or small the fraction of non-transport costs in final price, the elasticity for tons will be (minus) unity and the elasticity for ton-miles will be (minus) two.[13] We simply treat the non-transport cost per ton as a deduction from the price per ton—and the analysis is exactly the same as before. We conclude then that in the two limiting cases the results are not affected at all by the fact that factors other than transport enter into the production of the com-

---

port along the road. The following may easily be derived from the formulae already given:

	Tonnage	Ton-miles
Arc-elasticities of demand for road transport	$\dfrac{1}{\lambda}\left(\dfrac{\psi^2}{1-\lambda} - 1\right)$	$\dfrac{1}{\lambda}\left(\dfrac{\psi^3}{(1-\lambda)^2} - 1\right)$

The elasticity of demand for transport in terms of tons reduces at the limit to:

$$\epsilon_{\text{tons}} = \eta/(2 - \eta), \text{ i.e. } \frac{\text{elasticity of demand for commodity}}{2 - \text{elasticity of demand for commodity}}$$

This includes the previous results:

$$\epsilon_{\text{tons}} = -1 \text{ for } \eta \to -\infty, \text{ and } \epsilon_{\text{tons}} = 0 \text{ for } \eta \to 0.$$

See: A. A. Walters, "A Development Model of Transport," *American Economic Review*, (Proceedings), (May 1968).

[13] Strictly this statement is true only when the fraction of transport costs is finite.

modity. The original results still stand, and the fraction of non-transport costs does not affect the values at all.

41.   Now let us consider the "intermediate cases" where the demand is neither perfectly inelastic nor elastic. In order to examine the effects of transport improvement when only a fraction of the final price is transport cost, we shall consider first the case when the fraction is large and, secondly, the case when it is small. If the transport costs are a high fraction of final price, then the model is essentially the same as before—except that the reduction in area (the "shrinkage" factor Ψ at work) due to the lower price at the port will be slightly less. With other factors of production getting a small share of the price, the elasticity of demand for transport—both tons and ton-miles—will be higher (absolutely) than if transport costs constituted all outgoings. The second case, where transport costs are a very small fraction of total costs, will give rise to inelastic demand for transport. If we imagine that the transport cost is a minute fraction of the final price, it follows that the reduction in transport cost will have virtually zero effect in expanding output. But, of course, there will be the same *redistribution* of output along the road and so there will be an expansion in the ton-miles of road transport in response to the road improvement. Whatever the "intermediate" value of the elasticity of demand for the commodity, it is easily seen that, with a very small transport component in final price, there is zero elasticity of demand for transport in terms of tons, and -1 is the elasticity for ton-miles. In general, it is clear that the lower the fraction of the transport component and the lower the elasticity of produce demand, the lower will be the elasticity of demand for transport.[14] But the elasticity of demand for road transport in ton-miles will never drop below unity (absolute).

42.   This concludes the presentation of the basic model and some of its variants of non-congested roads. It is necessary to emphasize that it is purposefully simple and abstract in its formulation. The intention was to catch some of the important characteristics of reality—while ignoring others. This simplification makes a caricature of reality. The hope is, however, that our model has caught some of the constant, "essential" and

---

[14] When the elasticity of demand for the commodity on the market is η and the cost of factors other than transport per ton is f, we can find the "shrinkage factor," ψ, by writing out the elasticity:

$$\eta = \left[\frac{(a^{-1}b\psi^2 - 1)}{\psi - 1}\right]\left(\frac{k}{k-f}\right)$$

The term in the square bracket is exactly the same as the elasticity if $f = 0$; the term in the last bracket is the inverse of the fraction of transport cost in the final price.

ubiquitous features of the rural road, while ignoring the individual idio-syncratic elements in each special case. Further variants are briefly discussed in the last section of this chapter. They increase the analytical complications considerably—but do not alter drastically the qualitative conclusions reached in the main text.

43.   The extent to which one can trust this theory depends, of course, on whether the predictions made with the theory turn out to be better than those made with any alternative theory. The acid test of any theory is whether its predictions are consistent with the facts, and whether it predicts those facts better than any alternative equally simple and economical method. Unfortunately, we shall not be able to test the model by comparing its predictions with those of alternative theories. But some of the evidence, such as it is, will be briefly reviewed in Chapter VI.

44.   Meanwhile, in the following sections we shall explore some of the implications of this model. We want to know the distribution of the benefits of the road improvements, the effects of various tax policies and the consequences on real income and development.

4. Benefits of the Road Improvement

45.   For the basic Ellet model developed above we can easily draw the rent "surface." Thus we know that the rent associated with any location is simply the difference between the price at the port P and the transport cost. With the simplest model of all where there is only N-S and E-W transport, the rent surface is simply a pyramid with a summit W directly above P. Thus, before the road is constructed the existence of the port at P is sufficient to generate the rent pyramid shown in Figure 24. Rents are recorded vertically for each farm location. We know that the distance $PJ = PB = PA = k/b$. Similarly, the height of summit $WP = k$, since

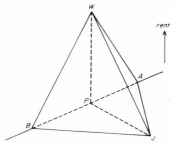

Figure 24.   The Rent Pyramid with No Road.

this is the value of one ton of output where there are no costs of carrying it to the port. Thus the volume of the rent pyramid without the road is

$$\frac{1}{3}k\left(\frac{k}{b}\right)^2 \quad \text{or} \quad \frac{k^3}{3b^2}$$

46.   Now when the road is built we observe the usual expansion of cultivation along the road. The rent pyramid is, so-to-speak, pulled out along the road—and J is stretched out to C as shown in Figure 25. All dimensions are the same as before except for PC which is of length k/a, and, of course, AC and BC which are given by $k\sqrt{a^{-2} + b^{-2}}$.

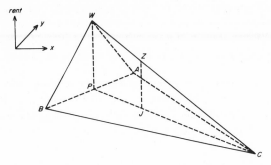

Figure 25.   Rent Pyramid with the Road.

47.   The increment of rent due to the road construction measures the benefits of the road. The benefit pyramid has no vertical surfaces. We obtain its shape by subtracting the old rent surface (without the road) from the new rent surface (with the road). The result is shown in Figure 26, transferring the benefits again into a pyramid with base ABC. The seaward side of the pyramid is "flapped down." The farm at J benefits most by the road construction: it is on the road and was previously just at the limit of cultivation. We can find the rent, which is just the same as the

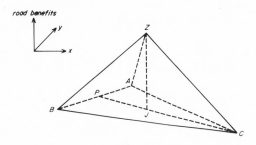

Figure 26.   Benefit Pyramid of Road.

136

benefit from the road, and is measured by: ZJ = price *minus* transport cost, i.e.

$$ZJ = k - a\left(\frac{k}{b}\right) = \frac{k(b-a)}{b}$$

dollars an acre. From this point the benefit tapers away to zero in each direction.

48. It is easy to calculate the total benefits due to the road by finding the volume of the benefit pyramid. A little algebra shows that the value of rents with the road is given by $k^3/3ab$.[15] If the ratio of a to b is 1 to 10 the rents are given by: $k^3/30a^2$, i.e. one-thirtieth of the cube of the price per acre output divided by the square of the motor cost. Thus the benefits are given by $k^3/(3ab) - k^3/(3b^2)$—the rent surface with the road less the rent surface without the road.

49. For most practical purposes it is convenient merely to examine *cross sections* of the benefit pyramid which are taken parallel to the road. This enables us to dispense with the complications of working with three-dimensional models. Let us first of all examine the cross section *along* the road. We are then simply recording the benefits of farms that lie along the road from P to the point C on the highway. The heights of the triangle PWJ show the cross section of rents along this route before the road was built. The maximum rent at W declines along WJ to zero at J, i.e. at a distance of k/b along the road. When the road is built the rent triangle becomes PWC, where C is at a distance of k/a along the highway. The benefits are measured by the vertical difference between these two triangles, i.e. by the triangle WJC. As we have seen, the height of ZJ is measured by $k(b-a)/b$.

---

[15] *Proof:*

$$\frac{\text{Rents}}{2} = \int_{x=0}^{\frac{k}{a}} \int_{y=0}^{-\frac{ax}{b}+\frac{k}{b}} (k - ax - by)\, dy\, dx$$

(It will be observed that the domain of the y integral is a function of x)

$$= \int_{x=0}^{\frac{k}{a}} \left\{ k\left[-\frac{ax}{b}+\frac{k}{b}\right] - ax\left[-\frac{ax}{b}+\frac{k}{b}\right] - \frac{b}{2}\left[-\frac{ax}{b}+\frac{k}{b}\right]^2 \right\} dx$$

$$= \int_{0}^{\frac{k}{a}} \frac{1}{2b}(ax-k)^2\, dx \qquad = \left[\frac{1}{6ab}(ax-k)^3\right]_{0}^{\frac{k}{a}}$$

$$= \frac{k^3}{6ab}$$

i.e. Rents $= \dfrac{k^3}{3ab}$

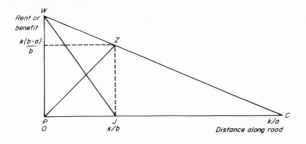

Figure 27. Cross Section of Rent Pyramid along the Road.

50.   Now consider another cross section of the benefit pyramid taken at some constant distance from the road and parallel to it. From an inspection of the benefit pyramid it is clear that these cross sections will all be similar triangles. The dimensions of the benefit triangle shrink proportionately in all dimensions the further we are away from the road. For example, at a distance of $k/2b$ from the road the cross section will have all the dimensions shrunk by a factor $\frac{1}{2}$.[16] The great convenience of this model is, therefore, that we can analyze one cross section in detail well knowing that all others are similar to it. Thus, a three-dimensional model can be transformed into a more manageable two-dimensional representation.

5. Taxes, Traffic, and Benefits

51.   The benefit pyramid or cross section benefit triangles enable us to investigate the "best" type of taxes. We can also use them to predict the effects of any type of tax which is related to the location of the farm or to road use.

52.   It might be thought that the optimum *total* tax to be collected should be related to the total benefits generated by the road. If this highway is worthwhile, and if these farmers are the only beneficiaries, then it follows that the benefit pyramid will exceed the total cost of the highway. The adoption of a "self-financing" rule for the highway may therefore require us to raise a revenue approximately as large as the benefit (and consumer surplus) generated. We shall not deal with such a restricted problem, however. It is much better to deal with the general problem of levying taxes with no rigid connection between the total benefit and the total tax yield

---

[16] It is recalled that the limiting distance from the road, when benefits become zero, is at A (or B), at a distance k/b.

138

to be extracted, although we shall always assume that the taxes to be collected are less than the benefits.[17]

Tax on Rents

53. It is clear that the "best" tax to levy is one that easily extracts a revenue proportionate to the benefits received without changing land use. A tax on the rent of land is the obvious, and indeed classic, form of impost that performs these tasks. These land taxes will merely extract the surplus and will not affect allocations of resources. Such a tax, however, must be of a kind quite different from those levies which are usually called land taxes. Strictly it would have to be a tax levied on the *increment* in rent due to the construction of the road. Then no one would be worse off than they were before and some farmers would be better off. This is illustrated in Figure 28 for the case of a 50 percent tax on the benefits of the road. Thus, we determine the mid-point of ZJ at Z', and then levy taxes according to the lines PZ' and CZ'. The *net* benefits to the farmers are then measured by the triangles PZZ' and $ZZ'C$.

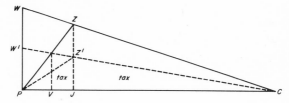

Figure 28.   Cross Section of Rent and Benefit Pyramid along the Road.

54. It is, however, very difficult to devise a land tax that falls on only the increments of rent due to the road. If, instead, one supposes that a general land tax were introduced to "pay for the road," it is clear that it would still not affect the area of cultivation. But it would mean that some farmers would be worse off than they were before the road was built, when there were no taxes. These farms are located only a short distance from P, i.e. with a general 50 percent tax on rents the farmers between P and V will lose, since the tax exceeds the benefit they get from the highway. We can draw a plan of those who suffer as in Figure 29. Farmers in the triangle ABV suffer from the land tax more than they gain from the road. They are worse off than before. All other farmers are at least as well off as before and some are better off.

---

[17] The question of investment criteria and taxation is best dealt with by using the truncated road model. But, as we shall see, there are many complications.

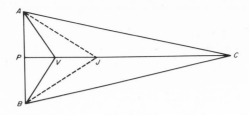

Figure 29. Plan of Development.

55. It is reasonable to suppose that, if land taxes are at all feasible, the levies will be imposed at more or less constant fractions of rent whether or not the road has yet been constructed. In other words, the land tax is likely to be constant as the road program is implemented. This will therefore mean that no one is worse off when the road is constructed, since the old cultivators were paying taxes equal to 50 percent of their rents before the road came and they continue to do so after the new facility is open. In many ways the tax on rents is an ideal one.[18] It does not affect any of the margins of cultivation and it ensures that no one is worse off than they were without the highway. But the transition from theory to practice appears to be particularly difficult with respect to the land tax.

56. It is difficult to avoid the fact that the actual assessment or the land tax will depend largely on the *actual output* of the land. In practice this will be determined by the energy and degree of application of the farmer. Thus, the land tax may have some of the disincentive effects of income taxes. Ideally, one would like to tax land according to its *potential* productivity, rather than the actual output, the cost of transport to the market would be subtracted from the potential productivity to obtain the appropriate assessment on the plot of land. But such assessments based on hypothetical notions rather than actual money flows are almost impossible to apply administratively. Experiences with assessments based on rental values are not happy.[19] This suggests that other taxes with less desirable theoretical properties but more chance of successful application may be preferable.

Ton-mile or Vehicle-mile Taxes

57. Probably the easiest tax to levy, and certainly the most ubiquitous, is the ton-mile or vehicle-mile tax. Gasoline and diesel oil levies are typical

---

[18] To avoid misunderstanding, it should be emphasized that this result is conditional upon the elasticity of demand being infinite. If it is finite then the consumers will enjoy rents and should be taxed at an appropriate rate according to the extent of their consumption. We return to this in Chapter VII.

[19] See Chapter VII for discussion of these aspects.

of those duties which have their main effects on ton-miles or vehicle-miles. Similar effects are achieved by duties on the purchase of new cars and on spare parts.[20] All these duties would normally be designated unequivocally as *user taxes* (or user charges) by transport economists. It is therefore important to have a general idea of the effects that they generate.

58. We may easily analyze the effects of a ton-mile tax in terms of a cross section of the benefit pyramid. Let us suppose that a tax of $\$t$ per ton-mile is levied. The tax line from P through X in Figure 30 is described simply as:

$$z = tx$$

where the height in the benefit direction is denoted by the z variable. When the mileage is so large that the tax exceeds the benefits of the road, cultivation ceases to be profitable. Thus where the tax line PX cuts the benefit cross section at X determines the limit of cultivation. Farms beyond the point C' are not worth cultivating, for the tax exceeds the rent.

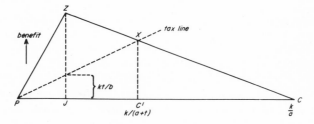

Figure 30.   Cross Section of Benefit Pyramid along the Road.

59. The effect on cultivation is simply the effect due to an increase in the ton-mile cost from a to $(a + t)$. The conditions of cultivation are now:

$$(a + t)x + by \quad \leq k \qquad y \geq 0$$

$$\text{and } (a + t)x + b(-y) \leq k \qquad y < 0$$

Thus in the plan of the area in Figure 31, the area of cultivation is represented by ABC'. The slope of AC' is given by the first equation above and the line AC is given as before by the same equation but with $t = 0$. Obviously the distance PC' is $\dfrac{k}{a + t}$.

---

[20] But they are not quite the same as fuel taxes, etc., since new cars depreciate over time as well as with respect to the mileage traveled.

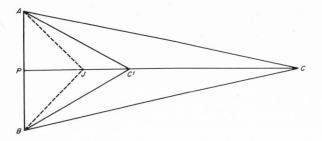

Figure 31. A Plan of the Area.

The Ton-mile Tax and Equity

60. Let us now return to the cross section of the benefit pyramid in Figure 30. Obviously the upper limit to the tax is given by:

$$a + t < b$$

or $\qquad t < b - a$

The tax must be less than the difference between the headloading and the motor cost. If the authority does charge a tax that is only slightly below this maximum tax rate, the authority will soak up almost all the benefits generated by the highway. No one will be any better off as a consequence of the road. But the more important result is that there will be no new traffic generated by the highway. The area of cultivation will remain as it was before the road was built (i.e. the triangle ABJ in Figure 29). The attempt to tax away all the benefits of the road by using a ton-mile tax will result, therefore, in the *maximum* restriction of output.

61. For tax rates which lie between $0 < t < b - a$, the authority will tax away the benefits of the road proportionately to the gross benefits for farms between P and J. For farms from J to C', however, the tax incidence runs counter to the benefit. For benefits decrease from J towards C', whereas the tax goes on increasing with the mileage from P. Those who gain most are, of course, still the farmers at J. The *net* benefit from the road of a farmer at J is measured by:

$$ZJ \text{ minus tax payment}$$

$$= k\left(\frac{b-a}{b}\right) - \frac{kt}{b} = \frac{k}{b}(b - a - t)$$

62. One might pause at this point to examine the equity of a ton-mile tax, and to compare it with the equity of the land (or strictly the rent) tax. The ideal aspect of the tax on rents was that it collected a tax propor-

tionate to the benefits of the road. It is often alleged that a tax according to the *use* of the road is an equitable way of paying for the road.[21] But it is clearly difficult to defend the ton-mile tax on equity grounds; for in our simple model the benefits are *not* simply proportional to the amount of use made of the highway. *A fortiori*, one may observe that, although the tax and benefit increase proportionately from P to J, after J the benefits *decrease* but the tax goes on *increasing* as we travel from J into the interior. Thus contrary to received opinion the ton-mile tax seems to score low marks on the grounds of equity.

The Yield of the Ton-mile Tax

63. It is of interest to examine the yield of the ton-mile tax. The *raison d'être* of many levies, such as the gasoline tax, is often to raise revenue rather than to price the use of the roads according to economic criteria.[22] It can be seen that the amount of revenue collected by a tax of t from

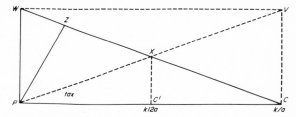

Figure 32. Cross Section of the Rent and Benefit Pyramid along the Road.

farms along the road is given by the area of the triangle PXC' in Figure 32. The distance PC' is:

$$\frac{k}{a+t}$$

and the height of the triangle is thus:

$$\frac{kt}{a+t}$$

The total taxes collected from farms along the road (T_r) then are given by:

$$T_r = \frac{1}{2} \cdot \frac{k^2 t}{(a+t)^2}$$

---

[21] This was suggested 200 years ago by Adam Smith, *An Inquiry into the Nature and Causes of the Wealth of Nations*, Book V, Chapter I, Cannan's 6th ed., (London, 1950). It has been echoed by other economists and statesmen over two centuries.

[22] There is good reason to suppose that budgetary needs determine the fuel taxes in the United Kingdom and India, for example, rather than any calculations about road costs.

This is the revenue secured from farms along the road from a tax of t a ton-mile.

64. Now let us ask what the level of the tax would have to be if the revenue from the tax were maximized. What tax rate would be imposed by a government whose interest lay not in getting the efficient prices for the roads but in milking the road traffic of as much revenue as could be extracted? We must then find a value for t such that T_r is maximized. It is easily found that the tax revenue is at a maximum when the tax per ton-mile is equal to the transport cost per ton-mile. The *ad valorem* ton-mile tax should be 100 percent on cost, or 50 percent of the market rate per ton-mile.[23]

65. This is such a simple result that it is worth exploring the implications a little further. Geometrically we see that, in Figure 32, the maximum tax revenue is obtained by "completing the diagonal." In other words, we impose a tax line PV which has the same slope as the rent line WC—except that it is positive, i.e. it increases as we go from P into the interior, whereas, the rent line WC declines as we go into the interior.

66. All this analysis has been carried out in terms of a cross section along the road. But we can translate these results into values for the total area affected. We can easily calculate the new (ex tax) tonnage and ton-mileage concerned. The range of haul is reduced 50 percent by the tax from k/a to $k/2a$. The tonnage is reduced from k^2/ab to $k^2/2ab$. The ton-mileage on the free road was $k^3/3a^2b$ and the ton-mileage on the road with a ton-mile tax of $t = a$, is given by $k^3/3(2a)^2b$, i.e. $k^3/12a^2b$. Thus, although the range of haul and the tonnage are only halved, the ton-mileage is reduced to a *quarter* of that on the free road.

67. Although this appears to be a silly policy for any government to follow there is at least superficial evidence that certain countries do in fact charge taxes which approach 50 percent of gross receipts. India, for example, has such high taxes on motor transport that one firm estimated that motor taxes approached 50 percent. But, of course, the model is not at all appropriate for such discussions—partly because of the existence of

---

[23] Differentiation gives:

$$\frac{dT_r}{dt} = \frac{k^2}{2} \cdot \frac{d}{dt}\left[\frac{t}{(a+t)^2}\right] = k^2\left[\frac{1}{(a+t)^2} - \frac{2t}{(a+t)^3}\right]$$

For stationary values of T_r, we have:

$$\frac{k^2}{2(a+t)^2}\left[1 - \frac{2t}{(a+t)}\right] = 0$$

so that: $\qquad t = a$

144

railways, etc. The moral if not the measure is, however, appropriate. Maximizing tax revenue does give rise to a great deal of waste of road capacity. But there is *less* waste than if the authority attempted, by ton-mile taxes, to soak up *all* the benefits of existing traffic, (cf. p. 142 above)—and there is more tax revenue to boot.

The Demand Curve Analogue

68.   It may also be useful to put this result in the context of ordinary demand and supply analysis. Let us measure the quantity of motor transport in ton-miles and the price in terms of $ per ton-mile. Obviously, the price of motor transport cannot rise above the price of headloading, since there would then be no use for a road for motor traffic. At b the demand goes down to zero. But if a price slightly below b is charged all the existing headloading traffic in the east-west direction will be switched on to the road—this amounts to a total of $k^3/3b^3$ ton-miles. This gives a corner at $k^3/3b^3$ in the demand curve. The rest of the demand curve is drawn with a constant elasticity of -2, as we proved above (if the road is not truncated). This gives the smooth "normal" slope as shown in Figure 33.

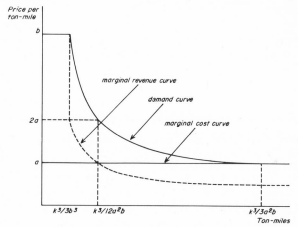

Figure 33.   The Demand and Cost Curves.

69.   We can also construct a marginal revenue curve for the road. Up to $k^3/3b^3$ the marginal revenue curve is coincidental with the demand curve. At the corner there is a discontinuity in the marginal revenue curve. The marginal revenue curve falls to a half of the price and remains at that proportion for the whole length of the demand curve. If the tax were zero the cost per ton-mile would be a and the number of ton-miles would be

$k^3/3a^2b$. If the government wished to maximize its tax revenue it would charge a tax of $a and collect from $k^3/12a^2b$ ton-miles. Thus the tax collected would be $k^3/12ab$ and this is the maximum. It can also be interpreted in the normal monopoly framework: the monopolist maximizes profit when marginal revenue is equal to marginal cost ($a per ton-mile).

"Covering the Costs" with a Ton-mile Tax

70.   It is convenient to use the demand curve formulation of the model for analyzing the consequences of a requirement for a balanced budget. In Figure 34, we have drawn the demand curve which was illustrated in Figure 33. We have also drawn the line $y = a$ which represents the cost of each ton-mile incurred by the vehicles along the highway—the average cost is constant so the marginal cost per ton-mile is also equal to $a.

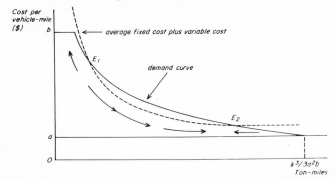

Figure 34.

71.   Let us suppose that the costs incurred by the road authority are constant—we can imagine that the variable maintenance cost has already been included in the value of $a per ton-mile. If the tax to cover the fixed costs of the road authority is levied on a ton-mile basis, we need to trace out the combination of ton-miles and tax rates which give rise to a certain fixed cost. These combinations are given by the formula:

$$(\text{ton-miles}) \times (\text{tax per ton-mile}) = \text{constant cost}$$

This equation will trace out a rectangular hyperbola—but with the important qualification that it is drawn with respect to the axis $y = a$ rather than the normal axis $y = O$. This is because the variable cost $a per ton-mile is always incurred and the ton-mile tax, required to cover the fixed costs of the road authority, must be added to it. An example of this curve is shown as the broken curve in Figure 34.

146

72.   It is clear from the calculated shape of the demand curve and from the known form of the cost curve that there will be two solutions, represented by E_1 and E_2, except in the accidental case when the cost curve just touches the demand curve. This dual solution follows from the fact that the elasticity of the demand curve is -2.0 over the range of price O to b, with respect to the axis $y = O$. The cost curve has an elasticity of -1.0 with respect to the axis $y = a$. The two curves must then cut twice—with the chance that for very low fixed costs the cost curve will cut the demand curve over the horizontal range (with price $= b$); where the tax for that solution is at $\$(b - a)$ a ton-mile, and thus frustrates all development traffic.

73.   For a very high fixed cost, however, it is conceivable that no possible ton-mile tax will give sufficient tax revenue to cover that fixed cost (the cost curve shifts upward and to the right, and is not cut at all by the demand curve). There is then no possibility of balancing the budget if one is restricted to ton-mile taxes. This is probably not an uncommon occurrence in developing countries. This suggests that either some other basis of taxation be used, or that the requirement of a balanced budget be dropped. We return to this point later.

74.   When there are two solutions such as E_1 and E_2 in Figure 34, one would expect the authority to choose the solution that gave rise to the largest amount of traffic. But the question remains whether the equilibria are "stable"; could the authority find its way to a budget equilibrium by "trial and error"? It is clear that E_2 is a stable equilibrium in the sense that, if the authority charges too low a tax it can approach E_2 by simply raising the tax. But this only applies for tax rates less than that implied by E_2. If the authority levied a tax higher than E_2 it would find that costs exceeded revenue—and so it would be tempted to increase the tax rate—which would merely result in such a large reduction of traffic that the average cost would rise even more than the price which people were willing to pay. Thus the movements are those shown by the arrows in Figure 34. This suggests that it is important for the authority to get the tax somewhere near the best level. But it is probably unrealistic to worry about the "stability" problem. The important point is the lack of uniqueness of the "balanced budget" requirement. If the two values of E_1 and E_2 are not too far from one another, it will not be obvious that the "correct" solution has been chosen. It is also conceivable—but again perhaps unrealistic—that the authority will choose a tax rate which gives rise to a lower tax revenue *and* a lower level of traffic (i.e. less than $k^3/12a^2b$ ton-miles) than

would be achieved by an authority whose aim was to maximize the tax revenue.

Ton-mile Taxes with Truncated Roads

75. So far we have dealt only with roads of unlimited length. Now it is necessary to see how these results carry over to the case of the road of length less than k/a.

76. One result is immediately obvious. If the authority is interested in maximizing its tax revenue and if the road is longer than $k/2a$, the solution is exactly the same as for the case of the endless highway. There will be no traffic, however, on the road at a distance of $k/2a$ or more. So it is clearly nefficient for the road authority to build a road of such a length. Indeed, the authority should clearly build a road of a distance much less than $k/2a$. The actual length of road will depend on two factors. The policy of the authority will determine whether the authority builds a road of a length that maximizes its net revenue or whether it builds a road so that the benefits of an additional 100 yards just equal its construction costs.

77. The number of interrelated policies on user charges and on investment suggest that a large number of alternatives need to be analyzed. Such a taxonomic approach, however, will not be adopted here, partly because one knows that policies pursued in practice are not clear-cut or even good approximations to the "ideal" form of the theory. General tendencies and broad conclusions are all that need to be drawn.

78. It is worth drawing a *map* of the effects. This is illustrated in Figure 35. When the road ends at x_0 the area of cultivation without the ton-mile tax is $AA'C'B'B$. When the ton-mile tax is imposed the area shrinks to $AA''C''B''B$, where $A''C''$ is parallel to $A'C'$ (and to AJ). By the arguments used above it is clear that a sensible road authority would not im-

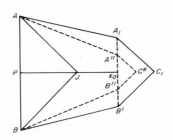

Figure 35.   Map of Development with Truncated Road.

148

pose a tax so that the slope of AA'' (and BB'') was such that it cut the road Px_o to the left of x_o. For in that case some of the road would be un-used—and so it is inefficient for the authority to build such a long road, *given* that it intends to impose such a high tax. The joint determination of the length of road and the tax to be imposed clearly shows that it is inconsistent to levy taxes that lead to the abandonment of road.

79. If the road is expanded by a small distance beyond x_o and the tax rate is held constant, one will observe a chevron-shaped area of additional cultivation as $A''C''B''$ is pushed out to the east, as illustrated in Figure 36 by the shaded area. If the benefit from this expansion of cultivation and the additional cuts in taxes which accrue to the existing triangle of culti-vation $A''B''C''$ exceed the costs of $(x_o' - x_o)$ miles of road, then the road is worth lengthening. Clearly the rents of the *additional* acreage are near enough zero if the increment $(x_o' - x_o)$ is small, for this land is just on the margin of cultivation. The land earns a surplus, however, and this is measured by the ton-mile tax paid per acre of additional cultivated area. With a tax rate per ton-mile of $\$t$, the tax paid by each acre (and each ton) of the chevron is $\$tx_o'$, which for a small change $(x_o' - x_o)$ is approxi-mately the same as $\$tx_o$. From the parameters given it is easy to calculate the new area of cultivation for a small increment $(x_o' - x_o) = dx_o$. With $b = 1$ this is given by:

$$2(1 - a - t)\{k - (a + t)x_o\} \qquad (a + t) < 1$$

and so the tax revenue from this expansion of acreage is given by:

$$2tx_o(1 - a - t)\{k - (a + t)x_o\}$$

in dollars.[24] Note that we have standardized the result so that the cost of headloading is unity.

---

[24] *Proof:*

At x_o $\qquad y = -(a + t)x_o + k \qquad (a + t) < 1$

So that the area of cultivation which is foregone by the truncation of the road at x_o is:

$$A = \{-(a + t)x_o + k\} \left[\frac{k}{a + t} - x_o - \{-(a + t)x_o + k\} \right]$$

$$A = \{k - (a + t)x_o\}^2 \left\{ \frac{1}{a + t} - 1 \right\}$$

$$\frac{dA}{dx_o} = 2\left(\frac{1 - a - t}{a + t} \right) (-a - t)\{k - (a + t)x_o\} = -2(1 - a - t)\{k - (a + t)x_o\}$$

which is, of course, negative.

149

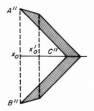

Figure 36.   The Expansion in Area as the Road Is Extended from x_o to x_o'.

80.   The existing triangle of cultivation beyond x_o, i.e. $A''B''C''$, will pay taxes equal to:

$$tdx_o \text{ (area of } A''B''C'')$$
$$= tdx_o\{k - (a + t)x_o\}^2$$

So that the total additional taxes collected are:

from new cultivators   *from existing cultivators*

$$2tx_o(1 - a - t)\{k - (a + t)x_o\}dx_o + t\{k - (a + t)x_o\}^2dx_o$$

And it is clear that if the road is relatively long (i.e. x_o is large) the taxes from new cultivators will dominate the result.

81.   It is important to note that the government's tax revenue does *not* represent all the benefits derived from the road expansion dx_o. Those in the existing triangle of cultivation $A''B''C''$ earn larger rents as a consequence of the road extension. For each acre (ton) the cost of transport is reduced by the difference between headloading cost (unity) and the ex-tax motor cost $(a + t)$ multiplied by the increased road space available dx_o, i.e. $dx_o(1 - a - t)$.

The number of acres in the triangle $A''B''C''$ is:

$$\{k - (a + t)x_o\}^2$$

So that the increase in rents of existing cultivators is given by:

$$(1 - a - t)\{k - (a + t)x_o\}^2dx_o$$

Thus the total benefits from extending the highway by dx_o are:

$$dx_o[2tx_o(1 - a - t)\{k - (a + t)x_o\} + (1 - a)\{k - (a + t)x_o\}^2]$$

This is the value that should be equated to the additional cost of the construction of dx_o miles of road. The alternative rule of expanding the roads

150

if the additional tax revenue exceeds the cost will give *too small* a road network.[25]

82. Thus, if the road authority adopts an investment policy of constructing roads when the additional tax exceeds the cost of the construction, the road should be extended beyond x_o if:

$$2tx_o(1 - a - t)\{k - (a + t)x_o\} + t\{k - (a + t)x_o\}^2$$

exceeds the marginal cost of road extension beyond x_o. This policy takes the tax rate per ton-mile as given. And it seems that this is a sensible policy to adopt if the government, for administrative reasons, can impose only ton-mile taxes and if it is not interested primarily in extracting as much net tax revenue (after allowing for annual expenditure on roads) as it can from the road users. But it is not the best policy, given the tax rate it has imposed, for a government concerned with optimizing its investment expenditures.[26]

83. It is easy to check these results by finding the total taxes collected. Integrating over the range of x from 0 to x_o, and then adding on the ton-mileage for the acreage beyond x_o we obtain:

$$\text{Tax revenue} = \frac{t}{2}\int_o^{x_o} x\{k - (a + t)x\}dx + tx_o\{k - (a + t)x_o\}^2$$

$$T = t\{kx_o^2 - \tfrac{2}{3}(a + t)x_o^3\} + tx_o\{k - (a + t)x_o\}^2$$

$$T = tx_o^2\{k - \tfrac{2}{3}(a + t)x_o\} + tx_o\{k - (a + t)x_o\}^2$$

And the marginal tax revenue when the road is expanded by a small amount dx_o is:

$$\frac{dT}{dx_o} = 2tx_o(1 - a - t)\{k - (a + t)x_o\} + t\{k - (a + t)x_o\}^2$$

This is the same as the result which we found by direct calculation of the economic effects. From this formulation it is also easy to calculate the effects of an increase in the tax rate by finding the differential $\partial T/\partial t$. By equating this differential to zero we can find the rate of tax that maximizes

---

[25] The difference in the length of road under the total benefit investment criterion and the length under the alternative rule is given by the difference in the solutions of the two quadratics in x_o for a given marginal cost of expanding the road by dx_o.

[26] It is also obvious that a road authority interested in maximizing the net "profits" in tax revenue from road construction would have a much more restrictive investment policy. It would be concerned with the *joint* determination of tax rates and road building, and, like any other monopolist, it would take into account the decline in marginal tax revenue rather than take the tax rate as given. But this seems an extreme case and will not be analyzed here.

tax receipts for a given length of highway. But the result does not have the pleasant simplicity of that which we obtained from the endless road case.

84. This cross section of the benefit pyramid of a truncated road can also be used to analyze the effects of various forms of taxation. In Figure 37 the normal benefit pyramid for the endless road is PZC. The tax rate is indicated by the slope of the line PZ'. The tax increases with the ton-miles up to the end of the truncated road at x_0. For traffic that feeds into the road at x_0 the tax paid is the same at the level $Z'x_0$ and TC''. We can determine the amount of traffic beyond x_0 by drawing the line $Z'Z''$ such that it is parallel to PZ; this line $Z'Z''$ represents the cost of headloading into x_0, and Z'', where it cuts the benefit pyramid, defines the limit of cultivation along the line beyond the end of the road, i.e. the point C''. Tax receipts are then represented by the shaded area.[27]

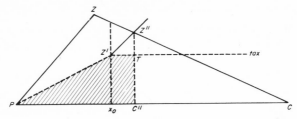

Figure 37. Cross Section along the Road of Benefit Pyramid with Endless and Truncated Road.

85. The analysis of the case of the truncated road is similar to that of the endless road. The additional complications with the ton-mile tax arise because of the "end-effects." And there is, additionally, the problem of how long the road should be. The reader will be able easily to translate the truncated road model into the ordinary form of demand and supply curves; as we did with the case of the endless highway. This will give a more readily understandable version of the end effects.

---

[27] It will be observed that the road need be considered as truncated for only a certain width—as one can see in the plan of the area below. For cross sections outside the range LM the road can be considered as endless. And as we approach L (and M) we note that the "truncated effect" declines; within the cross sections the absolute distance Px_0 is fixed and does not decline as we take parallel cross sections.

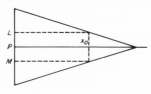

86. The fact that there is no marked difference between the truncated and the endless road results suggests that we may use the simpler model for most purposes without going far wrong. With this proviso, we shall proceed to examine the tonnage tax and compare it with the ton-mileage taxes.

The Tonnage Tax Compared with the Ton-mile Tax

87. It is of some interest to examine various alternative forms of taxation. The tonnage tax is one obvious possibility. One may imagine such a levy being administered by, for example, a percentage sales tax on the market. It will be recalled that such a sales tax is also useful if the elasticity of demand on the market is not infinite and if the consumers also benefit from the lower transport costs through lower prices on the market. So it is obvious that the tonnage tax deserves analysis in its own right.

88. The simplest approach is to analyze the cross section along the road—but as we shall see in a moment, such an approach has to be treated cautiously. In Figure 38 suppose that we impose a tax of VP per ton. This will then mean that it does not pay to till the soil beyond N. Cultivation is restricted to the section PN. The tax receipts are represented by the rectangle $PVXN$.

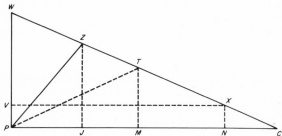

Figure 38. Cross Section of Rent and Benefit Pyramid along the Road—Illustrating Tonnage Taxes *vs* Ton-Mileage Taxes.

89. Compared with the ton-mileage tax represented by the line PT, it seems clear that the tonnage tax is much superior to the ton-mileage tax. First, the tonnage tax restricts cultivation much less than the ton-mileage tax. Secondly, it seems that the tonnage tax is more consistent with the normal concepts of equity than the ton-mileage tax. These two results are in fact borne out by the analysis—but they cannot be inferred directly from the cross section along the road. For it is important to observe that as we take cross sections at greater distances from the road the dimensions

of the benefit pyramid shrink proportionately *while the dimensions of the tonnage tax $VP remain constant.* The cross section result along the road is therefore not a proportional representation of the effects.

90. To examine the tonnage tax further let us draw a plan of the cultivated area. Clearly a tonnage tax of $c per ton will have the effect of reducing the area of cultivation to that described by the equations:

$$ax + by \leq k - c \qquad y \geq 0$$
$$ax - by \leq k - c \qquad y < 0$$

In Figure 39 the lines AC and BC describe the effects of a ton-mile tax. The broken lines $A'C'$ and $B'C'$ describe the effect of a tonnage tax.[28] It will be observed that the effect of a tonnage tax compared with that of a ton-mileage tax is to cut out of production the areas represented by the two shaded triangles.

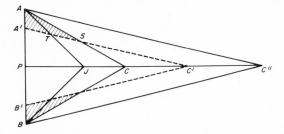

Figure 39. A Plan of the Cultivated Area.

91. This effect can be seen in terms of the benefit pyramid. The ton-mile tax essentially redefines a new plane for the zero benefit base. With no tax

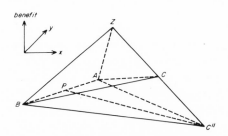

Figure 40. The Benefit Pyramid with a Ton-Mile Tax.

---

[28] For a tonnage tax of $c per ton, $\quad x > 0, y > 0$

$\quad ax + by \leq k - c$ describes $A'PC'$.

the measure of benefits is made vertically from a zero base plane ABC''. A ton-mile tax is shown by the plane ABC: the distance from this ABC plane to the plane ABC'' measures the tax per ton paid by farmers at the (x, y) location. The remainder, from the ABC plane to the surface of the benefit pyramid measures the benefit *net* of the ton-mile tax to the farmer.

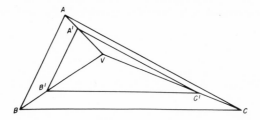

Figure 41. Aerial View of Benefit Pyramid with a Tonnage Tax.

92. A tonnage tax on the other hand simply raises the base of the pyramid by an equal distance at any point, i.e. by the amount of the tonnage tax which is independent of the location (x, y). As we can see, the farmers near the sea (in the $ABB'A'$ band) are worse off than they were before the road was constructed. The tax incurred (e.g. \$$c$ per ton) is less than the reduction in costs of transport due to the construction of the road. In this band the more distant ones from P are driven out of production by the tonnage tax. It will be observed, however, that if the tonnage tax were levied *only on commodities that use the road*, then no one would be worse off than they were before the road was constructed. Land which was cultivated before the road existed would continue to be cultivated and the road would not be used unless it reduced costs. Thus it would not be used by the coastal farmers where

$$x < \frac{c}{b - a}$$

But it is true that some land which would be cultivated with a ton-mile tax will lie fallow under such a tonnage tax—the triangle ATS in Figure 39 represents the area on the northern side of the road. There is some loss of production which might offset the seemingly larger gain in production in the interior from a tonnage tax as against a ton-mile tax—represented on the northern side of the road by the triangle SCC' in Figure 39.

Calculations of the Relative Advantages of Tonnage and Ton-mile Taxes

93. The issue, in theoretical terms, can only be settled by an extensive analysis. A start has been made here—but it is only a beginning. It is diffi-

cult to determine even the tax rates that give equal yields in the two cases.[29]

94. We have already seen that the ton-mile tax rate that will maximize revenue is $t = a$. This gives rise to a total tax revenue of $R(t = a) = k^3/(12ab)$. It is interesting to enquire what is the *tonnage* tax that will maximize revenue. This is given by maximizing $R(c)$—and the result is $c = k/3$.[30] Thus *when the tonnage tax is a third of the f.o.b. price at the port the total tax revenue will be at a maximum.*

95. It will also be observed that the maximum yield from a tonnage tax is much larger than the maximum yield from a ton-mile tax. In fact the maximum tonnage tax yield is almost 80 percent more than the maximum yield of the ton-mile tax. The much greater revenue yield of the tonnage

---

[29] Assuming that all tons pay for the road in the case of the tonnage tax, let $R(t)$ measure the tax receipts with a tax of $\$t$ per ton-mile and let $R(c)$ measure tax receipts with a tax of $\$c$ a ton.

$$R(c) = \frac{c(k - c)^2}{ab}$$

$$R(t) = \frac{tk^2}{3b(a + t)^2}$$

If $R(t) = R(c)$, we can write t as a function of c—and this turns out to be a quadratic so that:

$$t = -a + \frac{k^3 a}{6c(k - c)^2} + \frac{a}{2} \sqrt{\left[2 - \frac{k^3}{3c(k - c)^2} \right]^2 - \frac{4}{a}}$$

[30] Proofs of the propositions in the above two paragraphs:

(1) $$R(c) = \frac{c(k - c)^2}{ab} \qquad a, b, k, c > 0$$

$$\frac{dR(c)}{dc} = \frac{1}{ab}(k - c)(k - 3c) = 0$$

i.e. $k = c$ is the minimum

$k = 3c$ is the maximum

thus $c = \dfrac{k}{3}$ give maximum $R(c)$

i.e. $R(c) = \dfrac{k}{3}$ is maximum

$$R(c) = \frac{k}{3} = \frac{4k^3}{27ab}$$

(2) $$R(t) = \frac{tk^3}{3b(a + t)^2} \qquad t > 0$$

thus $R(t = a) = \dfrac{ak^3}{12ba^2}$

$$= \frac{k^3}{12ab}$$

tax is another powerful "financial" reason for preferring it to the ton-mile tax.[31]

96. It is also clear that these financial reasons for preferring a tonnage tax as against a ton-mile tax are not upset by arguments about the reduction in acreage. If we take the maximum revenue taxes as a standard of comparison we see that the tonnage tax that raises 80 percent more revenue than the ton-mile tax involves a cultivated area only 1/9th less.[32]

97. It is natural to conjecture that, for the same area of cultivation, the tonnage tax will always give a higher revenue than the ton-mile tax. First, however, one must find the taxes that give rise to equal areas. These are given by the relationship between c and t in the equations:

$$\frac{(k - c)^2}{ab} = \frac{k^2}{(a + t)b}$$

i.e.:
$$c^2 - 2kc + ak^2\left(\frac{1}{a} - \frac{1}{a + t}\right) = 0$$

So that:
$$c = \frac{2k \pm \sqrt{4k^2 - 4ak^2\left(\dfrac{1}{a} - \dfrac{1}{a + t}\right)}}{2}$$

$$\frac{c}{k} = 1 - \sqrt{\frac{1}{1 + \lambda}}$$

where λ is the *rate* of the ton-mile tax (i.e. $t = \lambda a$). Thus the tonnage tax rate c/k is expressed as a simple function of the ton-mile tax rate λ.

98. It is intuitively obvious that the revenue will always be larger for the tonnage tax than for the ton-mile tax, because the elasticity of de-

---

[31] Thus:
$$\frac{R\left(c = \dfrac{k}{3}\right)}{R(t = a)} = \left(\frac{4}{27}\right) 12$$
$$= 1.78$$
or almost 80 percent more.

[32] *Proof:*

$$\text{Area (with } c = \frac{1}{3}k = \left(\frac{2}{3}\right)^2\left(\frac{k^2}{ab}\right)$$

$$\text{Area (with } t = a) = \left(\frac{k}{b}\right)\left(\frac{k}{2a}\right)$$

$$= \frac{k^2}{2ab}$$

$$\frac{\text{Area }\left(\text{with } c = \dfrac{k}{3}\right)}{\text{Area (with } t = a)} = \frac{8}{9}$$

157

mand for tons is always less than that for ton-miles. So for the same area of cultivation the tonnage tax will give a higher yield. This result can also be proved.[33] A numerical illustration may serve to show the orders of magnitude involved. If the authority chose to maximize its revenue from ton-mile taxes it would fix $t = a$; and $(c/k) = 0.293$ would give rise to the same area of development. Let us compare the yield of the tonnage tax with that of the ton-mile tax. One can easily calculate that the yield of the tonnage tax is about 72 percent more than that of the ton-mile tax.[34] The reader can easily convince himself that this order of magnitude is not a fluke value. Indeed we can prove that the tonnage tax will always raise more than 50 percent more revenue than the ton-mile tax from the same area of cultivation.[35]

---

[33] *Proof:*

$$R(t) = \frac{tk^3}{3ba^2(1 + \lambda)^2}$$

$$R(c) = \frac{c(k - c)^2}{ab} \qquad \text{and } k - c = k\sqrt{\frac{1}{1 + \lambda}}$$

$$R(c) > R(t)$$

if $\qquad \dfrac{ck^2}{ab(1 + \lambda)} > \dfrac{k^3}{3ab(1 + \lambda)^2}$

i.e. $\qquad c > \dfrac{\lambda k}{3(1 + \lambda)}$

$$\left[1 - \sqrt{\frac{1}{1 + \lambda}}\right] > \frac{\lambda}{3(1 + \lambda)}$$

or: $\qquad \dfrac{1}{1 + \lambda} < \left[\dfrac{3 + 2\lambda}{3(1 + \lambda)}\right]^2$

i.e. $\quad 9 + 12\lambda + 4\lambda^2 > 9 + 9\lambda$

$$3\lambda + 4\lambda^2 > 0$$

And this will always be true for $\lambda > 0$. Thus the revenue from the tonnage tax always exceeds that from the ton-mile tax.

[34] The solution is then:

$$\frac{k}{c} = 3.414$$

and so $\qquad R(c) = \dfrac{0.1468k^3}{ab}$

$$R(t = a) = \frac{k^3}{12ab}$$

and the ratio of the two revenues is 1.72.

[35] Let z be the ratio of $R(t)$ to $R(c)$ when the two areas are equal. Then from footnote above, we seek a solution for z in the equation:

$$z\left[1 - \sqrt{\frac{1}{1 + \lambda}}\right] = \frac{\lambda}{3(1 + \lambda)}$$

158

99.   This "equal-area" test is probably the most important one for developing countries. And there is no doubt about the superiority of tonnage taxes to ton-mile taxes on this criterion. In examining the arguments for and against the two taxes, one may well regard this comparison as the critical one. The fact that one can always obtain at least 50 percent more revenue from the tonnage tax surely clinches the theoretical case, at least as far as the simple model is concerned.

100.   The only disadvantage of the tonnage tax relative to the ton-mile tax is the loss of production near the coast. The issue turns on how large this area is, relative to the gains in the interior, and whether this is likely to be a serious problem in practice. We have already examined the effects on area. Let us now deal with the latter aspect. One may conjecture that in practical cases the reduction of cultivated acreage near the sea, when the tonnage tax is imposed, will be of little importance. One reason is that it is likely that ports will be so close together (or barge and lighter traffic so cheap) that the catchment areas of ports will substantially overlap. The problem of peripheral areas of cultivation near the coast is then of virtually no importance. It is most likely that a tonnage tax will not give rise to any reduction in cultivated areas.

101.   This is also likely to be the situation when the road in question is a feeder road leading into an arterial road at P. Instead of the coast we have an arterial road. Thus the land which is adjacent to the arterial road will already be in the arterial's catchment area. It will not be affected by the construction and tax receipts of the feeder road. Essentially the tonnage tax drives development back into the interior; the ton-mileage tax concentrates it more around existing markets and the coast.

102.   This completes our discussion of the relative effects of the tonnage and the ton-mile taxes. The general conclusion is perfectly clear. The tonnage tax is superior to the ton-mile tax. It is superior on "financial" grounds, i.e. in terms of raising revenue. At least 50 percent more revenue

---

Simplifying we get:

$$z^2 - \frac{2z}{3} + \frac{\lambda}{9(1+\lambda)} = 0$$

Thus the solutions are:

$$z = \frac{1}{3}\left[1 \pm \sqrt{\frac{1}{1+\lambda}}\right]$$

Since λ is constrained to the range $0 < \lambda < 1$, it is obvious that z reaches the maximum as λ approaches zero. The limiting value of z is therefore $\frac{2}{3}$. I am grateful to Professor William Fellner for suggesting this approach.

can be raised. Its superiority is quite clear too on "efficiency" grounds. For the same revenue collected the tonnage tax will give rise to a much larger output. On equity grounds the issue is inevitably not perfectly clear-cut, but it seems likely that a tonnage tax, suitably adjusted for "end-of-road" effects, will be more consistent with common ideas of equity than will the ton-mile tax. In addition to its higher efficiency, the tonnage tax is also the better tax to employ when the elasticity of demand for the product is less than infinite. It will then soak up part of the benefit that accrues to the people in the form of "consumers' rents." The only remaining grounds on which one might still prefer the ton-mile tax are administrative "ease-of-collection" and various technical grounds. These will be deferred until a later stage of this study. The conclusions in this chapter, however, are derived from pure theory. Whether the theories are, or are not, useful depend on the facts. To these we turn in Chapter VI.

6. *Further Variants of the Basic Model*[36]

Free Movement of Headloaders in All Directions

103.   Hitherto we have assumed that the headloader was only permitted to move either N-S or E-W. He was not allowed to proceed diagonally. Let us now drop this assumption and see what results. Let the headloader be allowed to walk in *any* direction.

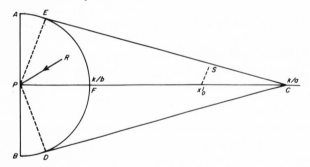

Figure 42.   A Plan of the Cultivated Area.

104.   Consider the plot at R in Figure 42. The distance to P is shown by the line PR and this will be the route taken by the headloader. If the co-ordinates of the point at R are x_R and y_R the distance is given by:

$$\sqrt{x_R^2 + y_R^2} \qquad \text{(positive root only)}$$

[36] This section may be skipped by those readers not interested in the technicalities of the model.

160

The area of cultivation before the road is built is therefore defined by the requirement that the costs be less than the price obtainable at P, i.e.:

$$b\sqrt{x^2 + y^2} \leq k$$

where b is the per mile headloading cost. The boundary of such an area is the circle around P with a radius of k/b.

105.   Now consider building a road from P—so that the cost per ton-mile along the road is $\$a$. The area of cultivation will clearly extend along the road. The question is what shape will be the new area of cultivation? To solve this, consider the route taken by a ton of produce originating at S. The commodity will be headloaded to the road at x'_o and then carried by motor vehicle to P. At what point will it be best to meet the road? Or what angle shall he walk from S? We can show that the angle at which he walks will be the *same* for all farmers in the new area of cultivation. This is intuitively obvious since the rate of exchange between headloading costs and motor costs per ton-mile is assumed to be constant. Therefore, the angle will represent the relative costs of the two modes.

106.   It might at first appear that the circle of cultivation will be expanded by the road into the form of an ellipse-like shape. But this is not the case. The new area of cultivation is described (in the north) by the small arc AE and the *line EC*, where C is at a distance k/a from P. In the south the area is described by the small arc BD and the line DC. It is not difficult to see why the lines EC and DC are in fact lines and not arcs as one's intuition suggests. The ability to carry diagonally compared with N-S movement by headloading reduces motor carriage costs more than it increases headloading costs, but the proportional charges remain the same. Thus the line simply swings out to reflect this reduction.

107.   To find the new area of cultivation one simply measures a distance along the road of k/a (i.e. the point C in Figure 42). This is obviously the limit of cultivation along the road since $ax = k$ when $y = 0$. From this point C one constructs the two *tangents* to the old circle of cultivation around P. The points of tangency are at E and D respectively. The direction of the line from the tangent point E to the port P describes the direction (relative to the road) which all headloaders take. Thus we know that the direction of the headloader from S to x' is parallel to the line EP. In the segments APE and BPD the commodity is still headloaded to the port at P.

108.   It is interesting to compare in Figure 43 this non-directional model with the model where headloaders were restricted to N-S *or* E-W move-

ment. Before construction of the road, our restricted model cut out the areas of cultivation in the arcs *AEF* and *BDF*. On the other hand when the road is built there is a gain in cultivation area, over the restricted model, represented by the areas *ACE* and *BCD*. The net effects are that the gains from the road are less than they would have been under the old restricted movement assumption.

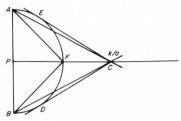

Figure 43.

109.   The net result in fact turns on the ratio of motor cost to headloading cost. As one can see directly, if *a* is very small relative to *b*, the distance *PC* will be large relative to the distance *PF*. The model will approximate to the restricted-movement one. If, however, *a* is only slightly smaller than *b* it follows that the restricted-movement model is a bad approximation. The gains in area of cultivation from the road will be much less than those predicted by the restricted-movement model. The gains in terms of rent increases will also be smaller than those in the restricted-movement model.

110.   These caveats, however, all refer to the case where *a* is not very much smaller than *b*. If, however, *a* is less than (say) one third as large as *b* they become of small importance. Furthermore, the uses we made of the restricted model above in measuring the elasticity of demand were for *an improvement of a given road*. In these cases we start out with a figure of the form of *AECDB* and extend the point *C* to the right by a small amount. It is clear that even when *b* is quite low relative to *a* (say, $b = 2a$) the difference in the new areas opened up for cultivation will be small in the two models. For motor cost which is less than $b/3$, the difference will virtually disappear. Thus we may conclude that the elasticity formulas carry over almost exactly when $b \geq 3a$.

111.   The case of a road of limited length is roughly the same as for the restricted-direction model. If the road ends at *X* we draw the lines $E'X$ and $D'X$ so that they are parallel to *EP* and *DP* respectively. The circular segment from E' to D' defines the limit of cultivation. The difference be-

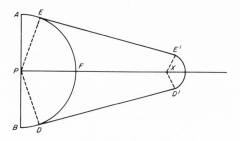

Figure 44.

tween this model and the short-road model with restricted directions is that the end is rounded instead of pointed.

Feeder Road Case

112. The feeder road example is one of considerable importance in development economics. It is easy to see, however, that it is merely a variation on the model considered above. Consider an existing arterial road RR' with a band of cultivation around it represented on the eastern side by

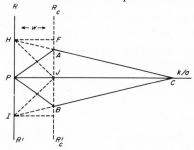

Figure 45.   A Plan of the Cultivated Area with a Feeder Road.

the broken line $R_cR'_c$.[37] Construct a road from P, a point on the arterial road as before. Now examine point A. If the land at A is just worth cultivating after the feeder road is built, and it is just worthwhile to use the road, the total cost of transport must be the same as before. If w is the width of the cultivated *band* before the feeder road is constructed, we must have the coordinates (d, y) at A satisfying the equation:

$$aw + by = k$$

i.e. $y = \dfrac{-aw}{b} + \dfrac{k}{b}$ at point A

---

[37] This has been constructed parallel to the road. In principle the cultivated band should get narrower or broader—but for the segment in question we have assumed that such narrowing is small enough to be ignored.

163

Farms between the line AP and the feeder road will find it profitable to use the feeder road to get to the junction at P. (This is similarly true for the mirror image between PB and the road.) The new area of cultivation opened up is represented by the triangle ABC where C is at a distance k/a from P. Note that this is considerably less than the area opened up in the case where there was no arterial road—this was represented by the triangle north of the road HJC (plus its mirror image to the south). Similarly, the area of farms that enjoy cost reductions on existing traffic is less: PAB instead of HJI. The benefit pyramid has four vertical faces instead of three—but it still has a maximum at the point J. The same conclusions about the effects of ton-mile and tonnage taxes carry over exactly to the feeder road case.

113.   The intuitive interpretation of the differences in benefits of the feeder road and those of the pure development case is that the feeder road obviously "wastes" rather more of its mileage going through the band by the road which is already cultivated. Consequently, *ceteris paribus* the benefits and the area of new cultivation will not be so great.

Network Models

114.   It is also relatively easy to see how this model extends to networks. Consider, for example, the crossroad model in Figure 46. (Again we ignore the efficient truncation of roads.) The overlapping of the development triangles defines an octagonal figure with its center P at the crossroads. The boundaries of the catchment area of each road is shown by the broken lines in the octagon. But, of course, the basic presumption of the model—that there is an infinitely elastic demand at P—makes interpretation very hazardous. Indeed it seems best to explore at this stage the effects of finite elasticities of demand on the reaction to transport provisions.

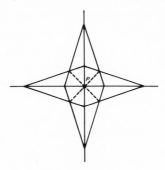

Figure 46.   The Cultivated Area with a Crossroad.

164

115. The model has so far been restricted to the single-crop case. This is no serious limitation since it can easily be extended to take account of a number of crops which have different transport characteristics. Consider two crops:

Crop (1) is difficult to headload but easy to roadhaul.
Crop (2) is easy to headload but relatively difficult to roadhaul.

We can describe the cost per ton-mile of crop (1) by road a_1 and by head b_1. The costs of crop (2) are analogously a_2 and b_2. The prices are respectively k_1 and k_2. It follows that the land will be used for the purpose which produces the greatest profit. The profit from crop (1) is given by:

$$k_1 - a_1 x - b_1 y \geq 0$$

and from crop (2) $k_2 - a_2 x - b_2 y \geq 0$

We can represent these regions on the road in the following figure:

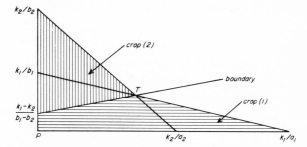

Figure 47. The Cultivated Area to the North of the Road When There Are Two Crops.

(we have not drawn in the boundaries to the south of the road since they are simply a mirror image of the northern half). The boundaries of the crops are shown by the vertically shaded area for crop (2) and the horizontally shaded area for crop (1). If when the road is improved headloading costs do not change, then the distance of the boundary north from P does not change. The boundary, however, swings around according to the intersection T of the two boundaries of marginal plots.[38] All the re-

---

[38] The equal profit boundary line is given by:
$$k_1 - a_1 x - b_1 y = k_2 - a_2 x - b_2 y$$
i.e. $y = (b_1 - b_2)^{-1}[(a_2 - a_1)x + (k_1 - k_2)]$
when $x = 0$, $y = \dfrac{k_1 - k_2}{b_1 - b_2}$
$$= \frac{\text{price difference}}{\text{difference in ton-mile headloading cost}}$$

165

maining analysis in terms of examining the effects of improved highways, of ton-mile taxes, etc. can continue exactly as before. The only difference arises from the allocation of land between crops and from the two rent slopes.

Alternative Models and Their Effects

116.   With many road developments there is also a competitive (as distinct from a complementary) mode. A road built by the side of a railway will have quite different effects from a road constructed into the bush. We can represent this diagrammatically as in Figure 48, where the railway has larger fixed costs and its ton-mile costs decline as mileage increases; this effect is shown by the "railway line" boundaries. Up to the boundary XY all the traffic is carried by road—the long-distance traffic beyond that boundary is carried by rail. And the building of the road extends the area of cultivation by making short-distance road traffic cheaper than rail.

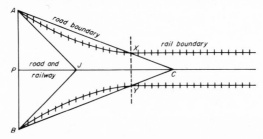

Figure 48.   The Plan of the Cultivated Area Where the Road and Railway Emanate Side by Side from P.

117.   The analysis of benefits and taxes is much more complicated than in the simple linear case. It can be pursued only with the aid of much mathematics. But the general tendencies are easily sketched by using the figure. They will not, however, be pursued here.

VI

EVIDENCE ON COSTS, CONGESTION, AND ELASTICITIES

1. *Introduction*

1. The purpose of this chapter is to review evidence on the theoretical magnitudes set out in Chapters III, IV and V of this study. No attempt is made to survey all published and unpublished material on costs and elasticities nor to evaluate carefully the quantity and quality of the evidence in each case. The basis and the reliability of much of the statistical material is usually doubtful and sometimes unknown. But if there is a consensus of opinion among engineers and practical transport men it is of some interest to know what it is. It is equally interesting to know if there appears to be *no* consensus and to hazard a guess why this should be so.

2. Our first task in Section 2 is to examine what evidence is available on the *journey cost* of vehicles. Journey costs are borne partly by the road authority in the form of an increase in maintenance cost—the so-called variable maintenance cost—but mostly by vehicle owners themselves in the form of *operating* and *congestion costs*. The first questions we ask are what is the level of variable maintenance cost and how does it vary with the type of road? And, of equal importance, how does it vary with the type of vehicle using the highway? The second set of questions are: what evidence is there of congestion (as we have defined it) on rural and inter-urban roads as well as on urban highways in developing countries? How

important is rural congestion and to what extent is it due to non-motor traffic?

3.   The next task is to examine the shape of the cost curve associated with building the highways and the annual fraction of maintenance cost that is not associated with the quantity of traffic. As we pointed out in the theoretical discussion, the question of whether economic user charges (EUC) would or would not produce sufficient revenue to pay for the total cost of the road system depends on the shape of the long-run average cost curve of roads. We conjectured that the shape was of the standard "S" type—with economies of scale for rural roads and diseconomies for urban roads (see Figure 6, p. 38). We here question whether this prediction is consistent with the facts.

4.   The last task attempted in this chapter is to review the evidence available about elasticities of demand for transport. This is a critical parameter for many policy proposals. The simple development model of Chapter V predicted that the elasticity in terms of ton-miles would be between -1.0 and -2.0. Non-development models suggest much lower (absolute) values. Statistical evidence on elasticities is so flimsy however that it does not help to discriminate between good and bad hypotheses.

2. *Variable Maintenance Costs*

5.   The first problem to be tackled in relation to journey costs is the estimate of the quantitative variation of road maintenance expenditure with the volume of traffic. Certain general precepts are currently taken into account by engineers in designing highways and in budgeting for maintenance expenditure. First it is well known that *overloaded* vehicles cause great damage to the surface of the highway.[1] The critical factor is the ratio of actual axle-loads to the design axle-load of the highway. Such overloading causes "washboarding" and a much more speedy break-up of the surface. No firm estimates of the cost of this overloading are available—but one engineer hazarded an opinion that a 50 percent overload on an axle would cause more damage than 1,000 properly loaded vehicles. Use of some earth and gravel roads by overloaded vehicles has destroyed the roads more or less completely. Clearly there is a consensus that overloading is very expensive. The appropriate way to treat this is to institute inspec-

---

[1] "Overloading" should be here defined as loads that generate larger costs to the road authority than the reduction in costs to the trucker. In practice and in law "overloading" is usually defined at a much lower level of weight in order to cover the safety margins of the design engineer.

tion systems and charge offenders very large fines. These fines should be at least as large as the sum of the damage and inspection cost divided by the probability of detection.

6. It is also commonly thought that an increase in the volume of traffic on the road will increase congestion and so cause many vehicles to drive on the side of the highway. This will cause damage to the edges and so increase the rate of deterioration of the highway. This suggests that the variable maintenance cost is an *increasing* function of the volume of traffic; as traffic increases the average variable maintenance costs increase. Again, there is no reliable quantitative information on this effect.[2] We shall therefore suppose that the relationship between maintenance cost and traffic is linear; but one must bear in mind that, for high traffic volumes, the maintenance cost probably increases more rapidly.[3]

7. The information available on the variation of maintenance cost with the traffic flow indicates that the lower the standard of the road the higher is the incidence of variable maintenance cost. This is of course consistent with the common observation that vehicles tear up the surface of earth roads much more than they do paved roads (assuming that the vehicles on the paved road are not overloaded). For the roads of Venezuela, a study revealed the following relationships between maintenance cost and average daily traffic volume.

Annual Maintenance Cost, Venezuela 1960[a]
(*per kilometer*)

Road	Bolivars	U.S. $ equivalent (US $1 = 4.5 bolivars, 1960)
Paved	10,400 + 1 (ADT)	2,300 + 0.2 (ADT)
Gravel	5,200 + 18 (ADT)	1,150 + 4 (ADT)
Earth	1,550 + 54 (ADT)	344 + 12 (ADT)

[a] Average daily traffic is here abbreviated as ADT.
Source: Richard M. Soberman, "Economic Analysis of Highway Design in Developing Countries," *Highway Research Record No. 115,* publication 1337, Highway Research Board, (Washington, D.C., 1966).

[2] This "edge-of-the-road" argument has important implications for the design of lane width. One informed observer has suggested that, with two-lane roads of proper width, motorists will merely go slower as traffic increases and will not drive on the edge.
[3] *Highway Research Board Bulletin 155,* Highway Research Board, (Washington, D.C., 1957) reports that maintenance costs should be regarded as increasing "sharply" when traffic reaches 1,000 vehicles a day. This "instruction" however, does not seem to have been the consequence of any statistical analysis.

These relationships were obtained by fitting regressions to data on maintenance expenses and traffic flow on roads in Venezuela.

8. Probably the most striking feature of these statistics is the enormous difference between the variable maintenance costs for different types of road. Comparing the earth and paved roads for example, it seems that the variable maintenance cost on the former is about fifty times as large as the variable maintenance cost on the latter! Transforming these values we see that the variable maintenance costs in Venezuela are (in U.S. currency):

Paved: 0.06 cents a vehicle-km or 0.1 cents a vehicle-mile

Gravel: 1.1 cents a vehicle-km or 1.8 cents a vehicle-mile

Earth: 3.3 cents a vehicle-km or 5.3 cents a vehicle-mile

Although one can clearly interpret these statistics only as orders of magnitude, the size of the variable maintenance cost on earth roads is quite startling. The incidence of motor taxation is much less—typically in the region of 1.5 to 4 cents a mile in most countries. Making a rough allowance for the additional fuel etc. used on earth roads, the tax a vehicle-mile would rarely be greater than 5 cents. This suggests that high taxes are indeed quite proper economic user charges on earth and perhaps also gravel roads.

9. There are however a number of reasons why it would be misleading to interpret these regression equations in this way. Apart from the difficulties of defining maintenance expenditure and the trade-offs between maintenance and capital spending, it seems clear that there is no simple one-way causal effect from traffic to maintenance cost. There is also a reverse effect; traffic will tend to be higher on well-maintained than on poorly-maintained roads. The level of traffic determines the amount to be spent on maintenance; the standard of maintenance determines the level of traffic.

10. It is, however, far easier to criticize than to collect statistics of this kind. Soberman's data, so far as I know, are almost unique. Soberman's parameters are derived from a statistical survey of actual experience with maintenance expenditures in Venezuela. But there are also many rules of thumb which are used to determine maintenance expenditure. One that is used in the old British colonies in West Africa is:[4]

Maintenance cost for
gravel road in £ Sterling
p.a. per mile   = 50 + 2 (Average daily traffic flow)

---

[4] R. S. Millard, *Roads, Road Transport, and Traffic in Developing Countries*, Conference on Civil Engineering, (London 1962).

Another example is the Cogeraf study of the Republic of Niger[5] where these formulas are used:

Maintenance costs for
surfaced road in
W.A. francs per km $= 130,000 + 0.88$ (Annual traffic—36,000)

and for gravel roads $= 40,000 + 4.44$ (Annual traffic)

The British West Africa rule is more or less the same as Soberman's equation for gravel roads. Cogeraf's rules are more complex—but again, there is no vital difference on the parameters for gravel roads. In exercises conducted by the Road Research Laboratory, variable maintenance cost was valued at one cent per vehicle-mile—but it is clear that no substantive research lay behind that value. Because of Britain's very high standard of maintenance, much heavier traffic volumes and inclement weather, this figure for paved roads does seem higher than the international average.[6] But this evidence, unlike the interpretative argument presented above, suggests that Soberman's figures are too *low*, not too high. On balance one is inclined to accept Soberman's estimates as the best available.

11.   The next problem is to measure the variation of maintenance costs with the mixture of traffic. It might reasonably be thought that heavy trucks and buses would cause greater maintenance costs per vehicle mile than light vehicles. A recent American inquiry,[7] however, generally found that on roads designed for heavy traffic there are virtually no differential maintenance effects between light and heavy vehicles. It has been argued instead that the presence of heavy vehicles occasions more damage partly because of the "probability of occurrences that will expose it (the road) to the risk of failure." Damage caused by the weather may be compounded more by heavy than by light vehicles. The passage of heavy trucks in the rainy season on earth roads may result quite quickly in the destruction of the highway.

12.   These arguments are not concluded. But clearly even if one accepts completely the proposition that there is no variation in maintenance cost according to weight of vehicle on pavements designed for that weight, the

---

[5] *Republique du Niger, Compagnie Général d'études et de recherches pour l'Afrique*, (Paris, 1963). This result is reported in a valuable survey by M. J. Betz, "Highway Maintenance Costs—A Consideration for Developing Areas," *Highway Research Record No. 94*, (Washington, D.C., 1965).

[6] Smeed Report, Appendix 2. It was also intended for *urban* roads which involve many additional complications.

[7] *Highway Cost Allocation Study*, Supplementary Report, House Document, No. 124, 89th Congress, 1st Session, Washington, 1965, pages 180 *et seq*.

171

brute facts are that in underdeveloped countries heavy vehicles *do* use inappropriate highways. And it may be difficult and expensive to provide administrative arrangements that prevent such misuse. It is therefore certain that heavy vehicles will cause higher maintenance costs than cars and light vans—but any precision regarding the amount would be unsafe.

13. The most reliable information on maintenance expenditures in advanced countries is contained in the reports of the United States Bureau of Public Roads. Maintenance costs are not analyzed as a function of traffic flow but only as general averages. The most striking feature is that the maintenance costs of the BPR are very much lower than those adduced by Soberman. Unfortunately no attempt can be made here to reconcile these estimates. Partly the differences are due to definition, and partly to the peculiarities of Venezuela. It is true that most other estimates of maintenance expenditures seem to approach the BPR estimates but it is very likely that they are not independent and are probably derived from the BPR figures. One cannot suppose that Soberman's estimate of the *variable* maintenance cost is discredited by the BPR figures.

Total Maintenance Cost per km per annum

Paved (Asphalt)	$800–$900
Gravel	$850
Earth	$300

(*Note:* The figures have been rounded to avoid the impression of spurious accuracy.)

3. Vehicle Operating Costs—Congestion Costs

14. We now turn to consider the *vehicle* costs as distinct from the road costs. Vehicle costs are incurred by the road user, whereas road costs are the legal responsibility of the road authority. Variation of vehicle operating cost with the type of highway is well known and has been recently documented and brought up-to-date.[8] The broad results need only be indicated here.[9]

Indices of Vehicle Operating Costs

	Paved	Gravel	Earth
Cars	100	128	165
Heavy Trucks	100	146–154	230–259

[8] Jan de Weille, *Quantification of Road User Savings*, World Bank Staff Occasional Papers No. 2, (1966).

[9] *Ibid.*, p. 28. It is interesting to note that Soberman's results for Venezuela do not differ markedly from these ranges.

172

There is, however, an obvious interaction between the maintenance standards of the highway and the operating costs of trucks using that highway. The measurement of such an interaction and its consequences on *optimum* maintenance expenditure and on traffic flow are interesting questions which are, however, outside the scope of this inquiry.

15. The important aspect of vehicle operating costs for the purposes of this study is their variation with the level of traffic. In other words we are interested primarily in the congestion effects as traffic is increased on a given highway. First let us make a broad survey of the general results. Obviously the easiest variable to observe is not cost, either operating or total cost, since it is conceptually difficult to define and requires detailed surveys of accounts. Consequently we use speed as a surrogate for cost; but this requires a transformation from speed to cost. Many such transformations are available for various countries and there does not appear to be any enormous variation among them. Here we shall use data for the United Kingdom, partly because of its reliability and partly because there is much ancillary information available. The Road Research Laboratory showed that the following equations gave good approximations to the cost-speed relationship:

$$c = 4.4 + 93/v \qquad \text{Up to 37 miles an hour}$$
$$c = 5.0 + 71/v \qquad \text{Between 37 and 45 miles an hour}$$

where c is the total average cost per vehicle (equivalent car)-mile in pence (approx. US cent) net of tax

v is the average running speed of traffic in miles per hour.

These results were obtained for a "normal" composition of traffic.[10] The figures for cost exclude any element of the valuation of non-working time. If this were included then the first equation would be (approximately):

$$c = 4.4 + 200/v$$

16. All these results are for *paved* roads in England; however, it would be relatively easy to construct "synthetic" costs for lower quality roads by using the de Weille study.[11] The composition of traffic on English high-

---

[10] These figures refer to 1963 values. See J. A. Bunce and J. O. Tresidder, *Characteristics of Rural Roads in Jamaica*, Conference on Civil Engineering Problems Overseas, Technical Session IV, (June 15, 1966), p. 35. (The data have been revised slightly.) See also for earlier data, Charlesworth, G., D. J. Reynolds and J. G. Wardrop, "Road Improvement; Choosing Priorities by a New Formula," *Engineering*, Vol. 188 (4873), (London, 1959), pp. 185–188.

[11] de Weille, *op. cit.* Such an exercise would have to ignore many of the interactions between road conditions—cost and speed; but it seems unlikely that such interactions would be quantitatively important.

ways is likely to contain rather a higher fraction of private cars than those of developing countries; but it is clear that the traffic mix on European highways is likely to be a closer approximation to conditions in developing countries than the composition on roads in the United States—the best alternative source of material.

17.   Now let us examine the relationship between speed in miles per hour (v) and vehicle flow (q), where q is expressed in "passenger car units" or p.c.u.'s per hour. The simplest approach is to assume that motor vehicle speed is a function of vehicle flow alone; that is to say we ignore non-vehicular road use. The broad results may be expressed as follows:

Urban traffic	$v = 25 - 0.014q$	w (width) $= 30$ ft., $v < 25$
or	$v = 25 - 0.42\ q/w$	$v < 25$
Rural Highways, three-lane	$v = 48 - 0.006q$	$v < 48$

The second equation for urban traffic has the road width (w) in feet as a parameter. We shall discuss various developments of these equations and their limitations later.[12]

18.   Now we put the cost equation and the speed-flow equations together to obtain cost as a function of traffic flow. Suitable substitutions give:

$$\text{Rural (three-lane)} \quad c = 5.0 + \frac{71}{(48 - .006q)} \quad 37 < v < 45$$

$$\text{Urban (30 ft width)} \quad c = 4.4 + \frac{93}{(25 - .014q)} \quad v < 25$$

Neither equation takes account of non-working time. For rural highways with three lanes we find the total cost of a traffic flow of q is:

$$qc = 5.0q + \frac{71}{(48 - .006q)}$$

To find out how much total cost increases as we increase the flow of traffic q, we obtain:

$$\frac{d(qc)}{dq} = 5.0 + \frac{71}{(48 - .006q)} + \frac{0.43q}{(48 - .006q)^2}$$

[12] J. C. Tanner, H. D. Johnson, and J. R. Scott, "Sample Survey of the Roads and Traffic of Great Britain," *Road Research Technical Paper No. 62*, HMSO, (London, 1962); and J. C. Tanner and J. R. Scott, "50-Point Traffic Census—the First 5 Years," *Road Research Technical Paper No. 63*, (London, 1962). See also: *Research on Road Traffic*, Road Research Laboratory, HMSO, (London, 1965); and T. M. Coburn, "Speed on 24 ft. and 30 ft. Wide Sections of A.5," *Road Research Laboratory Note RN/2905*, (Harmondsworth, England, 1956).

This expression has a nice interpretation. The left hand side is simply the marginal cost of additional traffic. The first two terms on the right hand side constitute the average cost. The third term is the *congestion effect*. This tells us the increase in total costs which is caused by vehicles getting in one another's way as the quantity of traffic increases. Thus we have:

Marginal social cost = Private cost *plus* Congestion cost

$$\text{of a three-lane rural road} = 5.0 + \frac{71}{(48 - 0.006q)} + \frac{0.43q}{(48 - 0.006q)^2}$$

where q is passenger car units flow per hour. Our main concern is with the congestion cost.

19. The first question which one may ask is whether the congestion cost is "large." As we argued in Chapter III if the difference between marginal social cost and private cost is not trivial, there is a good case for imposing a congestion levy. We may insert a few notional figures for vehicle flow per hour to see what results. Thus:

Three-lane rural

When $q = 100$ vehicles per hour, congestion cost = 0.025 pence
When $q = 1,000$ vehicles per hour, congestion cost = 0.36 pence

Typically rural roads in developing countries rarely have traffic volumes approaching 1,000 vehicles per hour. Probably the "normal" figure is nearer to 1,000 vehicles a *day*, so one may take it that the flow of about 100 vehicles (passenger car units) an hour is typical of rural traffic flow in developing countries. Indeed such statistics as are available suggest less than 100 vehicles an hour.

20. Clearly the upshot of these statistics is to suggest that *congestion on rural roads is of trivial importance* in developing countries. There is no need to take it into account in devising suitable user charges. This confirms the views of many practical observers of the traffic scene in developing countries; there is no congestion effect on the vast majority of rural and interurban highways.

21. Such a conclusion—however provisional—does emerge from a highly simplified model. One might reasonably ask whether the same results would come out of more complex models that take into account some of the factors so far omitted. Obviously one important effect is the size and character of the road. For higher volumes of traffic one would expect a

175

higher quality and larger capacity highway. The width of the road can be incorporated easily into the results for rural roads:

$$v = 51 - \frac{q + 1400}{6w} \text{ or 43 mph whichever is lower}$$

where w is the carriageway width in feet. This formula can be applied to roads with from two to six lanes.[13] The cost function is therefore:

$$c = 5.0 + \frac{71}{51 - \dfrac{q + 1400}{6w}}$$

But again it is easy to see that with the normal carriageway width associated with traffic flows, the congestion term is still quite trivial. This can also be observed from calculated speed-flow equations for different widths of road, as shown in the following table. It is easy to see that variation in the road width does not have a critical effect on the congestion cost. But the composition of traffic does.

Speed/flow Relations for Different Types of Vehicles on Rural Roads[14]

Road	Vehicle Type	Speed (mph) at flow q passenger car units per hour
2 lanes	Car	$41.9 - 0.0084\,q$
	Light commercial	$38.3 - 0.0068\,q$
	Medium commercial	$34.1 - 0.0048\,q$
	Heavy commercial	$29.2 - 0.0023\,q$
3 lanes	Car	$47.7 - 0.0062\,q$
	Light commercial	$40.5 - 0.0037\,q$
	Medium commercial	$33.9 - 0.0012\,q$
	Heavy commercial	$27.4 - 0.0002\,q$

22. As common sense suggests, heavy vehicles are less affected by traffic density than are light vans and cars. Since much of the traffic in developing countries consists of trucks and buses, this could be taken as further evidence that congestion costs are trivial. This effect is to some extent countered by the fact that the operating costs of trucks are so much higher than those of cars. Even so the congestion effect is still very small.

23. In certain countries the main culprits of congestion—even on rural roads—are pedestrians, carts, draft animals, farm implements, and a miscellaneous collection of other users. In rural areas perhaps the bullock

---

[13] *Research on Road Traffic*, p. 115.
[14] *Ibid.*, p. 115.

cart is the most serious impediment on the highway. One may attempt to reckon such carts at the equivalent private car units (p.c.u.'s). A heavy commercial vehicle or bus should probably be assessed at about 3 private cars for rural congestion purposes.[15] Pedal cycles count as 0.5 of a private car. It seems to me likely that bullock carts would have more congestion effects than two or even three buses or heavy commercial vehicles. This is merely a conjecture, there are no data available to provide a sound estimate. From personal experience, however, I would not expect any substantial disagreement with such a conjecture.[16]

24. As a rough approximation, therefore, one may suppose that there is no congestion on rural roads due to motor vehicle traffic. Delays in traffic flow are caused primarily by non-motor traffic, and in particular by the bullock cart, farm animals, pedestrians and cyclists. It would be interesting to calculate the cost of permitting bullock carts, for example, on the highway. This may be calculated either in terms of the delay occasioned to existing traffic or in terms of the amount of capital investment required to maintain the flow of goods and passengers.[17]

4. Congestion Costs in Towns—Some Generalizations

25. We have shown that congestion is a sizable problem only in the towns. In order to find optimum congestion levies, however, we need to know something about the elasticity of demand for motor transport, and about the cross-elasticities between one mode of transport and another. It must be admitted immediately that the data available on elasticities are worth practically nothing. What pass for measures of elasticity have shown very wide variations.[18] There is certainly no consensus of opinion to which one may appeal.

26. Whether it is critical to know the elasticity of demand with a fair degree of accuracy before calculating congestion levies depends on the sensitivity of such levies to variations in the elasticity. One must calculate and see. Oddly enough, from calculations made in connection with rerearch for the Smeed Report, the value of the elasticity of demand does not seem to have an important effect.[19] As the most extreme illustration,

---

[15] *Ibid.*, p. 201.

[16] Some supporting verbal evidence is contained in the *Report of Motor Vehicle Taxation Enquiry Committee*, (New Delhi, 1950).

[17] In addition one must also reckon the substantial damage inflicted on the road surface by the unshod wheels of a cart.

[18] See for example *Research on Road Traffic*, p. 480.

[19] J. C. Tanner, "Pricing the Use of the Roads: a Mathematical and Numerical Study," *Road Research Laboratory Note LN/319*, Department of Scientific and Industrial Research, (Harmondsworth, England, 1963).

consider elasticities as far apart as 0.25 and 8.0—a range that surely covers all conceivable practical cases. The optimum congestion levy for the low elasticity is between 1.3 and 2.4 times that for the high elasticity depending on the speed of traffic. (Note that this is for a thirty-two-fold difference in elasticity!) And for the speeds which one might consider normal in the cities of developing countries, the difference between the charges was on the order of less than 50 percent for these two extreme elasticities.[20]

27. It is therefore possible to fix the actual level of congestion charges without paying too much attention to variations in elasticities. But the reader should not conclude that elasticities do not affect decisions about the *desirability* of charging congestion levies. They do. If, for example, the elasticity is very low—say 0.25—then congestion levies will not much improve the traffic situation. People are willing to pay handsomely for the privilege of driving in the city; and there may well be large income effects which should be taken into account. These problems will be examined in the following chapters.

28. It is useful to have some idea of general orders of magnitude of the congestion levy. One may formulate these figures by using the speed-flow relationships for urban areas and the appropriate cost-speed equation. Substituting we obtain a cost-flow equation which is the basis of the calculated congestion levy. It is, however, useful to express this relationship according to the existing speed; speed is a good standard indicator of the extent of congestion in cities. The journey time or average speed is a measure of which many readers are directly aware; we judge congestion by the time it takes us to get from one place to another. From the data for urban highways in Britain we get the following broad picture of congestion levies:

Description of congestion	Present journey speed (*mph*)	Calculated congestion levy per vehicle mile (*U.S. cents*)
Severe	less than 10	10 to 20
Moderate	10 to 14	5 to 12
Mild	15 to 20	2 to 4

For vehicles on urban roads that achieve journey speeds of more than 20 mph the congestion levy would be less than two cents a mile.

---

[20] To some extent these results are misleading, since they do not take into account the "backward-bending" cost curve in conditions of extreme congestion (see Chapter III), and the use of speed as a standard of comparison also has some limitations. But one suspects that the general order of the results is not crucially affected by changing the assumptions, although it is clearly very difficult to check this suspicion.

29. These orders of magnitude of the congestion levy are derived entirely from measured relationships in urban Britain.[21] The congestion levy is calculated on the assumption that no taxes exist at present. Under conditions of severe congestion the valuation of non-working time has a considerable effect on the figures. In thinking about the applicability of these values to developing countries, one should therefore remember that probably a much larger fraction of cars, etc. is used for business purposes there than in Britain, and the amount of "working time" lost in congestion (per vehicle-mile) is likely to be higher.

30. The reader will no doubt be able to modify these figures so that they are not too atypical of cities in the developing countries. One critical difference is the much larger pedestrian and animal traffic in the cities of the developing world. It is impossibly expensive to institute a price system for pedestrians, so it seems that the best policy might be to take them into account as one of the "given environments" of the system of motor congestion levies. This does not mean accepting the number of pedestrians and the amount of animal traffic as a constant; on the contrary one must take into account the reactions of pedestrians in response to any system of congestion levies. Evidence on the effects of pedestrians on vehicle flow and speeds is available from very small and narrow samples.[22] For what it is worth, this evidence suggests that although there will be significant changes in pedestrian numbers associated with congestion levies, it does not seem to change the optimum value of the congestion levy on motor vehicles. We believe, however, that this result is of little use for many of the developing countries—partly because of the different standards of pedestrian behavior. The pedestrian reaction remains obscure—and perhaps it is the most important gap in the existing framework of knowledge.

5. The Total Cost Structure of Roads

31. One of the main reasons for classifying the roads as a public good arose because of the characteristics of the cost curves. The shape of the various cost curves set out in Chapter III was derived from *a priori* arguments. We now examine the extent to which such predicted cost curves are to be found in fact. The purpose of this review of the evidence is not, however, to provide numerical rules for investment nor, indeed, to furnish pricing rules which can be applied to a large number or even one particular country. Such guides to investment and pricing require extensive analysis

---

[21] See Tanner, *op. cit.*

[22] A. A. Walters, "Optimum Motor Taxes," *Applied Statistics*, Vol. X, No. 3, (London, November 1961), pp. 157–169.

of different categories of roads, variation in soil and climate, and differences in traffic and trade. Encyclopedias or manuals of this kind may be well worth compiling, but the purpose of this study is much more modest; we are concerned only with the broad pattern of road costs, not with the subtle distinctions required for road planning in practice. The broad pattern should be ubiquitous if it is to be useful for refuting or supporting a theory of road pricing.

Rural and Interurban

32. There is a consensus of opinion among engineers and other transport experts on the criterion for the improvement of almost all rural and interurban roads. This is the reduction in cost—both to the road authority and to the vehicle operator. Congestion or expansion in road capacity is almost never used to justify road investment. The only examples where congestion may be invoked as good grounds for investment are those where traffic is very dense on interurban roads. The almost universal justification for roads in rural areas where traffic is relatively light is the reduction in operating and maintenance costs, counterbalancing the additional fixed (sunk) costs. This consensus of opinion is not inconsistent with the form of the cost curve (for low traffic volumes) which we deduced from the "joint-product" argument in Chapter III. From the engineers' criterion one can derive a long-run cost curve which has the concave section for roads with low traffic volumes—just as we illustrated in Chapter III.[23]

33. One may be skeptical, however, of engineering opinion, and one may put more reliance on statistical demonstrations of the shape of empirical cost curves. There is a large quantity of statistical material on road construction and maintenance costs in developing countries. The figures usually tell broadly the same story although it is not always clear whether this is merely because they have been derived from similar sources, or whether they may be taken as supporting evidence. For this study we have chosen to use only one main source of statistics on road construction and maintenance: this is Soberman's study of Venezuela.[24] To some extent this information will be supplemented by some unpublished data from the Road Research Laboratory's work, in Sabah.[25]

---

[23] It is not clear that the engineers' criterion necessarily gives rise only to this concavity. To determine this would require a scholarly survey of engineering literature.

[24] Richard M. Soberman, *op. cit.* The reasons for choosing Soberman's data are first that it is independently derived, and second that it includes valuable information on variable maintenance cost, which we used earlier in this chapter.

[25] R. S. P. Bonney, *The Relationships between Road Building and Economic and Social Development in Sabah*, Part I, L.N./519, BOR 87, (Harmondsworth, England, February 1964).

180

34. The following data are for (flat) earth, gravel and bituminous two-lane highways in Venezuela. All roads are 7.2 meters and are for "design speeds" of 50 kilometers an hour. All prices are expressed in 1959 bolivars (and one U.S. dollar exchanged for 4.5 bolivars at that time).

TABLE 1: Costs of Roads in Venezuela, 72 meters wide, 1959

(*bolivars per kilometer*)

	Earth	Gravel	Bituminous
Construction cost	13,500	27,000	120,000 to 200,000
Invariate maintenance cost p.a.	1,500	5,200	10,400
Variable maintenance cost[a] p.a.			
(per truck per day)	54	18	1
Vehicle operating cost	1.782	1.465	0.717

[a] A certain number of bolivars a year is expended in maintenance cost, and this is shown to vary with the average daily traffic volume (in trucks). Thus an increase of one truck per day on an earth road will increase maintenance costs by 54 Bs a kilometer a year.

Sources: Construction cost: Soberman, *op. cit.*, Figures 13 and 14. Invariate maintenance cost: *op. cit.*, equations 4 and 5. Variable maintenance cost: *op. cit.*, equations 4 and 5. Vehicle operating cost: *op. cit.*, Table 4.

35. It is convenient to represent all these data on the same time basis. The normal way of describing costs is in terms of annual expenditures per kilometer or per unit of (average) daily traffic flow. First the construction cost needs to be converted into an equivalent annual sum. The simple procedure adopted here is to take 10 percent of the construction cost. More complicated techniques of reducing a capital sum to an equivalent annual flow—taking account of the different lengths of life of the roads, for example—may be used, but it is doubtful if the data are worth that much manipulation. The vehicle operating cost is also converted to an annual figure by multiplying by 365—so that the units are then bolivars per kilometer per annum for one daily vehicle. The data may be written as follows:

Annual costs in bolivars	Earth	Gravel	Bituminous
Fixed (per kilometer) Construction	1,350	2,700	12,000 to 20,000
Maintenance	1,500	5,200	10,400
Variable (per daily vehicle kilometer)			
Maintenance	54	18	1
Operating Cost	650	535	262

181

By combining the elements of cost the total cost equations can be formed. These are illustrated in the graph of Figure 49. Earth roads appear to give the lowest total cost for traffic up to about thirty-two trucks a day, then gravel becomes cheaper. It does not pay to pave the road until there are at least eighty vehicles a day.

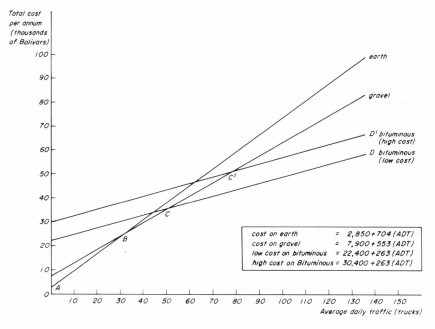

Figure 49. Cost of Rural Roads and Traffic (in Venezuela).

36.   Considering only these three roads (and assuming for the moment that bituminous roads are "low-cost"), one observes the typical form of long-run cost curve discussed in Chapter III. In Figure 49 *OABCD* describes the arc which appeared in the hypothetical long-run cost curve of Chapter III over the region where there were low levels of traffic. (If the bituminous road were high-cost, then we should merely substitute the "curve" *OABC'D'*.) It will be noticed that the capacity constraint does not appear on the diagram; these constraints become important only at traffic levels which are far in excess of those shown in the diagram. For all practical purposes they may be ignored.

37.   It might be suggested, however, that the absence of binding capacity constraints is merely a consequence of the pattern of construction we ob-

serve in Venezuela. Would not a "jeep-track"—a low standard road with poor alignment—be cheaper for very light traffic? On present evidence for countries which have considerable rainfall, the answer is no. In the Sabah study, it was shown that it was always better to build a well-aligned earth road than to build a jeep-track.[26] And even with a jeep-track it is unlikely that the variable cost would ever be lower than that with the earth road, and that the capacity constraint would ever matter.

38.   Other limitations are worth emphasizing. These data refer to countries which have considerable rainfall. For roads in desert countries one would find lower maintenance costs—probably only about 50 percent of those in wet climates, and especially lower on earth and gravel roads. The data used above apply only to flat country. With mountainous terrain the capital cost of the highway goes up considerably—between two- and three-fold for the same 50 kilometers per hour design speeds.[27] This suggests that all the cost lines in Figure 49 be moved bodily upwards. Such a transposition will affect the position of points B and C, but the basic shape will be the same as before. In mountainous terrain the curves in the road will mean that the capacity of the road is less than that of a highway of similar width on flat ground. Even so, for the volumes of traffic considered here, there is still no effective capacity constraint. Congestion may be ignored. The pattern of cost curves drawn in Chapter III is not discredited.

Urban Roads

39.   This concludes our discussion of the shape of the cost curves at the "low-traffic" levels. Now the shape of the curve at the "high-traffic" end should be examined to see whether the curve turns upwards. Much information has been collected on the variation of construction costs of urban roads and some data are available on the purchase of rights of way. But no study has been carried out to trace all the effects and interactions of increasing the urban road network to cater to an increase in traffic. And this is not surprising in view of the complexity of the task. The costs of increasing urban road capacity include not only the direct construction costs and rights of way, but also consequential changes in rents, the increase in congestion on the unimproved urban streets, the reduction in access,

---

[26] See *Road Research 1964*, (HMSO, London, 1966), pp. 135–136. This does not imply that there is a definitive case against constructing jeep-tracks. For "exploratory" purposes it may be a good idea to build one of these short-lived tracks to see what happens to development in that area. If little or nothing occurs then the capital lost is quite small—much less than would be lost by building a well-aligned earth road.

[27] Soberman, *op. cit.*, Fig. 13.

and so on.[28] All these vary enormously from one city to another, and it is unlikely that any broad representative figures are to be found.

40.   There is some evidence that construction costs increase more than proportionately to the size of the highway—partly because of the increased residential density.[29] The average cost of four-lane highways on the interstate system in urban areas of the United States was $1.69 million a mile whereas the average cost of eight-lane highways was $6.00 million a mile.[30] This suggests that there are increasing costs of construction in urban areas.

41.   What evidence is available on the costs of land also suggests that there is considerable variation with residential density—"from five percent or less at very low densities to 50 percent (of total costs or construction costs) or more at high densities."[31]

42.   The dangers of generalizing from conditions in cities in the United States to cities in the developing world need little emphasis; nor do the fragmentary and imperfect data available on costs. But for what the data are worth, the hypothetical pattern of costs of road construction and operation at high traffic volumes sketched in Chapter III is not discredited. The evidence suggests that there are in fact decreasing returns to road construction as traffic volumes become very large. But this is not a powerful test of the hypothesis and one's confidence in the postulated shape is not much increased by this review of the statistics.

43.   We conclude therefore that the provisional pattern of road construction and operating costs which was suggested in Chapter III has not been discredited by such evidence as we could bring to bear. In my view the shape for low traffic volumes has a high degree of credibility. And it is on the concavity (or non-convexity) at the low-traffic levels that the case for regarding the road as a public good depends.

---

[28] One must also beware of double counting.

[29] There is evidence that the *construction* cost for a standardized eight-lane highway increases according to the residential density:

   Construction cost (per mile) = $999,000 + $70,800 (residential density)

Hyman Joseph, "Construction Costs of Urban Expressways," *CATS Research News*, Vol. 4, No. 1, (December 1960), reported in J. Meyer, J. Kain, M. Wohl, *The Urban Transportation Problem*, (Harvard University Press, Cambridge, 1965).

[30] *Ibid.*, Table 62. We have used unweighted averages from this table. It must also be noted that these are *construction* costs only.

[31] *Ibid.*, p. 210. It is not perfectly clear what the authors mean by this statement—but the general drift is quite clear.

6. Discontinuities and Stage Construction

44. In Chapter III, we saw that discontinuities of investment and of cost functions played an important role in the formulation of policy. Some indications of the importance of discontinuities will now be reviewed. On the general level, however, it is of some interest to note that there are many dimensions to roads besides width and length. Curvature and alignment, pavement thickness and quality, standard of maintenance, and number of intersections are among the many factors that can be varied. The ability to vary these physical characteristics does not necessarily imply that discontinuities do not exist. It may still be relatively cheap to build certain standard roads—perhaps if only because engineering know-how and machines are adapted to such purposes. The facts only can answer this question.

45. Some general data are available for the United Kingdom. An analysis of information obtained by the Ministry of Transport on the costs of widening rural roads showed very wide ranges of cost per mile (thousand pounds sterling).[32] Perhaps the most remarkable feature of these statistics was the fact that the average cost of transforming a three-lane highway into a four-lane divided highway *exceeded* the cost of converting a two-lane road into a four-lane divided highway. It is clear, however, that the magnitude of the difference is not large enough to be taken seriously. But one must adduce that the cost of going from two to four lanes is about the same as going from three to four lanes. To build a road through the sequence two to three to four lanes (divided) one must incur (undiscounted) costs which are at least 50 percent more than the costs of expanding immediately from two to four lanes.

TABLE 2: Costs of Road Widening per mile, United Kingdom, 1958

(£'000)

	Normal range	Average
2 to 3 lanes	30 to 70	50
2 lanes to 4 lanes divided	60 to 130	90
3 lanes to 4 lanes divided	70 to 130	100

46. This is a sharp discontinuity. It suggests that it will rarely if ever be economic to build three-lane highways, given that a two-lane road already

---

[32] *Research on Road Traffic*, p. 206.

exists.[33] It is best to expand to a four-lane divided highway, without going through an intermediate stage. Furthermore, it implies that it is efficient to have uncongested divided highways for certain ranges of traffic—and these highways will incur deficits. But it is better to incur these deficits than to build a three-lane highway, suffer some congestion, and perhaps earn a small surplus (or at least incur lower deficits) with the congestion levies.[34]

47. Evidence of discontinuities on lower quality roads has been adduced in a study of road construction costs in Iran.[35] The authors there compared the stage construction operation of first graveling and then later paving and widening, with the single-stage construction of paving immediately to the final width. The difference was only about five percent of cost. This suggests that this particular discontinuity is not of very great importance and, as the authors point out, it may be offset by the postponement of some 40 percent of the investment.[36]

48. To sum up, therefore, one does find some evidence of sharp discontinuities in the construction of roads—although not quite so large as a naive interpretation of the data might suggest. In surfacing and widening there is also some evidence of discontinuities—but not so large, perhaps, as has been normally conjectured.

7. Relative Ton-mile Costs and the Development Triangle

49. The theory of Chapter V discussed the geographic consequences of transport development. Let us briefly and broadly review the results of that theory. The important ingredients or "inputs" of the model were the

---

[33] A rationalization may be made for the three-lane highway in terms of the lower level of maintenance costs required compared with the four-lane highway. But such a case seems implausible.

[34] There is a built-in implausibility about these statistics. For if it were really true that it was as cheap to build a four-lane divided highway as a three-lane road, why were *any* three-lane roads built at all? The implication is that any three-lane road that happens to be built is simply the result of mistaken planning. An alternative explanation is that the authorities constructed the best road in each set of circumstances. Thus in those places where a three-lane highway was built it would have cost more to have built a four-lane road. The high cost of such a hypothetical four-lane road is not included in the data. Similarly where it was relatively cheap to construct four-lane highways the authority was induced to construct them—and the even cheaper three-lane highway which they chose *not* to construct is not included in the table.

[35] H. G. van der Tak and J. de Weille, *Reappraisal of a Road Project in Iran*, World Bank Staff Occasional Paper No. 7, (1968), Chapter IV.

[36] It is necessary to add that an alternative expert opinion, based on the same data, suggested that the undiscounted difference in costs was on the order of 10 to 15 percent, rather than the 5 percent suggested by the authors.

relative ton-mile cost by motor and by non-motor transport—the *a* and the *b* of Chapter V. With this knowledge it was shown that the development would be of a triangular shape—with a broad base near the market and narrowing to a point on the road at a distance from the market dependent on the ratio of the market price of the commodity to the ton-mile cost of transport by truck.[37] Furthermore, the model predicts that the elasticity of demand for transport will be (minus) unity if transport is measured in tons and (minus) two if measured in ton-miles. Various qualifications, due to the truncation of the road, a finite elasticity of demand on the market, etc., modified these values to some extent. The other predictions about the amount to which traffic would be reduced by ton-mile and tonnage taxes, followed from the basic theory.

50. It is worthwhile first to give orders of magnitude of the ratio of "headloading" and animal transport costs to motor transport cost. In Nepal the cost per ton-mile of headloading (i.e. human porters) was about 15.0 Nepal rupees a mile, pack animal about 7.0, bullock cart 4.0, a five-ton diesel truck (half-loaded) 1.3 and rail 1.0.[38] In Liberia the cost of human porterage was between 50 and 70 cents a ton-mile, whereas the truck ton-mile cost was about 5 cents.[39] The general orders of the two ratios of human porterage cost to motor cost are not markedly inconsistent—a ratio of between ten and fifteen to one is the order of magnitude we seek. For pack animals the ratio is probably about five or six to one—but there is no alternative source to confirm this.

51. From these statistics one may predict the relative shape of the triangle of development. It should be about five or eight times as long in the direction of the highway as it is wide around the highway in the vicinity of the market. Evidence of a pattern of this kind appeared in maps of the rubber farms in Liberia—but the road distances were rather longer than those predicted by the theory.[40] This may be because the ton-mile cost by road tapers downwards with distance (a factor not incorporated in the simple model), but it is more probably explained by simple mistakes in the statistics.[41] At least one cannot claim that the Liberian evidence powerfully discredits the theory.

---

[37] The reader will recall that when there are other factor costs the distance is determined by the ratio of the difference between c.i.f. price and factor cost to the ton-mile truck cost.

[38] An IBRD report.

[39] *Economic Survey of Liberia*, (processed, Evanston, Illinois, 1963). See R. W. Clower, G. Dalton, M. Harwitz and A. A. Walters, *Growth Without Development: An Economic Survey of Liberia*, (Evanston, 1965).

[40] Some rubber was head-carried for distances of more than 60 miles to market.

[41] It was difficult to determine where the rubber came from, and which trees were not being tapped.

52.   In his study of road development in Sabah (formerly British North Borneo), Bonney also studies the effects of road building on the extension of the planting of cash crops.[42] Bonney's data do show the typical triangular form predicted by our model. Adjacent to the market, cultivation for export takes place at a depth of about 400 acres a mile, whereas 40 miles or so down the road from the market the area of cultivation of export crops drops to less than 200 acres a mile. But there are so few observations (only nine in all!) that one should perhaps regard it as an *illustration* rather than a test of the model.

---

[42] Bonney, *op. cit.*, Part III, "Agricultural Development, Traffic and Road Standards," L.N./648/RSPB, BOR 112, (July 1964).

VII

USER CHARGES AND TAXES IN PRACTICE

1. *Introduction*

1.   The purpose of this chapter can be simply stated: we seek practical ways of implementing the principles of user charges and taxes which were outlined in the first part of this study. Here we leave the tight logical relations of theoretical propositions. This chapter attempts the most difficult task of all: the translation of theoretical desiderata into a system of taxes and imposts that is administratively feasible.

2.   What is, or is not, feasible will vary from one country to another. We shall suppose that there are certain *standard* administrative difficulties which are ubiquitous. But we shall not recognize the existence of "political impossibilities." What can be done politically is so erratic and variable that it is best left out of account. We shall be concerned here with what is desirable *and* administratively feasible.

3.   The other main limitation is that one really only knows what is administratively feasible if one can observe it in practice. This would restrict our survey to the policy instruments at present in operation; and there is clearly more to be done than merely ring the changes on existing taxes. New types of taxes are required—one which will be suggested here is a

189

congestion levy in the form of a restricted license. The administrative feasibility of such a tax is a matter of conjecture rather than record; but one must use inferential evidence to examine estimates of the effects of such a tax.

4.   The main ingredients which we feed into the mixture of judgment, economic analysis and administrative generalization in this chapter are the orders of magnitude which emerged from the discussion of costs in Chapter VI. One cannot devise a general system of user charges without knowing which costs are important and which may be ignored as trivial. The degree of confidence which one may place in the cost estimates is, however, not large, so it is conceivable that new evidence may make necessary a significant revision in the prescriptions advanced here. The conclusions are provisional and conditional. And it is equally true that we have not explored the possibilities of new technologies and their influence on cost and demand. The results depend entirely on existing techniques.

5.   Naturally, it is not desirable to restrict the survey to the transport industries. Any form of taxation will have various side effects. For example, an export or import tax may have effects on the balance of payments—which will, in turn, induce other reactions by the public and private sectors. Some of these secondary effects are important and need to be traced and evaluated.[1]

6.   One further general point must also be made. The changeover from any existing system of taxation to those suggested here should be phased with some regard to the interim costs involved. It is important that government policy on user charges be perfectly clear with as few arbitrary and discretionary elements as possible. The rules must be closely defined and known well in advance. This does not mean that the user charges should be stable or fixed over periods of time. On the contrary we have argued that considerable flexibility is required in pricing the roads. The crucial stability is needed in government *policy* for user charges—not in the charges as such.[2]

---

[1] See, for example, the list of 17 desiderata set out in the Smeed Report, pp. 7–8.

[2] To illustrate this important distinction, it may be the stable policy of government to vary user charges according to the amount of congestion experienced hourly on the roads. Provided the rules of price variation are well defined and change slowly in a known predictable way, the policy is said to be stable. Instability arises when arbitrary "exclusions" are introduced, when the duties are changed "for balance of payments purposes" or "to protect the railways" or in response to any political pressure group. Stability and equality are required in the *rules*, not in the prices.

7. As we pointed out in Chapter III, the economic user charge (EUC) consists of two parts—the variable maintenance cost and the congestion levy. These values will vary between one highway and another, and between different types of vehicles. In particular, the congestion levy will vary according to the time of year and the time of day.

8. If there were no real costs involved in arranging and levying prices for road services, the economic user charge would be varied among roads, from one vehicle to another and continuously over time. But there *are*, of course, costs associated with the imposition of EUC's; for example, collecting tolls on toll-roads and parking charges from parking lots involve labor and capital costs. It is therefore conceivable that the costs of levying EUC's and policing them may be greater than the benefit derived from these charges.[3] The benefits of EUC's must be balanced against the administrative and policing costs involved. Unfortunately, we have only quite imprecise ideas about these costs. But it seems to be axiomatic that some considerable equalization of user charges over broad categories of traffic will be necessary. Indeed, our knowledge of EUC's is so scant and approximate that they can be described only in the most general terms.

9. The basic unit of both components of the EUC is reckoned in terms of vehicle-miles; the standard units of much transport economics—the ton-mile and the passenger-mile—are not so useful in the analysis of road use. But it is obviously important to distinguish between the various broad categories of vehicles. The private car, the light truck, the heavy truck, and the bus form perhaps the minimum classification list, although we shall occasionally abbreviate this to private cars and the rest. The truck and bus have much greater effects on congestion than the private car, and in turn are affected by congestion to a smaller extent. Non-motor traffic—such as pedal cycles, pedestrians, bullock carts and draft animals—needs to be distinguished also, partly because it does congest the roads and partly because of the difficulty of levying charges on it.

10. The next main classification—and in practice the most important one—is between urban and rural roads.[4] There is no unique way to classify

---

[3] Many examples of this exist in the private sector. Stores provide *free* parking although it clearly costs something to rent the land, and it may often be used by non-customers. The costs of policing exceed the costs of providing over-capacity in the parking lot.

[4] The term "rural road" is a traditional one—though it clearly covers roads of very different types and functions. It would be more useful to distinguish between *interurban* roads on the one hand and *rural secondary* feeder and access roads on the other. But the simplicity of the traditional dichotomy makes it useful occasionally for the purposes of this chapter.

roads as urban or rural; it is best to leave the distinction to be determined pragmatically by the administrative divisions of government. As a rough and ready rule we shall define urban areas as those where the vast majority of traffic is forced *by congestion* to travel at *journey* (not actual) *speeds* of 20 mph or less. Obviously, rural traffic may be constrained to travel at speeds as low as this, but we shall suppose that it is due to the nature of the road surface or hazardous curves or intersections rather than to the competition of other traffic on the rural highway. Apart from the general urban/rural distinction, it is also necessary to distinguish time of day variations in urban traffic and time of year (seasonal) factors in rural traffic.

11.   Now let us briefly examine the classification of administrative instruments available for effecting a system of EUC's. Taxes are the main instruments and may be broadly classified as follows:

Taxes on the Purchase, Ownership, and Operation of Motor Vehicles. These include excise taxes on the purchase of (usually new) vehicles (sometimes called purchase taxes), customs duties on the import of vehicles and parts; annual license fees which the owner must pay if he puts his vehicle on the state's highways; and taxes on fuels—both gasoline and diesel oil—and levies on lubricants and on tires. The most direct tax on vehicle operation is, of course, the toll.

"Non-user" Taxes. This useful but misleading title covers all taxes which are not directly associated with the ownership and operation of motor vehicles. They include taxes on land betterment due to transport, excise taxes and taxes on the export or import of goods typically carried by road transport.

Taxes on Non-motor Road Users. This might appear in the form of a tax on rickshaws or on carts drawn by draft animals.

12.   These classificatory systems will serve to give some general shape to the recommendations to be advanced in the next sections. A more detailed picture of the various techniques for taxing the purchase, ownership and operation of motor vehicles is given by Table 3, adapted from the Smeed Report. They have also been ranked in terms of their administrative simplicity—with the conditions to be found in underdeveloped countries particularly in mind. A low number indicates that there is relatively little administrative difficulty and cost in applying this particular form of pricing system; a high number suggests that it is prohibitively expensive either in administrative talent or in hardware. In the following section we shall review these methods.

192

TABLE 3: Methods of Charging for the Use of the Roads

Indirect				Direct					
Related to vehicle ownership	Related to vehicle usage			Charges registered off vehicles		Charges registered on vehicles			
	Related to amount of usage	Related to amount and place of usage	Related to place and time of usage	Manual scanning	Automatic scanning	Driver-operated meters		Automatic meters	
(a) ANNUAL LICENSES (b) PURCHASE TAX (c) IMPORT DUTIES	(a) FUEL TAX (b) TIRE TAX	DIFFERENTIAL FUEL TAX	(a) PARKING TAX (b) RESTRICTED LICENSES	TOLL GATES	Point pricing / Electronic recording	Clock-work meter / Continuous pricing	Electronic meter / Continuous pricing	Continuous pricing / Continuous systems	Point pricing / Point systems
RANK 1	1	3	4	5	10	6	7	8	8

Source: Adapted from the Smeed Report, p. 34. Ranks are allocated in this study according to difficulty and cost, the high ranking methods being the most costly.

3. User Charges for Variable Maintenance Costs

13.   In this and the following section we present the general framework of practical user charges which might be reasonably applied in most developing countries. In order to avoid clogging the description with countless limiting clauses the main recommendations are presented in an unduly dogmatic manner. But they should be interpreted only as general guideposts. In Section 5 we shall examine some of the more subtle variations and qualifications.

14.   The first task in this section is to find some form of tax which reflects the variable maintenance cost associated with each vehicle-mile. The obvious method of levying the maintenance cost is to impose a tax on vehicle operation. This suggests that a combination of gasoline, diesel, tire and lubricant taxes might be used. But the relationship is not at all simple. The statistical evidence suggests that the variable road maintenance cost per vehicle-mile differs considerably according to the type of road—paved, gravel or dirt. The costs per vehicle mile are of the order of 0.1–0.3 cents, about 2 cents and about 5 cents for paved, gravel and earth roads respectively. Even if we regard these figures as only indicators of orders of magnitude, it is quite clear that, although gasoline, lubricant and tire use are greater on earth roads than on paved highways, the variation is insignificant compared to that of the variable maintenance cost. In terms of rough orders of magnitude, we have the following vehicle operating cost relationships (cost on paved roads = 100):

		Paved	Gravel	Earth
Fuel	Car	100	120	140
	Truck (3-ton)	100	125	150
Tires	Car	100	200	350
	Truck	100	200	450
Depreciation and maintenance	Car	100	130	180
	Truck	100	150	250

Source: Jan de Weille, *op. cit.*, p. 70.

15.   It is indeed intuitively obvious that one cannot find a suitable combination of positive *ad valorem* taxes on fuel, tires, and depreciation and maintenance that will produce exactly the variable maintenance costs associated with each type of road.[5] The usual candidate for reflecting

---

[5] It is worthwhile to show that this is formally the case. Let $m(p)$, $m(g)$ and $m(e)$ be the variable maintenance costs on paved, gravel and earth roads respectively. Let λ_f, λ_t and λ_d be the *ad valorem* tax rates on fuel, tires and depreciation and maintenance respectively.

variable maintenance cost—the tax on fuel—is clearly the worst of the three. Fuel expenses do not vary sufficiently between the types of road. In terms of the amount of discrimination between one road and another the best tax is that on tires. The main trouble with an *ad valorem* tire tax is that the *rate* would have to be higher than that of a similar gasoline tax.[6] This suggests that the tire tax might be reinforced with the next best alternative—a tax which has its immediate incidence on depreciation and maintenance.[7] Such a tax is the duty on purchase of new cars and parts— or perhaps a general *ad valorem* tax on repairs to catch the labor component.[8]

16. There is, however, one important conclusion from these data; no simple system of positive *ad valorem* taxes can conceivably reproduce the pattern of variable maintenance costs. Indeed, one may go even further

---

Assume no substitutability of inputs, and suppose the fuel expenditure (net of tax) on paved roads is $f(p)$, on gravel roads $f(g)$, and on earth roads $f(e)$. Similarly, write $t(p)$ for tire expenditure on paved roads, etc., and $d(g)$ for depreciation on gravel roads, etc. Then we seek λ's so that:

$$m(p) = \lambda_f f(p) + \lambda_t t(p) + \lambda_d d(p)$$
$$m(g) = \lambda_f f(g) + \lambda_t t(g) + \lambda_d d(g)$$
$$m(e) = \lambda_f f(e) + \lambda_t t(e) + \lambda_d d(e)$$

Taking the $m(\ )$ values from Soberman (see p. 170 above) and inserting the values for $f(\ )$, $t(\ )$, and $g(\ )$, from de Weille, *op. cit.*, Table 11, p. 29, (for C speeds, average car and type II truck) we obtain (in units of US\$ per 1000 kms):

Average car

$$0.6 = \lambda_f 4.1 + \lambda_t 1.1 + \lambda_d 10.5 \qquad \text{paved}$$
$$11.0 = \lambda_f 4.5 + \lambda_t 2.5 + \lambda_d 13.7 \qquad \text{gravel}$$
$$33.0 = \lambda_f 5.2 + \lambda_t 4.5 + \lambda_d 18.9 \qquad \text{earth}$$

Truck (3.5 tons)

$$0.6 = \lambda_f 10.6 + \lambda_t 4.9 + \lambda_d 24.1 \qquad \text{paved}$$
$$11.0 = \lambda_f 12.8 + \lambda_t 10.7 + \lambda_d 36.8 \qquad \text{gravel}$$
$$33.0 = \lambda_f 15.1 + \lambda_t 25.0 + \lambda_d 61.7 \qquad \text{earth}$$

The solutions to these equations are not of the same orders of magnitude; nor does it help if we add another tax base, such as for lubricants. While it is possible to tax the depreciation and tires of trucks differently from automobiles, the substitution possibilities prevent this being carried too far. But the important point about the solutions:

	λ_f	λ_t	λ_d
Car	−45.7	−26.9	20.7
Truck	− 7.1	− 4.3	4.0

is that they involve negative values (i.e. they imply "subsidies" in the budgetary sense, for fuel and tires,) and very large positive values. We therefore reject these solutions as both administratively impractical and economically bad, since they would lead to much substitution and distortion.

[6] If, however, most of the traffic were trucks on earth and gravel roads this would not be the case.

[7] Depreciation and maintenance of vehicles, however, are less than proportionate to annual mileage. Part of depreciation depends on time, not use.

[8] High taxes on tires or repairs might be rejected on safety grounds.

195

and say that *ad valorem* taxes cannot even get reasonably close to the variable maintenance cost. It is only by arguing that Soberman's figures are not reliable as orders of magnitude that one can defend a tax system on relative incidence grounds; if, for example, the relative maintenance costs were in the ratio $1:2\frac{1}{2}:5$ on the three types of roads instead of Soberman's ratio of $1:15:57$, then it would be possible to levy a tire tax which would nicely correspond to the variable maintenance costs on each type of highway. Even so it would still be necessary to distinguish between truck tires and car tires—car tires paying a somewhat higher rate than truck tires.[9]

17. For illustrative purposes let us suppose that a tax of 100 percent of cost (i.e. 50 percent of purchase price) is imposed on car tires, and a tax of 50 percent of cost (i.e. 33 percent of purchase price) is imposed on truck tires. Then we would get the following results:

Road type	Variable mainte- nance cost	Tax on car ($ per 1000 km)	Tax on truck ($ per 1000 km)
Paved	0.6	1.1	2.5
Gravel	11.0	2.5	15.4
Earth	33.0	4.5	12.5

These taxes are about as close as we can be to the progression of costs— and they are nowhere near. But a number of cautionary remarks are in order: first, as we argued in Chapter VI, it seems very likely that the variable road maintenance costs of cars as compared to trucks are especially low on gravel and earth roads. Secondly, much of the damage to gravel and earth highways results from use in the rainy season. There is a very large variation in the maintenance costs of a vehicle journey according to the time of the year—at a rough guess the damage done by a journey to an earth road in the rainy season may be more than 100 times the damage done by a journey in the dry season. It seems impossible to discover any variation in user charges that would distinguish between use in the various seasons and the best procedure seems to be an outright administrative ban on the use of the earth roads during the wet season.

18. But these thoughts do naturally lead one to enquire whether there are any other taxes that would have the effect of producing a more eco-

[9] The argument of this paragraph hinges on the finding that the between-roads relative variation of variable road maintenance costs exceeds that of tire costs (the one with the maximum variation of approximately $1:2\frac{1}{2}:5$). Roughly speaking, this means that the statements made in the paragraph hold even though the relation between paved and earth maintenance costs as estimated by Soberman were up to a *tenfold overestimate!* The statements are therefore fairly robust.

nomic use of the earth road? Are there not groups of vehicle types which are used almost exclusively (or perhaps merely more intensively) on earth rather than on other types of highway? While it is probably true that four-wheel-drive vehicles (and perhaps also certain types of truck) are used on earth roads relatively more than private cars, it is clear that most of their mileage would tend to be either on paved or gravel roads, or else on private farmland, where upkeep of roads is a responsibility of the user. To tax them might mean cutting off the nose to spite the face.

19. Another sort of tax which might reasonably limit the use of the earth road is a general market tax. If most earth roads are of the farm-to-market variety, an *ad valorem* sales tax in the market would have some effect in cutting down the use of the earth road.[10] But if there was also a paved or gravel road supplying the market, such a tax would inefficiently impede traffic on these roads. Furthermore, it is often part and parcel of an agrarian policy to *encourage* by subsidies the marketing of cash crops as distinct from the consumption of subsistence crops. Thus the additional costs of the earth road might be regarded as an administratively effortless subsidy to stimulate marketing.

20. The upshot of all this discussion is clearly that one must make up one's mind whether the user charges are to be geared to the paved or to the non-paved roads. The nettle must be grasped for, so far as one can see there is no means of avoiding it. The answer must depend on generalizations. If a country has *only* rural earth roads and paved urban highways there may exist a nice solution where one fixes a tire or gasoline or vehicle tax suitably adjusted to the variable maintenance cost on the earth road. This value of tax per vehicle-mile (e.g. about 3 to 5 cents per vehicle-mile) might also roughly approximate to the congestion cost in the urban area during the normal daily traffic flows. (Or it might be necessary to raise an additional congestion toll to apply only during peak hours.)[11] Conditions like these appeared in Liberia in the late 1950's and early 1960's. The answer then is simple—impose high variable taxes for both urban and rural traffic, and congestion levies if necessary.

21. The nettle with the most painful sting is, however, the species where there is a mixture of paved interurban roads and earth interurban and farm-to-market highways. The decision must rest on the number of vehicle-miles traveled on each type of road—together with some estimate of the elasticity of demand when a vehicle-mile tax is in operation. In most

---

[10] This case was analyzed extensively in Chapter V.
[11] The congestion aspects will be discussed later in the next section.

countries it is a fairly safe generalization that, although the mileage of non-paved roads exceeds that of paved, the amount of traffic on paved highways is greater than that on earth and gravel roads. This suggests that we should use the paved roads as a standard, and let the earth-road users off cheaply. The extent of the inefficiency will depend on the elasticities of demand. The theory of Chapter V indicated an order of magnitude of the elasticity on development roads (predominantly of the earth or gravel type) of -1.0 to -2.0, but no data were available to check this conjecture. The elasticity on the interurban paved highways depends to a large extent on the availability of alternatives, such as rail and water transport, and there are no simple rules available.[12] In the absence of any other information it would seem worth examining the results if the elasticities were around unity.

22. As a general rule or "guideline," one may propose that, if the paved road traffic is over 75 percent of the total, it is wise to base the vehicle-mile tax on the paved highway costs. If, on the other hand, paved roads are so scarce that less than 40 percent of the traffic is to be found on them, there is a good *prima facie* case for basing vehicle-mile taxes on costs on the non-paved highways. But one should put only a very low degree of confidence in any such rule of thumb; each case ought to be examined on its merits. Maintenance costs will vary enormously between desert and heavy rainfall areas. And in particular one must bear in mind the advantages of low transport costs on earth roads in stimulating an increase in the fraction of land devoted to cash crops.

23. This completes our general discussion of the problems of reflecting variable maintenance cost in the system of user charges. We shall return later to the particular problems and aspects of the taxes suggested here, and to the effects of a balanced budget requirement. One of the conclusions of the discussion so far is that *taxes on fuels are clearly inferior to taxes on other inputs* which have their incidence in terms of vehicle-miles. This is a provisional conclusion because we need to inquire also into the administrative cost of such taxes, the distorting effects on vehicle design and use, etc.[13] Such a conclusion is quite inconsistent with views strongly held by

---

[12] In practice the elasticity has been found to vary between -0.6 and -3.4. But these refer to cases where a *particular* road has been improved, and apply almost entirely to passengers and particularly commuters. Little information is available about freight haulage.

[13] If the administrative cost and the distortion costs are, in sum, a linear function of the *ad valorem* rate, one may optimize the tax rates by using a linear programming formulation. Let these costs per unit *ad valorem* tax be $c(f)$, $c(t)$, and $c(d)$, respectively for fuel, tires, and depreciation and maintenance. Using the notation of footnote 5, page 194, we find:

$$\text{Minimize:} \quad \lambda_f c(f) + \lambda_t c(t) + \lambda_d c(d)$$

most transport specialists. Fuel taxes are normally regarded as very good ways of imposing user charges. But, of course, they need to be judged on other criteria than those which we have so far investigated.

4. *Congestion Levies*

24.   The two main components of the economic user charge (EUC) are the variable maintenance cost and the congestion charge. The former was levied in the form of a vehicle-mile tax applicable over the whole road system—with some attempt to deal with roads of different types. But earth, gravel, and paved roads are normally found together in each region; they are scattered all over the country. Congestion effects are quite different. Congestion occurs in large cities and is concentrated in one or two urban areas and conurbations. It is largely a local phenomenon.

25.   Like all generalizations this statement needs to be hedged with certain qualifications. As we saw in Chapter VI, the statistics indicate that interurban highways do not incur significantly high congestion costs until traffic reaches about 500 to 1,000 vehicles an *hour*. Even then the cost per vehicle-mile only rises to about 1 cent (US). These results, however, apply to the open road without steep grades and bends and with virtually no animal traffic—and, of course, to dry earth roads with no dust problem. Interurban roads that pass through many villages or small towns take on the characteristics of urban roads for part of their length.[14] Thus a typical interurban haul may involve a combination of rural and urban conditions. If, for example, 10 percent of the journey-miles of an interurban haul were in a zone of severe congestion (as defined in Chapter VI), the congestion cost per mile of journey would be about 2 cents. But this would be an extreme case—almost like urban traffic—and it does seem reasonable to suppose that for most interurban traffic there is no significant congestion cost. In the special case of dusty gravel and earth roads during the dry

---

Subject to: $\lambda_f f(p) + \lambda_t t(p) + \lambda_d d(p) \geq m(p)$
$\lambda_f f(g) + \lambda_t t(g) + \lambda_d d(g) \geq m(g)$
$\lambda_f f(e) + \lambda_t t(e) + \lambda_d d(e) \geq m(e)$

In words this simply says that we should choose *ad valorem* tax rates so that we minimize the administrative and distortion cost, subject to the requirement that the maintenance costs of each type of road are at least covered by the taxes collected. Obviously this formulation can be extended to cover other tax bases—such as different types of fuel, lubricants, etc.—and other complications of reality may be included. The pressing problem is, however, to make estimates of the costs of administration and distortion, i.e. the $c( )$'s. Although we shall turn to this problem later in the study, we find that there are no reliable data to be used.

[14] India is a typical case. A Bank mission has remarked on the fact that the congestion in villages is a handicap to truck traffic on interurban hauls.

season, traffic is impeded by the dust cloud caused by the passage of a vehicle. As we saw in Chapter VI, it is difficult to generalize about these congestion effects—but we might take the cost as a maximum at the lower end of the mild congestion bracket, i.e. about 1 or 2 cents per vehicle-mile. In spite of these qualifications we shall address our attention to congestion as a local urban phenomenon.

26. From Chapter VI we know the general orders of magnitude of the "ideal" congestion levies. In broad terms they are:

Severe congestion   —speed less than 10 mph   10 to 20 cents a mile
Moderate congestion—speed 10 to 14 mph   5 to 12 cents a mile
Mild congestion   —speed 15 to 20 mph   2 to 4 cents a mile

The large and difficult question is how such charges may be translated into administrative instruments which might reasonably be used in developing countries.

27. General fuel and tire taxes, and purchase taxes on vehicles, have already been discussed in connection with variable maintenance costs. They are among the least costly and most easily administered taxes, but unfortunately, they are of little use as congestion levies. There are certain differential effects between congested and uncongested traffic; for example, vehicles in severely congested conditions use more fuel per mile than vehicles in uncongested traffic streams. But the effect is much too small to be of any use; and it is likely that vehicles under mild conditions of congestion will use *less* fuel per mile than if they were on an open paved highway.

28. The main task with these two forms of taxes—on fuel and tires and on vehicles—is to ensure that no *perverse* effects are introduced. For example, a high fuel tax, which is not countered by other taxes, will lead to people choosing vehicles with a low power/weight ratio—and these are precisely the vehicles which give rise to most congestion in towns.[15] The manually operated rickshaw or cart is just the extreme example of this.

Differential Taxes

29. It is therefore natural to enquire whether differential *annual license duties, purchase taxes and import duties on vehicles* can help with the problem of congestion pricing. One obvious move is to adjust the duties so that they penalize the vehicles with a low power/weight ratio. The larger the

---

[15] The size and maneuverability of the vehicle also have some effect on congestion, but one suspects that the power/weight ratio is the most important and usually neglected factor. But, so far as I am aware, there is no evidence available on this aspect.

gasoline tax, the greater this differentiation should be. Normal arrangements for licensing, excise taxes, and tariffs differentiate in the opposite way. Taxation is often positively related to the horsepower—the low horsepowered vehicles having the cheapest licenses and levies.[16]

30. Yet another possibility, along the same lines, is to try to differentiate those categories of vehicles which are used almost exclusively in the urban area. For example, cars are typically used primarily in urban areas, while trucks are used primarily on interurban transits. Here then is a ready-made rationalization for charging cars a higher annual license fee than trucks. The disadvantages of such a differential license tax are that first, the categories are not nicely exclusive and, secondly, there might be considerable switching from one to the other according to the size of the license duty.

31. Another variant would be to charge the duty according to the location of the licensee. If I lived in the city or its suburbs I would have to pay a high fee to own an automobile, whereas if I lived in the wilds far from any urban sprawl, I would only have to pay a low license fee. There are obvious difficulties in administering such a scheme, and the loopholes for evasion—by using accommodating addresses, etc.—are not small. But provided the difference in the annual fee were not too large—say, $20 in the country and not more than $50 in the town—it does seem that it would be administratively feasible.[17] It would not go very far, however, towards differential charging of urban traffic. Taking the difference between the license fee figures suggested above (i.e. $30), and assuming a (low) mileage of 5,000 per annum, the effect would be only $\frac{3}{5}$ths of a cent a mile. But more important, the differential license fee (as distinct from an excise or purchase tax or a tariff) would affect only the decision whether or not to *own* a vehicle; it would have only an indirect and modest effect on the *use* of vehicles.[18] In sum, the differential license fee is of some use in congestion pricing, but even quite minor administrative difficulties would outweigh the small advantages of such a tax.

32. The instrument next in administrative complexity is the *differential fuel tax*. This tax would discriminate between fuel sold in urban areas and

---

[16] It may be administratively more efficient to use more draconian methods and simply ban certain types of congestion-causing vehicles; such a ban was introduced for manually-drawn rickshaws in Bangkok in 1959.

[17] The evidence for this conjecture is that in the advanced countries insurance companies do find it profitable to distinguish premiums on motor insurance according to residential area—and these variations are fairly large. Furthermore, the insurance companies have only limited ability to enforce legally their differential charges—cheating is not difficult. But the scheme is nevertheless successful.

[18] See paras. 68–77 for further discussion of the critical difference between license fees and other duties on the vehicle *purchase*.

their environs, on the one hand, and fuel sold in rural areas well away from the urban sprawl, on the other. The urban users would have to pay higher taxes a gallon than those in rural areas—so the differential effects of congestion could be at least partly reflected in the relative fuel tax.

33.   The efficacy of the differential fuel tax depends primarily on the ease with which it can be avoided. In a small country, like the United Kingdom, it can be shown that only very small effects are likely to be achieved by the differential fuel tax. If the difference in the tax is large there will be an incentive to engage in fuel-carrying (some may prefer to call it fuel-smuggling), and beneficial effects will be at least partly frittered away.[19] In small countries it is just not worth while. But in large countries it may well be possible to differentiate the fuel tax usefully between the region that contains the conurbation and regions that do not have any marked urban concentrations. In Thailand, for example, the present uniform tax on gasoline is Baht 0.80 a liter (or about US 14 cents a US gallon). It seems worth exploring the possibility of raising the tax in the area of Bangkok to (say) Baht 1.2 a liter.[20] As one leaves the area of Bangkok the tax could be *gradually* reduced, until in the country areas in the North it would be of the order of (say) Baht 0.4 a liter. The actual size of the progression and the level of the taxes would depend primarily on calculations about the incentive to avoid taxes and smuggle fuel, and the policing and administrative costs involved.

34.   The differential fuel tax provides a very rough form of congestion pricing. Although it does directly affect the cost of a vehicle-mile, it does not discriminate between different times of day, and it cannot distinguish between the congested center of cities and their less congested suburbs. Nevertheless, the possibility of differential fuel taxes does warrant further investigation in suitable countries.[21]

Charge Related to Place and Time of Usage

35.   We now turn to consider the charging systems that are related to the place and time of usage—but not directly to vehicle-mileage. The two ad-

[19] Some calculations of these effects appeared in the Smeed Report.

[20] This is about 120 percent of cost (Baht 1.00 a liter)—slightly less than the tax in many European countries. The bad effects on power/weight should be countered by varying the existing 100 percent import duty on simple c.i.f. value. (We shall also argue later than an *ad valorem* tax is better than a specific tax.)

[21] In most countries the price of fuel is lowest at the refinery—which is usually in or near the main conurbation. In transporting it to rural regions additional transport costs (and sometimes distributing costs) are incurred. As a minimum one might suggest that the tax be fixed such that it offsets these differential costs. There is then no problem of fuel-smuggling, but the wasteful purchase of fuel at remote locations by vehicles traveling to and from the city would be a source of inefficiency.

ministrative methods which we shall discuss in some detail are the parking charge and the restricted license. For parking charges we have, of course, a very large body of experience from the developed countries from which we may draw.

36.   The *parking charge* performs various functions, two of which are important in the present context. First, it rations the available parking space so that those who are willing to pay the price secure a parking lot. By comparing the price which people are willing to pay for parking with the cost one can see whether the amount of space allocated for parking should be increased or reduced. The cost of parking may be measured in the short run by the delays and increased costs of other traffic due to the occupation of the highway by a parked vehicle (as we saw and measured in Chapter VI), or by the increased difficulty of the parker in finding a place, and in the long run by the alternative use of the land and other resources used up in providing the parking facility. The second function of the parking charge is to reduce the amount of traffic in the central areas of large conurbations and other urban centers. It is supposed that, for a substantial fraction of urban traffic, there is a joint demand for a journey *and* a place to park. If the latter is made expensive it will reduce the number of journeys and so remove some of the congestion.

37.   As a method of rationing available parking space the parking tax is perhaps the single most useful device. It is clearly superior to administrative exclusions (discriminating according to employment, status, race, etc.) and to the queuing rule of "first come first served." But whether or not it is worth introducing parking charges depends on the administrative costs involved; the cost of queuing or the "first come first served" principle may in fact be lower than the cost of introducing parking charges.

38.   Since the facts and orders of magnitude are almost unknown, it is worth doing some very rough calculations of the costs and benefits of introducing parking meters. This must be regarded only as a "back-of-an-envelope" type of calculation, but it will indicate some orders of magnitude. The Road Research Laboratory found that when zones were metered in Central London the number of *parked vehicles was halved* and traffic speeds increased from 8.2 mph to 9.6 mph (16 percent).[22] Now let us insert this change in speed into the cost equation;[23] and to be on the low side let

---

[22] *Research on Road Traffic*, p. 333.
[23] See Chapter VI.

us also *ignore* the value of non-working time. Thus we obtain the decrease in cost as follows:

$$\text{Cost at 8.2 mph} = 4.4 + \frac{93}{8.2} \text{ in pence per vehicle-mile}$$

$$\text{Cost at 9.6 mph} = 4.4 + \frac{93}{9.6} \text{ in pence per vehicle-mile}$$

$$\text{Reduction in cost} = 1.8 \text{ pence per vehicle-mile}$$

Now let us multiply this gain by the total number of vehicle-miles traveled in Central London, which may be taken to be about 1.15×10^9.[24] Thus the total gain from increased speeds is valued at:

$$\$1.15 \times 10^7 \times 1.8 = \$21 \text{ million}$$

(one UK penny = one US cent).

There is some evidence that the gains in speed may have been overvalued because the evidence relates to one of the first metered zones but, at the same time, we have clearly chosen a low cost formula; one hopes that one bias may roughly offset the other.

39. On the cost side let us suppose that the real administrative costs per meter are of the order of 50 cents per working day.[25] There are 14,000 meters in Central London, so that the total administrative cost might be reckoned at about:

$$300 \times 14,000 \times \$0.5 = \$2.1 \text{ million a year}$$

We must also add something to the cost since about half of those who parked before in Central London, now do not find room to do so. If we suppose that the amount they would, on the average, be willing to pay is about 50 cents a day, then we know that the value of the parking foregone

---

[24] This figure is based on an unpublished paper by Newby of the Road Research Laboratory, No. RN/2476. Estimates of a similar order of magnitude are also to be found in the Smeed Report.

[25] Some evidence available on the administrative costs of introducing parking meters in recent years in Britain, suggests that administrative costs vary between about 30 percent and 85 percent of the gross revenue, a far higher fraction than that in the United States (though comparability is difficult because of different definitions). These costs should probably not be taken as representative, however, since the parking meters were, in my view, much over-manned. If we take the administrative costs as about 50 percent of gross revenue, this will serve as an order of magnitude for judging the desirability of schemes for the developing countries. Obviously, the fraction will be much lower in the center of cities, where the charge is high, than in the less congested areas; this indicates an order of priority for introducing parking meters.

is about another $2 million a year.[26] Thus the total cost of the parking meter scheme is about $4 million.

40. Clearly, on these figures the parking meter scheme amply pays for itself. The benefits are about $20 million and the costs about $4 million. This difference is so large that it is clearly "robust" with respect to quite large changes in assumptions of the actual numerical constants. Similarly, it seems likely that the broad orders of magnitude would be repeated in some urban centers in the developing countries. In many cities, such as Singapore and Istanbul, the combination of heavy traffic in narrow streets gives conditions so similar to those in London that the calculations must reveal a somewhat similar benefit for a parking meter system.

41. This does not necessarily mean that a parking meter system is the best of alternative schemes which have similar effects. For example, it may well be a good idea to sell parking rights to individuals, who may then retail them to the motorist. Provided that there is sufficient competition among the purchasers of the "rights," we could leave the price and the form of administration to be determined by the free competitive play of market forces. The "rights" operators may or may not find it profitable to use meters; it may conceivably be cheaper to employ parking attendants.[27]

42. The second function of a parking charge is to reduce the number of motorists using central areas because it increases the cost of the journey. Since the main culprit of congestion in the big cities of the developed world is the commuter by car, the parking charges should be organized so that they impinge heavily on the commuter.[28] It might reasonably be argued, however, that the private car commuter is not the main cause of congestion in the cities of the developing world. In some cities it is clearly the cyclist or pedestrian that slows the traffic to a walking pace; in others

---

[26] It will be observed here that the figures for Central London are broadly consistent with those obtained by the author for Slough—a small town on a main road near London. The cost, in terms of the interference to traffic, of one vehicle-hour of parking was about 50 cents. In London 14,000 meters provide about 140,000 hours of parking a day, or about 40 million hours a year. A total benefit of $21 million then gives a figure very close to 50 cents an hour. It should be emphasized that the data used in this check are *completely independent*, so that it serves as a real check on consistency.

[27] Yet another possibility is the so-called "disc system" employed in Paris. It does seem, however, that the administrative costs of such a system are large. See *Research on Road Traffic*, p. 331 *et seq.* But the low capital costs do not make it a possibility in developing countries.

[28] For example, if it were feasible, it would be a good idea to have the level of the parking charge determined by the time at which the vehicle is *taken out* of the parking place; the price would then increase enormously just before the peak traffic flow. Such a scheme seems, however, quite impossible to administer.

the taxis jam the streets. Each case must be examined and treated on its merits. But it seems likely that the general rules discussed above do in fact apply, in a rough and ready way, to some cities of the developing world. That is about as much as can be said here.

43.   The other major administrative instrument is the *restricted license*. This differs from the ordinary license since that does not restrict the operator or motorist in the use of the roads.[29] Restricted licenses do. A hypothetical example of a restricted license will make it reasonably clear how they work. The road authority may announce that any vehicle using the roads of Bangkok (or a suitably defined area) between the hours of 0700 and 2000 hours during any day other than Sunday must display a special "sticker" or license which may be purchased from the offices of the government (or perhaps some intermediary) for a cost of $100 for the year or $1 a day or $4 a week or $12 a month. The right to use the roads of Bangkok during these hours would be a privilege which could be bought at these prices.[30] Many variations are possible with this basic model. It is feasible to specify a "central area" for which a very high-priced license is required —say, $200 a year—and a "non-central area" for which the price is $100 a year. It is also possible to graduate the license fees even more finely—say, into five classes with prices ranging from $50 to $300. The city could also be split up into areas and, by suitable announcements beforehand, the authority could specify the degree of restriction imposed on entry. We shall not pursue these variations, however, partly because one conjectures that the frills may not be worth the administrative costs involved. We shall be concerned here with the simplest version of the restricted license system—a version which might be applicable in developing countries.

44.   Even with the simple restricted license scheme where there is merely one area—the city itself perhaps—there are many degrees of freedom left in deciding on a workable system. But, before doing so, it is wise to reflect again on the aims. In principle, the price paid per vehicle-mile of urban motoring should reflect all the costs involved and we wish to use the restricted license system to measure the social cost of congestion. But it is obvious that the restricted license does not have an immediate impact on the cost per vehicle-mile. It affects decisions about buying the *right* to enter the congested city. If the right sold is of annual currency, then once purchased a motorist would not thereafter be discouraged from entering

---

[29] Again this is not strictly true since there are license systems for the control and regulation of haulage in certain countries and these may involve restrictions on routes.

[30] The idea of restricted licenses has been investigated at some length and in detail for the United Kingdom in the Smeed Report.

the city and congesting its roads. If, on the other hand, licenses were only valid for the day the motorist would then be able to calculate each day whether it was worth taking his car into the city. This would provide a much closer and more relevant calculation of benefit and cost.[31]

45.   The upshot of this line of reasoning is that it is better, *ceteris paribus*, to have a daily license rather than an annual license system. This could be conveniently achieved by authorizing both types of license—but by making the purchase of an annual license only slightly cheaper than the price of 300 daily licenses. But much will depend on the relative administrative costs of selling both types of license and on the costs of policing the mixed system.[32]

46.   The precise method of selling licenses must depend to a large extent on the existing institutions in each country. Only the most general guides can be offered here. In principle, it would be possible for the transport authority to vary the number of daily licenses it sold to take into account special traffic conditions (such as troop movements, holidays, etc.), and to leave the price of a license to be fixed by the market. For example, authorizations could be sold wholesale to gasoline stations in the vicinity of the city, and motorists could buy them from the attendants at prices set by competition between the stations.[33] A large fraction of the administrative costs of the scheme are then recovered by the gasoline stations themselves—and they will have an incentive to keep these costs to a minimum. The transport authority (or the police) bears the costs of enforcing the system—though they would be considerably relieved by the reduction in congestion.

47.   The other simple technique of distribution is for the authority to fix the price of a license, and then issue as many licenses as people wish to purchase at that price. Gasoline stations may be required to sell them at the stated price with a certain commission on each one sold. Probably an appropriate rate of commission would be of the same order as that on the sale of postage stamps—between 5 and 10 percent.

48.   One main problem is that of enforcement. If it be accepted that no rigorous policing of the law is likely to occur, then, of course, we should

---

[31] But even so, once he has purchased a license for the day there is no additional cost incurred per vehicle-mile.

[32] Enquiries with the Metropolitan Police in London suggest that, with suitable automatic aids, the cost would not be prohibitively high; but such information is only of limited application in developing countries.

[33] In practice they could be sold wholesale to whoever wished to deal in these rights; the real difficulty is to avoid the cornering of the market.

have to rely on those instruments which require virtually zero police enforcement—such as the differential gasoline tax. Such a gloomy view is, however, a little extreme. In assessing the merits of the restricted license system one must realistically allow for a certain percentage of wastage for graft and corrupt administration.

49.   A second problem is that of boundaries. This is primarily a difficulty with the "one-zone" simple system which seems most applicable for the developing countries. It is not at all easy to find the "natural" boundaries of the zone of congestion. And when they are drawn it will be observed that certain motorists may need to get to their office which is located just over the boundary in the congested zone—and yet for these few yards they have to pay the full daily fee.

Tolls and Sophisticated Metering Systems

50.   Now we turn to some of the more sophisticated systems of levying congestion charges. But before doing so we should examine probably the best-known and well-tried method of charging for the use of the roads— the toll. There are numerous examples of toll-roads in both the developed and the developing countries of the world. But there are very few which apply to highways that are congested.[34] Most tollways are, naturally enough, interurban highways with limited access. It is indeed the limited number of points of entry and egress that enables a tollgate system to be introduced with some degree of efficiency.

51.   This requirement does imply that tolls have few applications in urban traffic. It is true that they may be used for special purposes—such as for urban expressways where there are a limited number of access points.[35] But they cannot be used for levying congestion charges on the users of downtown streets. There are too many intersections to make tolls at all feasible. Nor would it be sensible to set up tollgates at the very numerous entrances to central areas. It is likely that vehicles would make only one daily journey into the area. So the toll system would have essentially the same effects as the restricted license system—except that tolls would be much more expensive to administer, and they would induce their own special form of congestion before the tollgate.

52.   The conclusion is clearly that toll-roads have a very limited place in the implementation of congestion charges. Particular cases can be made

---

[34] In the United States the New Jersey Turnpike, Merritt Parkway, and Lincoln Tunnel in New York might be considered congested urban toll-roads.

[35] Tolls are used for certain new urban and suburban expressways, in Chicago, for example. See paras. 80–86 for a more detailed discussion of toll-roads.

for tolls on urban expressways—by arguing that the toll-road will provide a differentiated speedy transit for those who are willing to pay the higher price, and by keeping congestion down on the expressway. But in general tolls of the conventional type are no good for congestion pricing.

53. Much ingenuity has been lavished on devising *other systems of levying congestion taxes*.[36] Broadly speaking, the devices may be classified according to whether the recording is on the vehicle or at some central agency and whether the charging mechanism is operated by the driver or by some automatic device. All these mechanical and electronic systems of charging have two features in common; they are relatively expensive in terms of equipment and administrative supervision, and all are untried. These two considerations together suggest that they are not suitable for developing countries. It is surely the best policy for the developing countries to wait until they have been tried out by one of the advanced countries where there is a relative abundance of capital and administrative talent.

5. *Administration, Incidence, and Side Effects of User Charges*

54. So far in this chapter, the emphasis has been placed on general types of taxes—such as levies on inputs into motoring, restricted licenses on the use of central areas, etc. For the most part we have discussed these taxes in terms of *ad valorem* rates, since this was the simplest way in which to couch the problem; it avoids all discussion about the relative incidence of tax for a given expenditure. But such a simplification also avoids an important problem, to which we now must turn.

55. Taxes can be broadly divided into direct and indirect. Indirect, or outlay, taxes can be divided again very broadly into *ad valorem* and specific taxes. There are many variations of both *ad valorem* and specific taxes according to the point at which they are collected, the range of application of different rates, the specification of levies, and the form of collection.

Fuel Taxes

56. The first tax to be examined is at present perhaps the most important form of "user charge," the *tax on fuel*. The great attraction of the fuel tax is its simplicity and ease and cheapness of collection. Administratively the easiest form of the fuel tax is simply a *specific* levy on the quantity sold, such as X cents a gallon. Such a tax can be levied at the refinery, at the

---

[36] The details of most existing schemes and an appreciation of their relative advantages will be found in the Smeed Report.

port, or at the production, importing, or wholesale stage of distribution. No distinction is made between different qualities of fuel—and sometimes diesel fuel is taxed at the same rate as gasoline. The tax is simply a flat rate per gallon.

57.   The taxation of motor fuel by this simple specific levy is the most common form of taxation in both developed and developing countries. In the United Kingdom, for example, in 1967 the tax was normally about two shillings and nine pence (US 33 cents) an imperial gallon. This is levied on all fuel—whatever the octane rating, whether diesel oil or petrol.[37] Such a tax costs very, very little to collect. The revenue officer merely has to ascertain the number of gallons and levy the tax accordingly. There is only a small opportunity for graft and evasion. The collection points are concentrated at the refineries (or ports) and supervision and control are easy. Such specific taxes are suitable for levying road user charges since roughly the same mileage is to be obtained from a gallon of high or low octane fuel. The super gasoline gives higher "performance" but hardly any more miles per gallon. Diesel fuel however gives many more miles per gallon than gasoline—and if the tax is designed primarily to reflect road use, the specific diesel tax should be higher than the gasoline levy. Simple specific taxes then seem to be best on the grounds that they reflect closely road use and that they are simple to levy and supervise.

58.   The administrative simplicity of such a specific tax per gallon of fuel is, however, bought at the cost of some inefficiency in fuel use and distribution. Low octane fuel and diesel oil are much less expensive to produce than high octane fuels—probably about 12 to 15 US cents an imperial gallon compared with about 25 cents a gallon for the high octane fuels. For simplicity let us suppose that the cost ratio is 1:2, 12.5 cents and 25 cents respectively. If we add the specific tax to get the selling price we obtain values of 44.5 and 57 cents. The ratio of prices is thus 1:1.3, which is much less than the cost ratio. Thus the use of a specific tax per gallon, irrespective of the quality of the fuel, encourages the undue use of the more expensive gasolines which require complex and costly refining. For efficiency, prices on the market should reflect relative costs; the higher the specific tax the greater the discrepancy between relative prices and costs.

59.   Furthermore, the specific tax does limit the effectiveness of competition in the distribution of fuel. The fuel retailer who cuts his price by (say) 5 cents a gallon will only effect about a 10 percent reduction in the price of fuel; but if it is low octane petrol, the percentage reduction in the

---

[37] It should be observed that the diesel oil used by railway locomotives is not so taxed.

ex tax receipts per gallon is *40 percent* (using the U.K. data). The incentive to cut prices and compete is then much dampened by this form of specific tax.

60. In sum, then, the specific form of taxation of a standard rate for all motor fuels does distort price/cost relationships and inhibits the efficient distribution of fuel.[38] It is, of course, possible to avoid some of the unfortunate effects by varying the tax rate according to the type of fuel. Probably the simplest approach is to have a different tax rate for diesel fuel. It is relatively easy to identify diesel fuel from gasoline and no great opportunities for chicanery are opened up by differentiating the tax rate. In Thailand, for example, the tax on gasoline is Baht 0.80 a liter—giving a selling price of Baht 1.80, whereas the tax on diesel fuel is only Baht 0.12 a liter—giving a price of about Baht 0.80 to 1.00 a liter. This is a large differential—indeed, it is larger than the variation in relative costs, so that diesel fuel is made cheaper relative to cost than gasoline.[39] The important point, however, is that such a differentiated fuel tax seems to have been administratively successful; but it is difficult to judge the effects in terms of the extent to which the slightly enlarged opportunities for graft have been seized. One may conjecture that the effects have been small—but evidence is difficult to elicit.

61. A differentiated tax between gasoline and diesel fuel seems both administratively feasible and desirable. The minimum extent of the specific tax differential should be set by the relative costs of diesel fuel and gasoline. If, furthermore, a case can be made for classifying gasoline-using vehicles as the main culprits of congestion, there will appear to be a case for differentiating even further as in Thailand.

62. One might reasonably enquire whether it is also desirable to levy different rates of specific taxes on fuels that have different octane ratings. For example, the rate of tax on high octane (97 plus) might be 35 cents a gallon while the rate on low octane (less than 92) might be 20 cents and the rate on medium octane might be 28 cents. These tax levels would roughly reflect the relative costs of production and so the final selling prices would be roughly in line with costs. Such a tax system would elimi-

---

[38] It seems to me plausible to explain the persistence of oligopolist price fixing by the major oil companies of the United Kingdom partly in terms of this very high specific tax.

[39] This is, as we have seen, a sensible policy for trucks and other vehicles that use diesel fuel as they are run primarily on uncongested interurban roads (paved) while vehicles that consume gasoline are used mainly on congested city streets. Casual observations support this generalization.

nate the present discrimination in favor of the high-octane-using car and against the low-octane-using van and truck.

63. However desirable in principle, such a differentiated tax would encounter many difficulties of administration. Identifying an octane rating is not a simple matter. In practice octane ratings are found by actually using the fuel in a standard engine and observing the effects. They cannot be tested simply by means of a hydrometer (as in the case of the specific gravity of alcoholic beverages). Thus the opportunities for evasion and fraud are expanded considerably. It is not difficult to think of safeguards which might be employed in practice. For example, the gasoline might be colored at the refinery, so that everyone, from the refinery onwards, could easily identify the three classes of petrol.[40] Thus the tests of octane rating would be necessary only at the refinery. Such a coloring system would also help prevent fraud at various levels of retail distribution; the quality of petrol would be easily recognized by the purchaser. It could be combined with the "weights-and-measures" function of government.

64. Differential specific taxes, according to octane rating, are practiced with apparent success by a number of countries. Peru, for example, charges a tax of about 4 cents a (US) gallon on regular gasoline and a little over 5 cents a (US) gallon on "extra" gasoline. (There is, incidentally, no tax at all on diesel fuel.) Venezuela differentiates even more drastically between the three types of fuel:

"Standard" gasoline	Bs 0.0304	a liter, US 2.4 cents a gallon
"Premium" gasoline	Bs 0.0609	a liter, US 4.8 cents a gallon
Diesel fuel	Bs 0.00323	a liter, US 0.3 cents a gallon

Clearly these are good examples of the feasibility of differentiating. But it will be noted that the actual level of the tax in both cases is rather low—much lower than the level of tax in Western Europe and even lower than the 8 to 11 cents a gallon in the United States. Thus in Peru and Venezuela the payoff for corruption and graft is very low—only 2 cents or so a gallon—so it is perhaps not surprising that the system has worked reasonably well. With a bigger absolute differential—such as that discussed above—the incentives for evasion would be much greater. It seems wise to insure against such practices by some means such as coloring the gasoline.

---

[40] Identification by color was practiced in Britain immediately after the war of 1939–45, in order to implement the petrol-rationing system. The identification seems to have been administratively successful.

65.   A differentiated fuel tax does not, however, mitigate the other major disadvantage of a specific tax—the lack of incentive for price cutting and efficient retail distribution. This can be achieved only by changing over to an *ad valorem* tax base. In principle, the *ad valorem* tax may be levied at any stage of the production and distribution process. It is often convenient to collect the tax at the *wholesale* stage as the fuel leaves the refinery. There are then few points of collection and the administration is not difficult. Problems arise, especially in the not uncommon cases where the refining firm also has interests in distribution, because the *ad valorem* tax may be assessed on low *book* values; the policing of reasonable or proper prices is not an easy matter. Furthermore, taxing at the wholesale stage will still mean that competition among retailers is inhibited by the (to the retailer) fixed tax.

66.   The natural extension of this argument is then to levy the tax on the *retail* value. The filling stations themselves would collect a certain percentage in tax from the customers. Administrative difficulties aside, this is clearly the most efficient form of gasoline and diesel taxation. But the costs of administration are indeed formidable. The tax must be collected at every filling station. The opportunities for graft, corruption, evasion and avoidance are enormous. No simple device—such as coloring the fuel—will help. The authorities could keep a continuous check on the *amount* of fuel delivered to each filling station and combine it with spot checks on prices. But the latter would be expensive to administer. Clearly the *ad valorem* tax will be useful only if the rate is quite low—as a rough rule let us say less than 20 percent. For relatively high rates of tax on fuel it is best to employ the differentiated specific tax.

67.   It is clearly possible to use the specific fuel tax for the purpose of reflecting relative differences in congestion in different parts of the country. Specific taxes could be set for each locality—largely as they are now for different states in the United States. There are no difficulties in using specific differentiated fuel taxes for the purposes of levying congestion charges—in spite of the fact that most of the discussion we pursued there was in terms of *ad valorem* taxes.[41]

Import Duties and Excise Taxes

68.   Now we consider the *import duties on motor vehicles and parts*. It is convenient to examine also the *excise duties* (or *purchase tax*) on new ve-

---

[41] Note, however, that in countries which have persistent inflation an *ad valorem* tax is administratively best.

213

hicles produced domestically. Both these levies fall on *new* vehicles and parts.[42] This distinguishes these taxes from the annual license fee. Then the levy is extracted from all vehicles, whether new or old.

69. Import duties on vehicles have unending complexities. They may be broadly classified into the following categories:

(i)	*ad valorem* straight percentage	—may take the form of a simple X percent duty on declared or official valuations.
(ii)	*ad valorem* progressive	—may be 50 percent up to $2,000 and 75 percent for vehicles above $2,000 and so on.
(iii)	by size of vehicle	—may take the form of a tax rate specified according to the weight of the vehicle, its length, its horsepower, or some combination of these various components.

The import taxes on motor vehicles exhibit the desire of governments to encourage local fabrication industries—particularly local assembly of vehicles and the production of tires, batteries, and trimmings.[43] They may also be used as short-term instruments to prevent or cure balance of payments disequilibrium.

70. For the purpose of levying user charges the import duty is inferior to an annual license system. Import and excise duties are levied on new cars only. An increase in import duty, unaccompanied by increases in license duties, will give rise to windfall benefits to existing owners of motor vehicles. A smaller number of vehicles will be imported and the expanded demand will face a relatively smaller stock of vehicles. So the value of vehicles will be higher than it would have been in the absence of the increase in import duty. It is obviously sensible to tax this unearned windfall away by the use of the vehicle license duty.

71. But it is natural to inquire whether the same effects could not be achieved simply by raising the annual license fee. This would cut down the demand for new vehicles. And the government could then appropriate virtually all the windfall receipts due to this restrictive policy; none would

---

[42] Even if there is an extensive importation of secondhand vehicles, they are clearly new to the country concerned.

[43] The amount of protection accorded to these ancillary industries is often inefficiently large because of the escalation of the percentages.

214

accrue to the private vehicle owner. Clearly this is a much better technique for achieving this objective than a discriminating tax against *new* vehicles. It would not cause distortion of patterns of replacement and repair—such as occurs where there is a very high tariff or virtual ban on imports of vehicles.

72.   We conclude therefore, that whatever the validity of the "infant-industry" argument for levying tariffs, their use for collecting user charges is inefficient and inferior to the license system.[44] The only advantage of the import duty, as opposed to the license fee, is that it does fall to some extent on the *operating* costs of the vehicles. The import duty (and its domestic cousin, the excise duty or purchase tax) increases the price of new cars. Insofar as the depreciation of a motor vehicle is determined by the mileage run, as distinct from those depredations which are caused merely by the passage of time, the import duty exerts its incidence on the *operating* costs of vehicle-miles. The license duty, on the other hand, is not closely related to the mileage run. Thus, if it were necessary to have duties on operation of vehicles, in addition to the gasoline or tire tax, there would be a case for employing the tariff and the excise duty. We have, indeed, argued that a combination of tire and "depreciation and maintenance" taxes was the best reflection of the relative costs of damage to the surfaces of different types of road. In application much will depend on the relative use of different vehicles on various types of road. But it is important not to vary the rates of tariff and excise levy, unless these are offset by suitable movements in license rates, so that the windfalls of existing owners are appropriated by the government and correspondingly, windfall losses are not suffered by private owners. One's natural preference is for *stable* rates of duty, and the employment of other methods to solve balance of payments problems; but this is probably too much to ask.

License Duties

73.   First, let us discuss the effects of the *general license duty*—leaving until later the problems of the differential *restricted* license. The general license confers on the holder (or strictly on a specific vehicle owned by the holder) the right to use the highway. A license fee of a flat rate for each class of vehicle is the normal kind of levy. The disadvantage of such a flat rate is that it discourages the licensing (and so the use) of low quality "stand-by" vehicles. This disadvantage can be to some extent avoided by

---

[44] There is no need to discuss extensively the relative administrative costs of the two systems, since the licensing system will be in operation in any case; the problem is the use to be made of it.

making it administratively easy to acquire short-term licenses—such as the daily license arrangements discussed in connection with the congestion levy. But even with a daily license system there are costs of administration and there is still the lump-sum payment to be made to get the vehicle on the road for any given day. Furthermore, a flat rate tax for each class of vehicle has a very different incidence; the owner of a Rolls Royce pays a very much smaller fraction of his total expenditure on motoring in the form of license duty than does the owner of a Volkswagen (about 1/10th as much). Many people would argue that such an arrangement is inequitable.

74. The obvious alternative is to relate the general lincese duty to some measure of the value of the vehicle. But an *ad valorem* license duty is not without administrative difficulties. New vehicles are relatively easy to assess for an *ad valorem* license duty. With old vehicles, however, the authority would find it necessary to fix depreciation and amortization schedules for each class of vehicle—and perhaps also for each make and type of vehicle, as in the list prices used for the vehicle excise tax in most states of the USA.

75. Let us now examine the efficiency aspects of the licensing system. It is obvious that it is necessary to consider the licensing arrangements in conjunction with the gasoline and tire tax. If the authority decides on a high gasoline tax then, *ceteris paribus*, people will choose vehicles with a low power/weight ratio where the gasoline consumption per ton-mile is low. Apart from the technical inefficiencies involved, such vehicles give rise to much more congestion than the high-powered vehicles. To some extent this effect may be offset by charging high license duties for vehicles with a low power/weight ratio.

76. The weight of a vehicle is easy to determine and causes no important administrative difficulty. But the measurement of power does. The natural measure of power is the "brake-horse-power"—but this is not easy to determine in practice, and the makers' figures vary according to specification. The most clear-cut measure is the cubic capacity. This is closely related to the power of the engine and is easy to determine. Thus, one suspects that the best measure of the power/weight ratio is, in fact, the ratio of cubic capacity to weight.

77. The problem of linking the *ad valorem* duty (on new values) to the cubic-capacity/weight criterion is one of detailed administration. The precise form of the taxes and the actual figures employed must vary, not only according to the cost of enforcement and policing, but also according to

the extent to which the daily (congestion) license system is used. And the existing institutional arrangements must play a large part in deciding the shape of the tax system. As a general rule, however, it is wise to use the *ad valorem* (new) duty as a base. The cubic-capacity/weight ratio (and any other criteria which the authority decides to use) could be employed to determine a "points" system which would credit or debit the vehicle on the *ad valorem* scale. A low cubic-capacity/weight ratio, for example, would send a vehicle higher up the *ad valorem* scale. For administrative purposes, however, the points system must depend on criteria that are easily observed and readily recorded. All subjective elements and even merely lengthy calculations must be avoided. The system should be applicable by persons who have a competence of the level attained by Post Office counter clerks.

Tire and Lubricant Taxes

78.   The gasoline and license duties are the two most important user taxes at present applied in both developed and developing countries. But, as we discussed in an earlier section of this chapter, there are many taxes on the operation of vehicles other than fuel taxes. The problems of, for example, *tire taxes* are similar to those of fuel taxation. Tires may be measured according to the weight of rubber. A specific tax per pound of rubber is the simplest of all levies. This is the form of the tire tax in the United States and it seems to have been quite successful. But the rates of duty are low—far below those which we envisage as necessary for reflecting the variable maintenance costs on earth roads. Tires are also an obvious candidate for an *ad valorem* levy. Levying a tire tax at the retail stage raises all the well-known administrative objections. Instead, it would be sensible for developing countries to consider an *ad valorem* tax ex works or an import duty on the declared or official value. This would reduce drastically the number of points of collection. And the tied retailer is not so important in tire distribution as he is in the oil business. Heavy protection of the tire industry in certain countries results in an implied tax on the user (and a disguised subsidy to the producer—or strictly to the owners of scarce talents used in the industry). Of course, it would be useful to keep the accounts of the tire industry separate from that of the transport industry, so that one knew what sort of tax was being paid by the road user to subsidize the producers of tires. But this is clearly too much to expect. Tire levies may give rise to the greater use of unsafe tires. It may be possible to devise a combination of taxes and regulations (for example low taxes on high quality tires) that improve the accident statistics; but this has not been pursued here.

217

79. Taxes on *lubricants* are also similar to the fuel levies largely because there is a simple quantitative measure available—the number of gallons or liters. Specific taxes per gallon or liter are possible and, one suspects, are the most desirable of the alternative forms available. It is, however, difficult to differentiate the lubricants used by trucks and heavy vehicles from those employed in cars and light vans. On the other hand, it is possible to distinguish between tires used for trucks and tractors and those used for automobiles. Furthermore there is much variation in the oil consumption of vehicles per mile; and since the revenue collected is so small there seems to be a good case for not taxing lubricants at all.

Interurban Toll-Roads

80. We noted earlier, in discussing congestion charges, that an ordinary toll system is quite impractical for the ordinary urban streets of a city.[45] Tolls are necessarily feasible only for interurban highways or urban motorways with limited access. These characteristics are typical of the toll-roads which are at present in operation. The limited access aspect has led some transport experts to suggest that there should also be a free road alongside the toll highway. Furthermore, if there is a free road alongside the users will have a choice of paying the toll and enjoying a speedy journey, or of not paying the toll and suffering all the congestion and interference with traffic flow occasioned by numerous intersections, etc. The combination of tollway and free road therefore provides a superior "mix" of road services than simply one type of road service on one highway. Each motorist can choose the service appropriate to his circumstances.

81. Whether or not this mixture of tollway and freeway is efficient, however, depends on whether or not the tollway is congested. If the tollway is not congested it is inefficient to levy tolls and to keep traffic off the uncongested tollway. It may well still be efficient to construct a limited access road so that there is a fast highway available, but if vehicles do not get in one another's way it is best not to levy tolls.[46] And it seems that congestion is unlikely to be important on such limited access "thruways." On limited access highways very large traffic flows are possible without mutual interference of vehicles—as may be attested by many toll-roads in the United States. Thus, there is no occasion for tolls where there is no congestion.

---

[45] It is, of course, possible that in the not too distant future automatic computerized methods of charging will be introduced which will eliminate these objections; see the Smeed Report.

[46] Note that for a free road with limited acess, the cost of access points is lower than that for a tollway because tollgates do not have to be provided and manned. Access to a tollway is often unduly restricted because of the need for concentrating the collection of tolls.

82.   We conjecture that there are very, very few cases where tollways are justified in developing countries. The only cases one can imagine are those urban tollways in the main cities where there is some likelihood of congestion. But for interurban transits it seems probable that even the construction of free roads with the very limited access attributes of toll-roads is not worthwhile. Such duplication of facilities is expensive and must be carefully justified.[47]

83.   The institution of tolls on limited access highways may not, in fact, restrict to any great extent the amount of traffic using the tollway if the demand is sufficiently inelastic. If, for example, the highway is used mainly for carrying a raw material which is a small fraction of the total cost of a final product, then the demand is likely to be inelastic for a toll which is less than the difference between the cost on the alternative free road and the cost on the tollway. In practice, however, roads are rarely as specialized as this; typically, there is a mixture of traffic. In developing countries, the elasticities are unlikely to be so low that the toll does not matter.

84.   One further feature of toll roads is that the authority is usually required to recover the cost of the road over a certain number of years. And the normal method is to charge a constant money toll over these years. Clearly, it is likely that the road begins by being not congested for the first years—but a toll is levied. As traffic grows the road may eventually become congested—but the toll may well be eliminated if the road has "paid for itself." The analysis of this study suggests that the best pattern of tolls is, in fact, the *opposite* to this! There should be very low or zero tolls in the early years and higher tolls as the congestion increases. Whether or not the total receipts have or have not paid for the road is not relevant. If road space is scarce it should be priced.

85.   The desirability of a toll depends on the administrative cost of levying tolls and the costs of the reduced number of access points which make tolls possible. Much evidence is available on the costs of administration of interurban toll roads in the United States, and the facts suggest that a substantial fraction of revenue is devoted to administration.[48] There does not seem to be any direct evidence on the costs of forgoing access points. However it may be conjectured that restriction on access is fairly impor-

---

[47] There seems to be a good case for arguing that most of the investment in limited access motorways in Britain was wasted in the sense that almost the same journey times could have been achieved by a much lower investment in bypasses around congested areas.

[48] Wilfred Owen and Charles L. Dearing, *Toll Roads and the Problem of Highway Modernization*, The Brookings Institution, (Washington, D.C., 1951).

tant, since additional access points are so costly in terms of administrative expenditure that the tollway authority will keep the number down.

86. As a general conclusion to this discussion of toll-roads, it seems likely that urban expressways are the only obvious candidates for toll methods of pricing and finance. And even then the case must be made carefully in terms of the elasticity of demand and the probable congestion effects. As for proposals for rural toll-roads one may conclude that if there is a case for a rural tollway there is usually an even better case for a rural freeway.

Non-User Taxes

87. So far we have been concerned with the typical "user charges" of the roads. Taxes on fuel, lubricants, licenses and so on, and tolls are all the direct responsibility of the vehicle operator. But, as we argued in Chapter V, there is a case for considering various other forms of *"non-user" taxes* to finance road development. Since the benefits of road development appear in the form of "rents" either to owners of fixed factors of production or to consumers, it is natural to seek methods of eliciting from these people the windfall gains they receive from the lowering of the transport price.

88. *A land tax* is one obvious form of exaction that fits neatly into this category. The administrative problems of land taxation are, however, formidable even in developed countries. We argued in the theoretical discussion that land taxes should be determined by the maximum productivity of the land if it were used efficiently. Land should be taxed according to its *potential* rather than its actual production. Such hypothetical values can rarely be used for a tax base, however, and they can be dismissed at this stage. Some other base must be sought.

89. The obvious administrative base is simply the acre of land. But land is not homogeneous either in its productive potential or in terms of accessibility. The variations are so enormous that a standard specific tax an acre would clearly be inefficient and would not collect the unearned surplus from the road construction. Some differentiation is required. Both factors, inherent productivity and accessibility to markets, must be reflected in any feasible system of land valuation.

90. Where there is a free commercial market in land and a substantial number of tenant farmers paying a commercial rent, the problem of valuation is not insuperable. In Australia and New Zealand there has been a land tax since the turn of the century. The bases of the tax are the "improved capital value," the "unimproved capital value," and the "assessed

annual value."[49] The capital values are the amounts which would be secured by sale on the free market. The assessed annual value is the rent which the land would earn in a free market. The valuation of land and property for assessment is, however, a formidable task and, in Australia, it probably engages a staff of 1,500 to 2,000 skilled persons—both in the central state valuation offices and in private practice. The standards of assessment, however, are judged to be good.[50]

91.   The relative success of the land tax in Australia and New Zealand depends much on (a) the existence of a free market in land and in tenancy arrangements, (b) the availability of a staff of expert incorruptible valuers, and (c) the relatively low rates of tax imposed. From the evidence available these three conditions seem to be prerequisites for any successful system of land taxation.[51] To illustrate this one may take the example of the local property tax (the local "rate") in England and Wales which is based on the assessed annual rent at which "the hereditament might be reasonably expected to let from year to year." Of the three conditions listed above only (b) holds. The market in real property has become so distorted by subsidy, controlled rents and various other forms of restrictive legislation, that the assessment is now quite hypothetical.[52] And the rates of payment are not low.

92.   For the developing countries it is clear that, at least, the second condition is unlikely to be met. The number of trained valuers (usually they are also surveyors) is small and they would perhaps be wastefully employed on such valuation tasks. But even if there were a sufficient supply of valuers, there are few developing countries where there is a free commercial market in land. The absence of cadastral surveys makes it difficult to purchase and sell land if one has no clear idea who owns it in the first place. For many tribal communities indeed the concept of ownership and permanent alienation of land is foreign. Even in communities of peasant

---

[49] In recent legislation in Jamaica, Trinidad and Barbados, where they have adopted a somewhat similar system of land taxes, the "unimproved value" is called more appropriately the "site value."

[50] See A. M. Woodruff and L. L. Ecker-Racz, "Property Taxes and Land Use Patterns in Australia and New Zealand," *Tax Executive*, Vol. XVIII, No. 1, (Baltimore, Maryland, October 1965), pp. 16–63.

[51] Again from Australian experience, one is tempted to add that the government must also have the political courage to enforce this tax without granting numerous political exemptions. Many such fiscal monstrosities are to be found in the Australian (and the English) system of property taxes.

[52] Certain aspects of the monstrous inequities and inefficiencies of the existing system were set out in *Report of the Committee of Inquiry into the Impact of Rates on Households*, (HMSO, London, 1965).

proprietors, there is often no simple market in land—for ownership involves all sorts of peripheral obligations or rewards. Everything is sold, if at all, as a "package deal." Similarly, with peasants as tenants, the rent paid is often associated with ritualistic or kinship functions. Simple impersonal market transactions in land are in fact quite a rare phenomenon of certain kinds of Western societies.

93. For these reasons, therefore, one must reject any general form of land and property taxation as a method of financing major highway systems. For small "farm-to-market" roads, however, where the impact and the benefits are very localized, some primitive form of local land levy may be used to finance the development in part. Whether or not this form of finance is a good thing depends to a large extent on the institutions of the community. Anthropology here takes over from economic analysis.

94. In Chapter V we showed that if the demand for the produce that travels down the road to market is less than perfectly elastic, some of the benefits accrue to consumers in the form of lower prices; the "rents" are in fact rents of location of consumers. This naturally suggests that the *consumers* in urban areas be taxed—in the form of a general income or sales tax—in order to pay for the road that brings the goods to market in town. The actual form of such a tax should be judged in terms of the ordinary canons of taxation. The simplest form would be a poll tax for residents of the city—but there are many others which have an appeal of administrative simplicity and efficiency, and which are not so inequitable.

6. A Review of the User Charge Proposals

95. To end this chapter, let us review the tax proposals made and let us see how they would look as an integrated program. The two dominant themes of the user charge system are, first, the "normal" charge per vehicle-mile to reflect the variable maintenance cost and, secondly, the congestion levy, over and above the "normal" charge, to reflect the cost imposed as vehicles get in one another's way.

96. The suggested best way of levying the normal vehicle-mile charge in terms of correlation with roadway costs is by taxing tires. But this still depends on ensuring that the tire tax does not result in lax safety standards. The vehicle purchase tax and the gasoline tax are the next best alternatives. The proposed way of levying congestion charges is more complex. Differential gasoline taxes may help distinguish between congested and uncongested traffic. Other methods such as non-restricted licenses associated with the location of the operator are also possible ways of differen-

222

tiating between vehicles that generate congestion and those that do not. Subsidiary tax variations such as those which take into account the power/ weight ratio or differentiate against cars and in favor of trucks would also help. For the large cities it seems likely that a system of parking charges could be usefully introduced. Much experience is available from the developed countries on this form of charging.

97. The main instrument of congestion charges, however, must be the restricted license. Any motorist must pay for the privilege of entering a congested area. It is of great importance to realize, however, that what we have suggested is no more than a guideline or framework of ideas with which to confront any real situation. This is not a cut and dried prescription for immediate application. It is, indeed, quite possible that a more detailed study of any particular country may suggest quite strongly that some of the particular taxes which we have here suggested are inapplicable or inefficient. Whether that is, or is not, the case does not affect the main framework of approach; it merely influences the particular way in which the principles are applied. The principles themselves remain the same. The urban traffic should be charged more for using paved highways than the rural user. Any system of taxation or pricing that does not involve this principle is *prima facie* inefficient.

98. Whatever the taxes chosen, it is necessary to select those forms of levy which have good effects on efficiency of production and distribution. This discrimination requires a judgment of the effects of *ad valorem* levies and specific taxes. In particular, much will depend on the likelihood of evasion. This can be judged only in terms of the particular institutional and social ethos of the states concerned.

99. We have left many loose ends in discussing this general framework of taxation. One important question which we have not yet discussed is whether or not the system of taxes we have suggested will "cover the costs" of the road system. Will the congestion levies in urban areas balance the "losses" on the rural and interurban roads? This question is taken up in the next chapter—though we do not pretend to give any general answer, for there is none.

100. The other main question on which we have only touched is that of finding taxes to supply public saving. This question again we take up in the following chapter. But the important point is that the distribution of the tax between urban and rural traffic should follow the principles laid down above.

223

101.   It is unfortunately the case that the forms of taxation prescribed in this chapter are comparatively new in their form and incidence. They differ radically from those usually prescribed by many informed experts.[53] The system suggested here can only finally be judged by its results. Meanwhile, the case must stand on its merits as a consistent argument.

---

[53] See, for example, Meyer, Stenason, Peck, and Zwick, *The Economics of Competition in the Transportation Industries*, (Harvard University Press, Cambridge, 1959).

VIII

USER CHARGES, BUDGETARY CONTROL, AND EQUITY

1. *The Road Budget—a Calculation*

1.   One of the enduring objections to the propositions advanced through-out this study is that such a policy is likely to generate a deficit in the road budget, and that this will have to be made good by general taxation. Such a deficit is not bad *per se*. It may simply be better to use forms of taxation other than the normal "user charges" in order to finance the highways; all taxes and expenditures should be judged in terms of their effects. But it is clearly of some administrative and political interest to know whether the system of charges suggested in Chapter VII will give rise to a deficit or not.

2.   The only way to decide on the likelihood of deficits is to do the arith-metic and see what results emerge. Again this approach really requires a detailed survey of countries in different stages of development and under varying geographical circumstances. But the data are not available and the evidence is difficult to collect. As an imperfect and inferior substitute we present some calculations for Thailand. This is a country which is in many respects typical of a large fraction of the developing world—but it is better off than its neighbors in Southeast Asia, having about one vehicle for 200 persons (1964). Thus it may be thought to be in the van of most developing countries.

3. There were about 170,000 vehicles registered in Thailand and roughly one-half of the vehicles were concentrated in the Bangkok area (about 2 million in population). In Bangkok there was a very high ratio of car ownership—roughly one car for twenty-three persons. Let us suppose that the 85,000 or so vehicles in Bangkok each run about 14,000 miles a year. (Since there are many taxis this figure seems to be an underestimate—but there are no data to check this conjecture.) This gives a total annual vehicle mileage in and around Bangkok of about 1.2 billion vehicle-miles. It seems likely that the vehicle-mileage of the 85,000 or so vehicles outside Bangkok is much larger—at least 2.0 to 2.5 billion. It thus seems reasonable to assume that about 1.2 billion vehicle-miles per annum are run in the congested conditions of Bangkok and about twice that number in the country.

4. There are no neat studies of congestion and speed-flow relationships in Bangkok. From personal observations of journey times in the city, I would judge it to be under conditions of moderate congestion (journey speeds 10–15 mph) for some four or six hours of the day, with severe congestion during the hour or two of the peak. But in order to "play safe" with the calculation, let us suppose that the congestion charge takes only *mildly* congested conditions into account—such as those which are encountered by some traffic in the suburbs, i.e. journey speeds of about 18 mph. As we have seen in Chapter VI, this would involve a tax of about 3 US cents or so a mile for the private car.

5. When such a congestion tax is imposed—whatever the combination of administrative instruments used—there would be a reduction in the vehicle mileage in the city. Suppose that it fell from 1.2 to 1.0 billion vehicle-miles.[1] The gross yield of the congestion tax would therefore be of the order of $35 million. This is between two and three times the level of taxation at present levied on city traffic.

6. Most of the existing revenue is extracted from the interurban and rural road users—about $45–50 million. Our proposals require a reduction in the existing gasoline tax (about 14 or 15 US cents a US gallon); the actual reduction would depend on the feasibility of "fuel-fetching" journeys, etc., but let us suppose that the tax went down to about 7 cents a US gallon. The largest reduction is required in the level of import duties (including municipal and excise taxes) which amounts to about 100 percent of the c.i.f. value of cars and about 46 percent for trucks. A reduction to 30 percent and 15 percent, together with the lowering of the gasoline tax, would give rise to a reduction in revenue from the existing $45–50 million

---

[1] This implies an elasticity of demand of less than unity (absolute value).

to about $27–30 million, allowing for expansion due to the lower price. These are only very rough orders of magnitude, but the suggestion is that the incidence of tax on the rural and interurban user would be about halved. The phasing of such a policy must be carefully designed; in particular, to avoid windfalls, the reduction in the import duties should be carefully phased.

7. From these calculations, therefore, there is no evidence that deficits on the road budget would arise from the user charge system we have suggested. A total revenue of $62–65 million would be more than sufficient to cover Thailand's road expenditure as conventionally defined.[2] Indeed, it is clear that, if congestion taxes were levied at an appropriately high level (and given the relative inelasticity of demand by urban users) a "profit" would result from the existing road system. This may be considered *prima facie* evidence for expanding and improving the road system—but the actual decisions must depend on the additional cost and benefits involved.

8. It must be emphasized that these actual figures should not be taken too seriously; but the orders of magnitude should be noted. On the usual calculations there would be a deficit on rural and interurban roads and a surplus on the city streets; overall there should probably be a surplus. A Bank study of transport in Central America also suggests that there would be a surplus of revenue over costs if the EUC's were levied. The provisional conclusion to be drawn from this arithmetic is that deficits on the road budget are not necessarily a chronic weakness of the system of user charges which was outlined in the previous chapters.[3]

9. Granted that the economic user charges are being levied, we might now turn our attention to the other side of the coin—the level of government expenditure on the roads.

---

[2] The aggregate expenditure on roads in Thailand (excluding city streets) for the seven years 1960 to 1966 was US$315.4 million. (This value includes investment in the year in which the expenditure was laid out and does not use depreciation or amortization figures.) Taking the simple average we find that annual expenditure was $45 million approximately. An informed expert suggests that the city streets might cost about 20–25 percent of the nonurban expenditure; so total expenditure would be in the region of $54–56 million.

[3] Two criticisms (*inter alia*) have been leveled at this calculation. First it is suggested that the number of vehicle-miles in congested urban areas (Bangkok) has been overestimated. Second, a recent observer in Bangkok has argued that the congestion levies suggested above are much too low; Bangkok is the "most congested city" he had ever seen. Both criticisms seem to be valid, and the statistics should be amended accordingly. The tax revenues have not been recalculated here, however, largely because the two amendments offset one another.

Evidence from certain countries in East Africa, however, does suggest that there would be a shortfall in the road budget if EUC's were levied. Probably road user charges would there only amount to some 10–30 percent of the existing taxes, and perhaps less than 10 percent of the "costs" of the road budget.

227

2. Controls, Rules, and Discretion

10. In Chapter VII we discussed the practical problems of implementing systems of user charges. Attention was concentrated on the microeffects of each form of taxation. We were concerned with the effects on the use of roads, on the design and utilization of vehicles, and so on. But, as noted in Chapter IV, there is another major aspect of user charges. This is the problem of budgetary control and the associated macroeconomic effects including effects on the distribution of income.

11. The level of expenditure on the highways is probably the most difficult and, at the same time, the most important decision made by government in the general field of transport policy. It is normally perhaps more important for the government to pursue the best investment policy than for it to levy the ideal user charges. Departures from the ideal user charges do give rise to some misallocations—but these can be corrected in a relatively short time, whereas a road in the wrong place is there for its lifetime. Furthermore, it is much more difficult to assess the effects of road building and improvement than to provide for a workable and sensible system of user charges. Great expertise is required in judging the desirability of investment projects—and each one must be treated separately on its merits.

12. Even if there is agreement on the criteria of investment, as set out, for example, in Chapter III of this study, great difficulties occur in applying such criteria in practice. Different investigators will come up with widely different results. In addition, such decisions are not taken in an abstract disinterested way; they are political decisions in which interested pressure groups play an important part. Even in the United States, where there is the greatest concentration of expertise in this field of analysis, some serious misallocations arise, because, one suspects, of the interplay of pressure groups in the political machine. In developing countries similar misallocations appear. One of the recognized rewards of political success is a payoff to the supporters in the form of public works. Is it possible to define some simple administrative arrangements or, perhaps, a "rule" which would serve to prevent much of the misallocation?

13. There are, of course, a wide variety of devices that could be used to ensure government discipline in road spending. In degree of sophistication they range all the way from complex voting mechanisms to simple "ceilings" and "floors," or even "guidelines." Two such devices have been employed in practice and deserve some consideration. The first is an en-

shrined constitutional rule that the government spend a fixed percentage of the total government budget on roads. This is an earmarking of expenditure. The main advantage of such a rule is its unambiguous administrative simplicity. Probably the main objection is that road expenditure would then grow at broadly the same rate as national income—whereas the number of vehicles and the demand for roads tend to grow faster than national income. And just suppose that road transport was superseded by some other mode—then the rule would wastefully keep on ploughing money into the roads. An obvious alternative is to fix the relationship between expenditure on roads and the stock of vehicles, so that spending grows as the number of vehicles expands.

14. It is quite a short step from this proposal to another main alternative—the "road fund." Often it is proposed that road user taxes, however defined, should be paid into a fund to be used solely for road expenditure. Certain variants of a road fund are similar to the requirement of a nationwide balanced road budget. But a road fund need not only include taxes that fall on road users. *Any* earmarking procedure can be adopted so that specific revenues are tied to road expenditure. In some countries, for example, general import duties are paid into the road fund. There may be no reason why the expenditure on roads should be linked to user taxes as conventionally defined. It might give a better path of expenditure if road spending were tied to some other form of revenue. The discipline on aggregate expenditure would be as efficient, and the lack of discipline over local and particular expenditure would be the same.

15. To avoid misunderstanding, it should be stated unequivocally that a rational disinterested government with perfect knowledge of existing relationships could improve greatly on the behavior implied in any of the "rules." Even with imperfect knowledge one suspects that a rational disinterested government could outperform any "rule." But in the imperfect world in which we live—and especially considering the nature of the political and administrative process in many developing countries—a "rule" may well be the best of all possible solutions.

The Road Fund

16. The concept of the "road fund" is one of the most enduring ideas in road finance. There are, as we saw in Chapter IV, many versions of road-fund financing. The common thread is some fixed relationship between the amount of revenue collected in what are defined, for budgetary purposes, as user taxes and the expenditure, however defined, on the highways.

Somehow the roads are thought to pay for themselves.[4] In many versions of the road fund, the receipts from user taxes are paid into the fund and are not channeled through the normal Treasury or Exchequer accounts. On the expenditure side the fund does not have to compete with all other forms of government expenditure. Fund revenues are to be spent only on highways and the trustees of the fund (the road authority) can spend without fear of the Treasury raiding their resources. (This insulation from the fiscal process is sometimes described by the horrible word "defiscalization.") The road authority is not subject to direct political pressures from the government and legislature in developing the road spending program and in deciding on the distribution of road expenditure.

17.   One interesting aspect of the road fund is that it is widely accepted as a "good thing" by electorates. Furthermore, there is an additional twist to the road-fund idea that has received much informed approval; that we should "pay-as-we-ride" and not incur any considerable debt to finance highway construction. The most influential and significant debate on this issue took place in the United States during the enactment of the law establishing the interstate highway system in 1956. With some exceptions, Congress has adhered to the "pay-as-we-ride" principle. This version of the road fund we shall distinguish by calling it the "no-borrowing road fund," or for short NBRF.

18.   Experience with road funds is mixed. Britain operated a road fund from the beginning of the motor era to 1926. In that year the Right Honorable Winston Churchill, then Chancellor of the Exchequer, carried out one of his less celebrated raids—on the road fund. And so road taxes were siphoned off into the coffers of the Exchequer. That was the beginning of the end. Although the road fund was not formally wound up until the mid-1950's, the sporadic raids quickly turned into annual excursions. Motor taxation far exceeded annual expenditure on the highways, and the road-fund concept became as dead as the dodo.

19.   The experience of Britain compared with that of the United States illustrates another aspect of the administration of road funds. In Britain control of expenditure and taxation *de facto* is in the hands of the executive branch of government. In the United States control is partly the responsibility of Congress—the legislative branch of authority. In Britain the appropriation of road taxes is easy, but in the United States the President, in order to raid a road fund, would have to inveigle Congress to pass appropriate legislation—no easy task. Thus, a road fund is more likely to retain

---

[4] This is enshrined in the old "tale of the tub." "Each tub must stand on its own bottom." The dimensions of a tub are physical, but the scope of the road budget is only in the mind.

its integrity where there exists some separation of powers or similar constitutional guarantee of non-interference. A cursory survey of the constitutional characteristics of developing countries does suggest that governmental conditions are not auspicious for the establishment of road funds. But if there is a strong commitment by all parties to the concept of a road fund, then the constitutional difficulties will not much matter.

20.　This appears to be the case in New Zealand. There is a general commitment to the concept of road-fund financing. Roads are constructed and maintained by the National Roads Board. The law specifies those taxes which are to be paid into the National Road Fund; these include vehicle registration fees, license fees, tire taxes, the diesel vehicle-mileage tax, 15 pence out of the 17 pence per (imperial) gallon gasoline duty, and finally sales and import duties on road vehicles. The Board makes grants to local authorities for approved maintenance and construction work. The Board has no power to borrow—and so the system is an archetype of the NBRF type. The balancing of the books is almost perfect. In 1960/61, for example, the total revenue from road user taxes was £NZ36.7 million and the total expenditure on road construction and maintenance was £NZ36.5 million.

21.　Has the NBRF resulted in about the right level of spending on New Zealand's highways? It is, of course, impossible to find any informed and independent answers to such a question. There is some evidence that it would be efficient to spend in aggregate rather more than is anticipated over the years 1962/63 to 1970/71.[5] There is, moreover, a widespread dissatisfaction with the "no-borrowing" stipulation—since it is clear that large expenditures in particular years—such as those occasioned by building a bridge—would inefficiently cut down other normal expenditure. To phase work properly it might be better to borrow.

22.　One of the most important features of the New Zealand transport system, however, is that goods transported by road are severely restricted by licensing. The prime object of this legislation is to protect the traffic and the revenue of the railways. It succeeds. But the cost is very large. It is very difficult for a public haulier or even a trader carrying only his own goods to get authority to run more than 40 to 75 miles, when there is also a rail connection. Such controls greatly restrict the use of roads (which are usually uncongested) and much reduce the revenue that would be obtained from road taxes if the trucking industry were left free to compete with the railways. If, alternatively, the motor tax system were used in-

---

[5] This is my interpretation of a Bank report on New Zealand—but the evidence is clearly not strong.

stead to reduce competition with rail to a level similar to that generated by the present system of bureaucratic controls, a very large revenue would be available for spending on the highways. This would ensure that the state appropriated the revenue derived from the restriction on road truck traffic, instead of the lucky truckers who secured authorizations.

23. The essential point is that the road revenues are artificially and, I believe, inefficiently restricted by the rationing system. In the absence of this system much more revenue would be available for spending on the highways, and it seems likely that there would be at least some modification of the existing suspicion that too little is being spent.

24. The case of Argentina, on the other hand, illustrates the difficulty of operating a road fund when there is not adequate support for the integrity of the fund. The National Highway Fund of Argentina derives 90 percent of its revenue from user taxes, largely by means of a 50 percent *ad valorem* tax on gasoline and oil (1961). These taxes were to be collected by the state petroleum company and paid over to the National Highway Fund. But at the same time the state fixed the price of petroleum at M$N 5.4 a liter, which implied a tax of M$N 2.7. The balance of M$N 2.7 was less than the production costs of M$N 3.48. So the state petroleum company did not hand over the M$N 2.7 per liter tax to the National Highway Fund. Eventually the tax per liter was reduced so that it was consistent with the cost and the controlled price—the tax went down from M$N 2.7 to M$N 1.74 a liter. And, of course, the National Highway Fund incurred a deficit.

25. It is difficult to imagine a road fund serving any useful purpose when it is possible to play ducks and drakes with its receipts. (The restriction on the revenue of the fund did not much affect road expenditure.) This has led informed observers to suggest that the best policy in Argentina would be to "refiscalize" highway funds and road expenditure, to bring them back into the budget.

26. To sum up, therefore, the experience of Argentina with a road-fund form of administration is much less happy than that of New Zealand and the United States. And it appears that the difference arose largely from a divergence in the degree of commitment to the accounting discipline of the fund, rather than from any fundamental fault in the road-fund idea.

Coordination

27. One of the most important objections to the road-fund form of administration is that it results in decisions about intrastructural road and

rail investment being taken without any formal system of coordination. This was, indeed, one of the important objections taken by informed experts to the operation of the pseudo-road fund in Argentina. The implication is that with political governmental control of both road and rail expenditure on track (and perhaps also rail equipment), there is a better chance of avoiding wasteful expenditure and unnecessary duplication of facilities. In their report on *Options in Transport Tariff Policy*,[6] the experts of E.E.C. have suggested that coordination was the main reason for keeping both road and rail investment in infrastructure in the hands of the central government.

28. But even if control is vested in the central government it does not necessarily follow that "coordination" will take place. In a report on Turkey, for example, it seems that both road and rail investment were the responsibility of the government but, so far as one could discover, there was no coordination between the two. Road investment and maintenance were the responsibility of the Minister of Public Works. Rail investment was carried out by the nationalized railway undertaking which was responsible to the Minister of Transport and Communications. There was no coordinating Minister. Such coordination could not take place through decisions on the budget; the expertise and knowledge were not present in the budget departments. Even in the United Kingdom with its highly centralized administration the extent of coordination of road and rail investment has, in fact, been very small, although efforts have been made in recent years to remedy this. Coordination is a delicate flower that must be carefully cultivated in a suitable environment; it will not blossom just anywhere.

29. Whether the flower is worth cultivation is another matter. The presumption by most administrators is that coordination is a "good thing." Building a road, for example, at the side of an existing railway will obviously affect the benefits from the railway. It may be that the two facilities are complements to one another—so that each may be better off with the presence of the other. But it is more likely, perhaps, that the facilities are competitive. Thus an authority that controlled both road and rail investment could take into account the *total* effects of any investment program. The coordinating authority could act for the national good and prevent "wasteful" competition and duplication of facilities.

30. It is undoubtedly true that a rational disinterested coordinating authority, supported by a highly competent and independent research staff,

---

[6] Maurice Allais *et al.*, *Options in Transport Tariff Policy*, (Brussels, 1965).

could make great strides in sieving and streamlining investment programs. The practical danger is that the authority will not be disinterested and will not be supported by a suitably high-level team of fact-finders and analysts. Bad coordination may be worse than no coordination at all.

Earmarked Revenues and Other Rules

31. One of the main advantages of the road-fund approach is that it does provide the road authority with a steady stream of funds available in future years. The authority can plan efficiently the future expenditure on the highways with the assurance that the necessary finance will be forthcoming. Furthermore, all truckers, bus operators, traders, farmers and industrialists will be more or less perfectly certain about the future aggregate spending on the highways, and they can plan accordingly. The value of such certainty to road builders and users is clearly high.

32. Many other simple earmarking arrangements are possible which would give rise to somewhat similar effects. It is possible, for example, to earmark some of the tariff receipts for spending on the highways. In judging the desirability of tariff earmarking, there are many aspects to be taken into account. But the underlying requirement is that the tariff rates, the volume of imports, and so the revenue from tariffs must be relatively stable. The obvious disadvantage is that it will encourage greater road investment when, for countercyclical policy, one should be cutting expenditure.[7] It will be argued later in this chapter that road spending should not be used to attempt to counter the pressures of aggregate demand. But surely administrative arrangements should not add fuel to the flames of inflation. For these reasons tariff receipts should be rejected as a possible base for an earmarking rule.

33. Instead of determining the income of the road authority in terms of earmarked taxes, one may fix it by a simple rule. One such rule that has some practical appeal is that the authority should get a sum of money per vehicle registered. The simplest rule of all is a constant sum (which, of course, must be defined in real terms) per vehicle. For example, it might be sensible to allocate, annually, say, $150 per car, $400 per medium truck and $1,000 per heavy truck. Even more complicated rules are possible, distinguishing between the regional location of the vehicles, whether urban or rural, and so on. Having settled on a rule, it is of the

---

[7] Consider, for example, an inflationary situation in a country with a fixed exchange rate. The pressure of demand will lead to more imports and so tariff receipts will rise; this will put money in the hands of the road authority to spend on the highways. Additional government spending will make the inflation even worse; the signal is green when it should be red.

utmost importance to stick to it. Rules are only of use if they are observed and if everyone believes they will be observed. Then there will be all the advantages of certainty to both road builder and trucker; they can plan confidently on the basis of safe expectations.

34.   So far as I know, no governments have ever guaranteed formally to provide road expenditure in this way. But it is not unlikely that intra-governmental budgetary bargains of this kind are struck. Some rules of thumb are often used for making difficult decisions on the allocation of funds.

3. Equity—the Beneficiaries and the Losers

35.   It seems likely that one of the main reasons for the longevity of the road-fund concept is the "built-in" principle of equity; the road users are the main beneficiaries from the improved highways, so they should foot the bill. They are an easily identified group and charges can therefore be exacted from them directly for the advantages conferred. This is not the case with many forms of public expenditure.

36.   This is, however, a naive view of the incidence of the user charges. The duty will be "passed on." The simple model of Chapter V showed that the burden of the ton-mile tax will be passed on to the owners of the land. If one grants the assumption of the model, including a perfectly elastic supply of transport and of marketing facilities and an infinitely elastic demand for the commodity at the port, the analysis of the benefits and of the incidence of taxes of the normal ton-mile or vehicle-mile type clearly shows that landowners are not taxed in proportion to the benefits they receive from the highway. Indeed the great disadvantage of the ton-mile tax is its high incidence on marginal lands. If this model is useful for analyzing problems in the real world, it clearly shows that user charges do not have the attractive equitable properties that are usually claimed; other feasible taxes have effects that most people would consider more consistent with principles of equity.

37.   It may be argued, however, that the model cannot be used in certain practical cases. For example, in countries where the quantity of trucks is controlled by licensing regulations—such as in South Africa or New Zea-land—it is quite wrong to assume that there is an infinitely elastic supply of motor transport at the going rate per ton-mile. In the extreme case when the regulating authority does not authorize any increase in the number of new vehicle journeys, a decrease in transport costs will be entirely absorbed by the trucking firms. If the regulating authority controls only

the quantity of trucking services and permits the trucking rate per ton-mile to be fixed by market forces, the rate will not fall, but costs will. All benefits from the road improvement are distributed in the form of increased profits to the truckers who have authority to operate on that route.

38. This result is no more than a manifestation of the general rule that the benefits of the road (and the incidence of the tax) are passed on to factors that are fixed in supply. With this kind of regulated trucking, the authorization-to-carry is the "factor" that is fixed—and so, assuming that the regulating authority provides no room for maneuvering, all the benefits of road improvement appear as the rents or profits of the owners of the authorizations.

39. In this case a ton-mile tax levied on road users will simply soak up the unearned surplus of those who possess the authorizations. In principle one could fix the level of the ton-mile tax so that it siphoned off all the unearned rent, and the amount and distribution of cultivation would be the same as before the improvement. The same traffic would be on the highway. The only difference is that the real costs incurred by the trucks will have diminished by an amount equal to the cost-saving on the improved road—and this will have been replaced by a ton-mile tax exactly equal to the cost-saving per ton-mile; so the government appropriates the benefits. It is also easy to see that the same result could have been obtained without regulation. Provided that the government levies ton-mile taxes just high enough to soak up all the benefits accruing to *existing* traffic, the effect will be to transfer all the benefits to the government and the amount of traffic and the extent and distribution of cultivation will remain the same.[8]

40. If, for some reason, there is such a policy of restricting the expansion of road transport, the analysis suggests that a ton-mile type of tax may be an efficient way to regulate the amount of transport and to appropriate the private benefits jointly generated by these restrictions and the improvements in the highways.[9] Such a "package" of policies does, however, have the crucial disadvantage of throwing away all the development benefits; and it is not difficult to devise better "package deals."

41. Let us therefore leave the "no-development" case and examine the effects where there is a market demand which is less than perfectly elas-

---

[8] This is the case where in the figures of Chapter V the tax line is coincidental with the "next-to-the-sea" surface of the benefit pyramid in the simple development model.

[9] We shall observe that, in practice, it is probably best to levy taxes on the ownership of vehicles.

tic—but where there is no restriction on entry into the road haulage business. If the good is exported then there is a clear case for an export tax; in the extreme case where there is a rigid quantity demanded, whatever the price, the case for taxing the foreigner is overwhelming.[10] In practical cases, however, the elasticity is likely to be high. But we argued that even when the demand was *perfectly* elastic an export tax would be a good way of raising revenue; so it is clearly a presumption that for intermediate elasticities the same policy should be used. The danger of such a tax is that the reduction in the domestic price at the port will encourage the transfer of resources to other (domestic) uses and there will be a consequential loss of foreign currency.[11] Judgments must be made of the possibility and extent of such transfers, and the importance of the loss of foreign currency in each case.

42.   The equity argument for an export tax per ton is reinforced by the consideration that the export demand is less than perfectly elastic. The inelasticity of demand modifies the loss of rents which would be entailed in a tonnage tax under conditions of infinitely elastic demand. If one can ignore the moral implications of the international distribution of income, the principle that "the foreigner should pay" seems to command a wide degree of support. And often, of course, the foreign importer is a relatively rich industrial country.

43.   Now suppose that instead of being exported the commodity is sold entirely in a domestic market where the demand is inelastic. Then the domestic consumers will reap most of the benefit of the reduction in transport costs—and it is efficient and equitable that they pay tonnage taxes. Again it will be observed that the basis of the tax is quantity on the market and there is no discrimination according to distance. If the commodity is in part used domestically and in part exported, then *ceteris paribus*, both exports and domestic consumption should bear the same tax. In fact, however, such decisions are likely to be dominated by the twin needs to stimulate domestic industry and to earn foreign currency. We return to these problems in their macroeconomic setting in the last section of this chapter.

Urban and Rural Incomes

44.   The main burden of the theoretical discussion, however, was to show that there was a good case for taxing the vehicle-miles of urban motoring

---

[10] The only argument, and it is a serious one, for moderating behavior is the fact that one might invite retaliation.

[11] The reader will recall that in our formal model this contingency was apparently ignored; the alternative of domestic (subsistence) production was, however, present in the land that was not used for market production.

more heavily than the vehicle-miles of the rural and interurban road user. Taxes should be high where traffic is congested and low where the highways are not congested. The effects of a switch to this policy will depend on the precise form of the existing system of taxation. In order to focus discussion it is useful to assume that the existing system results in the same tax per vehicle-mile whether on the rural roads or on congested city streets. Our policy requires an increase in urban taxes and a reduction in rural taxes—let us assume that urban taxes are doubled per vehicle-mile and that the rural tax per vehicle-mile is halved. Furthermore, in order to standardize the comparison, let us also suppose that the aggregate amount collected in taxes does not change; we have merely changed the distribution between urban and rural (including interurban).

45. A naive interpretation of incidence would conclude that the urbanites would suffer and the rural population would gain. The higher cost of motor transport in the town would make it more expensive to live there, but, on the other hand, the expansion of the area of cultivation in the country would increase rural incomes and employment. If this naive conclusion were correct, there would be strong grounds for labeling the resulting redistribution of income "a good thing." It would ameliorate rural poverty, one of the main reasons alleged for the "drift to the towns," and at the same time it would make the towns somewhat less attractive to footloose labor.

46. Such a naive interpretation is unlikely to be correct. Consider a situation where the rural and interurban transport is predominantly by truck, and the intra-city traffic largely by private car. The immediate incidence of the proposed tax system is likely to be detrimental to the car and beneficial to the truck traffic. If economic user charges are levied (with no tonnage tax to balance the budget) on a ton-mile basis, it is obvious that both rural and interurban transport will be cheaper. But as we argued above, the effects of cheap rural transport may be manifest in the lowering of the price of produce and the expansion of the quantity marketed in the urban areas. Clearly the urban consumers gain from the reduced prices; and it is conceivable that, if their demand is sufficiently inelastic, their gain may exceed that of the farmers (considered as a group). Those urbanites who consume relatively large amounts of the rural produce gain most; and since this is probably often foodstuffs, it is likely that it will benefit relatively the least well-to-do. On the other hand the gain to the farmers may be siphoned off to the landlords in the form of higher rents.

47. The lower rates and fares for interurban traffic will permit more specialization in the towns. Distance, between raw materials and factories

and between factory and market or port, will be less of a barrier than before. Such gains will be widely distributed but they would probably be more concentrated in the towns than among the rural community. It is not clear that this will benefit the rural farmer and laborer to any considerable extent.

48.   Thus, contrary to the naive impression, the lowering of ton-mile taxes on rural and interurban transport will tend to benefit both town and country dweller. It is difficult to conjecture who will gain most; one suspects that if most of the traffic is carrying food to the urban area, the urban population will be the larger gainers. If, on the other hand, the commodity is exported through the port, as in our simple model, the rural community will be the main beneficiary. In the first case, the urban working class would benefit most, in the second case the rentiers or farmers.

49.   The effects of increasing ton-mile taxes in the city are somewhat less difficult to trace. In developing countries car owners in urban areas are usually taxi firms, the professional middle class and the wealthier members of the business community. Some of the incidence will be passed on in terms of increased marketing costs of produce in the urban areas. But probably the main effects would be borne by personal accounts, partly in the form of increased taxi fares.

50.   Although it seems as though the urbanite will suffer from this increase in urban motor taxes (leaving aside for the time being any gain from a reduction in rural farm-to-market taxes), it is not certain that this will be the outcome. One extreme example is where the city is so congested that more or less continuous traffic queues slow down traffic to such an extent that the flow is very small. After the imposition of taxes, the queues may be dispersed and the flow actually *increased*.[12] It is conceivable, therefore, that, in spite of the doubling of tax per mile, the reduction in congestion costs is so large that the money costs (including taxes) of urban motoring are actually reduced! Everyone gains. Although this may appear to be a most unusual situation, there is some evidence that in very highly congested conditions (Singapore, Saigon, Bangkok), it may be a correct picture. But for the vast majority of urban areas in developing countries, such a description may be appropriate only for the peak hour.

---

[12] This is the so-called "backward-bending" section of the speed-flow relationship, which one may interpret as a transform of the supply curve. See A. A. Walters, "The Theory and Measurement of Marginal Private and Social Cost of Highway Congestion," *Econometrica*, Vol. 29 and for a more readable account: C. D. Foster, *The Transport Problem*, (Blackie, London, 1963). See also A. C. Dick "Speed/Flow Relationships within an Urban Area," *Traffic Engineering and Control*, (London, October 1966), and A. A. Walters, "Road Pricing: Some Technical Aspects," *De Economist*, (North Holland, Amsterdam, 1968).

51.   When congestion is moderate, but not severe in the sense discussed above, then the immediate impact on the urban motorist is that he pays more in the increment of taxation than his costs fall because of the reduction in congestion. Again, however, one may observe that those motorists who value their time relatively highly may gain from this arrangement. I may be willing to pay $3 to save an hour of my time from being spent in traffic queues, consequently I will be better off paying $5 for a taxi journey that hitherto cost $4 if I save 30 minutes because of the reduction in congestion. The "price" to me of a taxi ride has gone down, for we must reckon as part of that price the value of the time I waste in the taxi.

52.   With urban congestion levies, therefore, the people who value their time relatively highly will be better off than they were before. On the other hand, those persons who put little value on their time will generally be injured by the congestion toll; though much depends on the cost of avoiding it by traveling off-peak. The net effect is then to make the relatively rich better off and the poor worse off than without the congestion tolls. This is, in other words, the opposite effect to that of reducing rural motor taxes where there was a benefit for the urban working classes.

53.   The net results of this discussion are inconclusive. There does not seem to be a powerful argument to show that any one general class of persons, such as the urban poor, will be on balance injured by the move to the suggested tax structure. The gains and losses seem to be diffused relatively widely over the population. This conclusion in turn suggests that there is no urgent question of the desirability of compensating, by suitable taxes or budgetary transfers, any general section of the populace. Each particular case must be judged on its merits.

54.   The general lesson to be drawn from this discussion is that the government should move slowly but surely towards the new user charge policy. Users must have time to adjust to the new charges; industrialists should know the future policy well in advance so that they can make appropriate decisions about location. An inexorable progress towards the new system of user charges will provide that air of certainty and stability essential in the broad framework of economic life.

4. *Macroeconomic Problems—the Shortage of Capital, Balance of Payments, and Inflation*

55.   The system of taxation adopted has implications for the supply of savings, the use of existing capital and the demand for additional capital. Let us examine first the *utilization of capital*, and in particular, the use of

cars and trucks. Consider the license duty and the gasoline tax, which may be used to raise a certain amount of revenue, and let us suppose that these are the only two taxes between which we must choose.[13] If the revenue is raised solely by means of a gasoline tax, it will be relatively cheap to own a vehicle but relatively expensive to run it. If the roads on which these vehicles run are paved and not congested, it is clear that the gasoline tax is indeed a bad one, for it induces people to hold a relatively large number of vehicles and to underutilize them. The result is that few services are extracted from a lot of capital.

56. Now consider the license duty as the only source of revenue. The total incidence of the tax will now fall on the *ownership* of capital—the vehicle. The high shadow price of owning capital can be reflected in the license duty imposed. The marginal cost of providing services with the vehicle will be low, since there is no gasoline tax. While each vehicle must earn sufficient revenue to pay the license duty, each vehicle operator will be induced to use his vehicle much more intensively than if he paid no license fee and a high fuel levy. By the use of the license fee rather than the fuel tax, we tend to get the same or even a larger quantity of services from a substantially smaller number of vehicles used more intensely.[14]

57. As a general rule, therefore, one would prefer licensing to gasoline taxes, and the greater the capital shortage the more marked that preference would be. *A fortiori* license fees rather than restrictive regulation should be used to control the number of vehicles. We have also argued that license fees are in general preferable to import duties—but this must be examined again in terms of the balance of payments problem.

58. We now examine the differential effects, if any, on *savings*. As far as private saving is concerned it is difficult to believe that the difference between a gasoline tax and a license fee will have any significant effect. There is more to be said about motor taxation as a general source of public saving.[15] If it be decided that the road user is the best source of revenue, it is necessary to devise taxes that are as efficient as possible and consistent with the other aims of government policy. Again, license duties must be

---

[13] We could argue this case with any tax on vehicle-miles—the fuel tax is a useful illustration.

[14] Similarly, it is important to ensure that regulation and control do not lead to the inefficient use of vehicles. In India there are many striking examples of inefficiency and waste caused by the various regulatory bodies. Such hardships are not necessary and could easily be avoided by a suitable system of license fees.

[15] We remind the reader that much of the case for "covering the cost" of the road system by motor taxation can be much better and more honestly argued in terms of using motor taxes to increase public saving and so public investment.

considered high on the list of desirable taxes. The analysis of the theoretical models also suggests that tonnage (and passenger) taxes are preferable to levies which have their incidence on a ton-mile basis. In principle, one should choose taxes that interfere as little as possible with development. For countries such as those in West Africa that produce rubber and iron ore for a world market, it seems to be a good policy to impose an export tax per ton. This will then not result in the stringent limitations of exploitation which would occur with a ton-mile type of tax. We have shown that paradoxically, an export tax would be less restrictive on exports than a ton-mile tax that collects the same total revenue. For a given level of development the export tax would produce at least 50 percent more revenue than a ton-mile tax. Whether it would also produce more public and private savings is another rather large question, the answer to which depends on the consumption-investment behavior of the farmers and exploiters concerned.[16] It seems to be a sensible provisional conjecture that the export tax would result in larger savings unless the savings schedules of farmers and others followed rather curious patterns; but this matter will have to be left for further analysis. At this stage we may conclude that there are no "public saving" grounds on which one may automatically rely in order to justify the typical ton-mile taxes on the transport industries.[17]

59. It must also be said unequivocally that user-charge policy should not be regarded as a major instrument for correcting *balance of payments* disequilibria or for attempting to dampen the fires of *inflation*. One of the constant themes of this chapter has been the need for stability in road expenditure. Schemes of highway improvement are long-term operations and they take time to plan and schedule efficiently. They *can* be turned on and off annually but only at a very large cost. Similarly, small businessmen will be very reluctant to invest in trucking and bus firms if they are

---

[16] Certain West African countries do have export taxes in the form of the surpluses collected by marketing boards. In the case of Nigeria, for example, the proceeds from the marketing boards have been used to finance agricultural research, universities and modern manufacturing as well as roads: see Gerald K. Hellener, "The Fiscal Role of Marketing Boards in Nigerian Development," *Economic Journal*, Vol. LXXIV, No. 295, (Cambridge, England, September 1964), pp. 582–610. In Hellener's judgment the boards have achieved remarkable success as revenue collectors; he concludes "the mechanism of export taxation through earnings of marketing board trading has worked well. . . ."

[17] The argument can be easily transformed to take account of those countries where the main centers of consumption are domestic markets (towns and cities) rather than overseas industries. Instead of an export tax, we should have a market tax of so much per ton. In practice, this tax per ton might be efficiently combined with the congestion levy. The argument suggests that it may be efficient, in order to generate public savings, to charge even higher levies for entering congested market areas than those implied by the calculation of optimum congestion taxes.

likely to be subject to large changes in taxation, regulation, and road provision. The great advantage of rules is that they may provide such stability.

60. The main provision which must be written into the rules is that they should not result in making an incipient inflation blossom or a fine balance of payments topple. If they have any effect at all it should tend to be corrective rather than destabilizing. In particular the government should not attempt to damp down rises in the general level of prices by pegging user charges. Such Canute-like behavior will give rise only to wet socks and cold feet.

61. Another general principle may be drawn from this discussion. If an economy gets into such a state with its balance of payments that it is forced to adopt restrictive measures, it is best to use license fees rather than restrictive import quotas and other quantitative restrictions. The license fee will enable the state to appropriate the surplus instead of the lucky people who get the quotas. The elimination of bureaucratic procedures, red tape, bribery and lobbying will also be a significant advantage of the licensing system. But if the license fee is used for this purpose, the link between license revenue and road spending must be severed. As a formal arrangement it may be a good idea to distinguish between the "normal" license fee which may be paid into the road fund, and the license "surcharge," or general revenue tax, which accrues to the general budget. Many other arrangements are possible.

62. It is important to emphasize that this discussion of the inflationary and balance of payments effects of various rules of road finance is no substitute for a full and detailed analysis of the probable effects of any likely rule. The strains and pressures to which any rule is subject must realistically be taken into account in framing it. Foresight may prevent critical weaknesses and even breakdowns. In this section we have illustrated some of the questions that might reasonably be asked; many more have been omitted or glossed over. In practical cases a full detailed inquiry is necessary.